W9-BUS-216

barcode
is on
title page

NEW YORK

Published in cooperation with
The Museum of the City of New York,
The New—York Historical Society,
The New York Public Library, and
The Municipal Art Society
with financial support from
Furthermore, the publication program
of The J. M. Kaplan Fund,
The Susan and Elihu Rose Foundation,
The Emigrant Savings Bank, and
The Seymour Durst Old York Foundation.
Massimo Vignelli, design consultant.

NEW YORK

An Illustrated History of the People by Allon Schoener

FINKELSTEIN
MEMORIAL LIBRARY
SPRING VALLEY, N.Y.

W. W. Norton & Company   New York • London

Copyright © 1998 by Allon Schoener

All rights reserved
Printed in Italy
First Edition

The text of this book is composed in
Century ATFBQ Expanded
The display is set in Century ATFBQ Bold
Composition and layout by Gina Webster
Manufacturing by Arnoldo Mondadori
Editore, Verona, Italy

Library of Congress Cataloging-in-
Publication Data
Schoener, Allon.
New York : an illustrated history of the
people / by Allon Schoener.
    p.   cm.
Includes bibliographical references and
index.
ISBN 0-393-04581-1
1. Ethnology—New York (State)—New
York—Pictorial works. 2. New York (N.Y.)—
Ethnic relations—Pictorial works. 3. New
York (N.Y.)—Race relations—Pictorial works.
4. New York (N.Y.)—Emigration and immi-
gration—History—Pictorial works. I. Title.
F128.9.A1S36   1998
974.7'1004—DC21   98-10533
                              CIP

W. W. Norton & Company, Inc.
500 Fifth Avenue
New York, N. Y. 10110
http://www.wwnorton.com

W. W. Norton & Company Ltd.
10 Coptic Street
London WC1A 1PU

1 2 3 4 5 6 7 8 9 0

The author gratefully acknowledges permis-
sion to publish the following:
Selection from *The New York Sketches of
Stephen Crane and Related Pieces*, edited by
R. W. Stallan and E. R. Hagemann, copy-
right © 1966 by New York University Press.
Selection from *Manhattan Transfer* by John
Dos Passos, Somerset Books, 1925.
Reprinted by permission of Henry Holt and
Company, Inc. Selections from *Black Man-
hattan* by James Weldon Johnson, reprinted
by permission of Ollie Sims Okala, Executor
of the Estate of Grace Nail Johnson.
Selection from *O America: When You and I
Were Young* by Luigi Barzini, © 1977 by
Luigi Barzini, reprinted by permission of
HarperCollins Publishers, Inc. Selection from
Dark Ghetto: Dilemmas of Social Power by
Kenneth B. Clark, copyright © by Kenneth
B. Clark, copyright renewed 1993 by
Kenneth B. Clark, reprinted by permission
of HarperCollins Publishers, Inc. Selection
from *Sticks and Stones* by Lewis Mumford,
© copyright 1955 by Dover Publications,
Inc. Reprinted by permission of Dover
Publications, Inc. Selection from *Daily News*,
November 1, 1929, reprinted by permission
of *New York Daily News*. L.P. Selections
from the *New York Times*, January 1, 1927,
January 1, 1937, and June 22, 1937, © copy-
right 1927 and 1937 by The New York
Times Co. Reprinted by permission.
Selection from *New York Herald Tribune*,
August 15, 1945, © copyright 1945 by New
York Herald Tribune, Inc. All rights
reserved. Reproduced by permission.
Selection from "Notes and Comment" by E.
B. White, *The New Yorker*, June 11, 1955.

Reprinted by permission. Selections from
Marjorie Morningstar by Herman Wouk, ©
copyright 1955 by Herman Wouk. Used by
permission of Doubleday, a division of Ban-
tam Doubleday Dell Publishing Group, Inc.
Selection from "My Dungeon Shook" by
James Baldwin, collected in *The Fire Next
Time*, © copyright 1962, 1963 by James
Baldwin. Copyright renewed. Published by
Vintage Books. Reprinted by arrangement
with the James Baldwin Estate. Selection
from *At the Edge of Harlem* by Edward
Wakin, published by William Morrow and
Company, © copyright 1965 by Edward
Wakin. Reproduced by permission. Selection
from *The Feminine Mystique* by Betty
Friedan, © copyright 1983, 1974, 1973, 1963
by Betty Friedan. Reprinted by permission
of W. W. Norton & Company, Inc. Selection
from *Letters of the Lubavitcher Rebbe, Rabbi
Menachem Schneerson: 1956–1980*, Kehot
Publishing Company, 1981, reproduced by
permission. Selection from *Commentary by
A. Bartlett Giamatti* appearing in *The
Italian Americans* by Allon Schoener.
Reproduced by permission of Toni Giamatti.
Selection from *Wise Guy: Life in a Mafia
Family* by Nicholas Pileggi, published by
Simon and Schuster, © copyright 1985 by
Pileggi Literary Properties, Inc. Reproduced
by permission of the author. Selection from
"Keep America's Door Open" by Rudoph
Giuliani appearing in the *Wall Street
Journal*, January 9, 1997. Reproduced by
permission. Selection from *Delirious New
York* by Rem Koolhaas, © copyright 1994
by Rem Koolhaas and The Monacelli Press.
Reproduced by permission.

Contents

In 1524, Giovanni da Verrazzano, surveying the east coast of North America in the service of François I, king of France, was the first European known to enter New York Harbor. His square-rigged *Dauphine,* armed with cannon, caused consternation among the Native Americans who inhabited the area. Verrazzano said that they "passed from one shore to the other in order to see us."

In the same year, Pope Clement VII proposed that Michelangelo prepare drawings for the future Biblioteca Laurenziana in Florence. Both Verrazzano, born near Florence, and Michelangelo were products of sixteenth-century Italian Renaissance culture. With a maritime tradition of nearly two millennia, the Italians were in the vanguard of explorers seeking a sea route to the Orient.

The European encounter with New York was not an accident, nor was it an isolated event. Sixteenth-century Europe, experiencing a period of economic expansion and population growth, was emerging from a long period of contraction. Trade was increasing and cities, as centers of industry and commerce, were thriving. In 1500, four European cities—Paris, Milan, Naples, and Venice—had more than 100,000 inhabitants. To maintain this rate of growth, new markets and new sources of raw materials were needed.

The existing land routes to the Orient were difficult to traverse and fraught with territorial problems. A maritime link seemed faster and more desirable. Although Europeans had been fishing off the coast of North America, they had limited knowledge of the land masses to be found on the western edge of the Atlantic Ocean. Europeans assumed that there would be a way of reaching the Orient by navigating through or around these areas.

European objectives shifted from exploration intent upon trade to the exploitation of people and natural resources. Hernando Cortés's conquest of Mexico between 1519 and 1522 established a pattern replicated by the Spanish throughout Latin America and the Caribbean and emulated by other European powers seeking to establish colonies in the Americas. Conquest followed by colonization had been central to European history. First the Greeks during the Hellenistic Period, and later the Romans when they established their empire, conquered foreign territories, transforming them into Greek and Roman colonies. The Greeks, Romans, and their European successors had no monopoly on conquest leading to colonization; this practice had been common throughout history in all parts of the world.

The Aztec city of Tenochtitlan (Mexico City), at the time of the Spanish conquest, was one of the world's largest cities, having a population estimated to be in the neighborhood of 150,000 people. In 1492, the Inka ruled the largest empire in the Americas, rivaled only by the concurrent Chinese and Ottoman empires. From its capital in Cuzco, the Inka Empire ran southward to central Chile and included the northwestern part of Argentina as well as the highlands of Peru, Bolivia, Ecuador, and Columbia. The native people who inhabited the east coast of North America had a long history, diverse cultures, and networks of settlements that embroidered the region. Native American people had been living in and around New York City for an estimated 11,500 years.

In 1609 Henry Hudson, with the backing of the Dutch East India Company, set sail from Amsterdam seeking a passage to China. He proposed a voyage along the northern coast of Russia and Siberia. Having problems with ice and a potentially mutinous crew, Hudson decided to turn westward toward the coast of North America. When Hudson dropped anchor in what is now the harbor of New York City, this signaled the beginning of a Dutch presence in the region.

In 1625, a Dutch settlement, Fort Amsterdam, was established on Manhattan Island. It was settled by some thirty families, mostly French-speaking Walloons. Peter Minuit, possibly of Dutch or Walloon ancestry, arrived in 1626 with a new group of immigrants who proceeded to build thirty houses. In the same year, he purchased Manhattan Island from Native American chiefs. Following the Walloons, Dutch, German, British, and Scandinavian immigrants began to arrive. Fort Amsterdam became New Amsterdam. Hardly a time of ethnic or religious tolerance, this was the period of the Reformation and Counter-Reformation in Europe, when religion held a central place in the lives of most people. Protestantism was shaking the foundations of the Catholic Church. Jews had been exiled from Spain and Portugal and were denied equal rights in other countries. The African slave trade,

Chapter One
Colonial City: 1514–1824
The Dutch and British Build a
Base of Diversity

initiated by the Portuguese and expanded by the British, Dutch, and French, was uprooting millions of Africans and transporting them to the Americas.

Although the Dutch ruled New Amsterdam only forty years, they left an indelible imprint on the future city. Perhaps their most lasting legacy is two of the city's passions that persist today: its absorption with commerce and its dedication to religious and ethnic heterogeneity.

New Amsterdam was founded as a commercial colony administered by the Dutch West India Company. The Plymouth Company, an English consortium that developed colonies in New England, permitted a Puritan oligarchy to dominate. In Pennsylvania, Quaker theology and business practices meshed. In New Amsterdam, commerce was foremost with religion a subtext. There was a reluctant tolerance of people representing varied nationalities and religions contradicted by open racial and religious discrimination. Active in the African slave trade, the Dutch introduced slavery to New Amsterdam in 1626. At the same time, they initiated a pattern of racially segregated housing. African slaves did not live within the Dutch compound, they lived along the East River opposite what is now Roosevelt Island. As a consequence of the Portuguese conquest of Brazil, a group of Sephardic Jews who had been residing in Recife came to New Amsterdam in 1654. Reverend Johannes Megalpolensis, minister of the Dutch Reformed Church of New Amsterdam, known to be intolerant, described the colony's religious heterogeneity in 1655 saying, "we have here Papists, Mennonites and Lutherans among the Dutch; also many Puritans or Independents and many other atheists."

When New Amsterdam became New York following the British conquest in 1664, the city had an estimated population of about 1,500. In 1685, Captain William Byrd, a visitor from Virginia, described the city's inhabitants as "about six-eighths Dutch, the remainder French and English." Although the British controlled the city, they did not dominate its population. In 1692, Charles Lowdich lamented that "our chiefest unhappyness here is too great a mixture of Nations, and English ye least part." With increasing immigration from the British Isles, the situation changed. By 1703, it was reported that less than fifty percent of the 818 heads of households were Dutch. In 1744, Dr. Alexander Hamilton, a visitor from Annapolis, commented that the Dutch were still entrenched in government and that their language and customs had begun to die out. Here, we find the first evidence of the often repeated phenomenon of ethnic succession so much a part of New York's history. At a particular moment in time, one ethnic group establishes its prominence; as its numbers dwindle, the next group of new immigrants replaces it in civic importance.

Another pattern, intermarriage, emerged. The British, Scots, and French found no difficulty marrying one another. On a rare occasion, a Jew would marry a gentile, but this would generally be scorned by both groups. There was no intermarriage of African-Americans and whites.

The Dutch prohibited public worship by Jews, Lutherans, and Quakers; the British allowed them to erect their own houses of worship; however, they excluded Catholics from this privilege.

New York became an American city when the revolutionary committee took over the municipal government in 1775; however, the British captured the city in 1776 and seven subsequent years of occupation delayed the process until 1783. When the British evacuated in November of that year, they left a physically and economically devastated city. In the period between the Revolutionary War and the War of 1812, New York was more an American city, in the sense that its ethnic population reflected the nation as a whole, than at any other time in its history. Between 1790 and 1820, the city's population soared from 33,131 to 123,706. Two groups contributed to this growth: New Englanders and Irish immigrants.

As New York's population continued to grow, the city's ethnic diversity became a magnet for immigrants who saw it as a place where they could associate with their own people while gaining access to economic opportunity. What immigrants found in the early nineteenth century holds true today.

p. 10: Depiction of a sea monster thought to be inhabiting the North Atlantic, 1550; LC. Below: A seaman taking the altitude by observing a star with a cross-staff, also about 1550; LC.
Preceding pages: New York as seen from Brooklyn Heights, about 1717, drawn by William Burgis; NYPL.

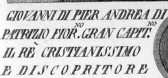

GIOVANNI DI PIER ANDREA DI   BERNARDO DA VERRAZZANO
PATRIZIO FIOR. GRAN CAPIT.^{no}   COMANDANTE IN MARE PER
IL RÈ CRISTIANISSIMO   FRANCESCO PRIMO,
E DISCOPRITORE   DELLA NUOVA FRANCIA.
nato circa il MCDLXXV.   morto nel MDXXV.
Dedicato al merito sing.^{re} dell' Illmo e Rev.^{mo} Sig.^{re} Lodovico da Verrazzano
Patrizio, e Canonico Fiorentino Agnato del Med.^o
Preso dal Quadro Originale in Tela esistente presso la sud.^a Nobil Famiglia.
G. Zocchi del.   F. Allegrini inci. 1767

1.

The European Encounter with New York

2.

New York City is a product of the Western European Age of Exploration, which began at the end of the fifteenth century. For years European fishermen had sailed to the North Atlantic, searching for cod. Although territorial land wars continued to be fought by emerging European nation-states, changing social, economic, and political conditions gave impetus to the search for non-European areas for trade and conquest. In the Western Hemisphere there was a north-south division: The Spanish and Portuguese explored the Caribbean and Central and South America, the English, Dutch, and French explored the east coast of North America. The Spanish and Portuguese pursued silver and gold, while the English, French, and Dutch sought fish and furs. Soon after Columbus's voyages, the Spanish and Portuguese had established colonies in the Caribbean and Central and South America. While the others were exploring the unexplored, the Spanish were building cities with elaborate churches and civic buildings. The Europeans shared an attitude toward native peoples: They were to be conquered and exploited.

Products of the Italian Renaissance, Italian explorers were engaged by the British (John Cabot), French (Giovanni da Verrazano), Portuguese (Amerigo Vespucci), and Spaniards (Christopher Columbus) to lead their voyages of discovery. Verrazano, a member of a prominent Florentine family with wide trade and banking connections, was an expert navigator. In the service of François I of France, he made an exploratory voyage along the east coast of North

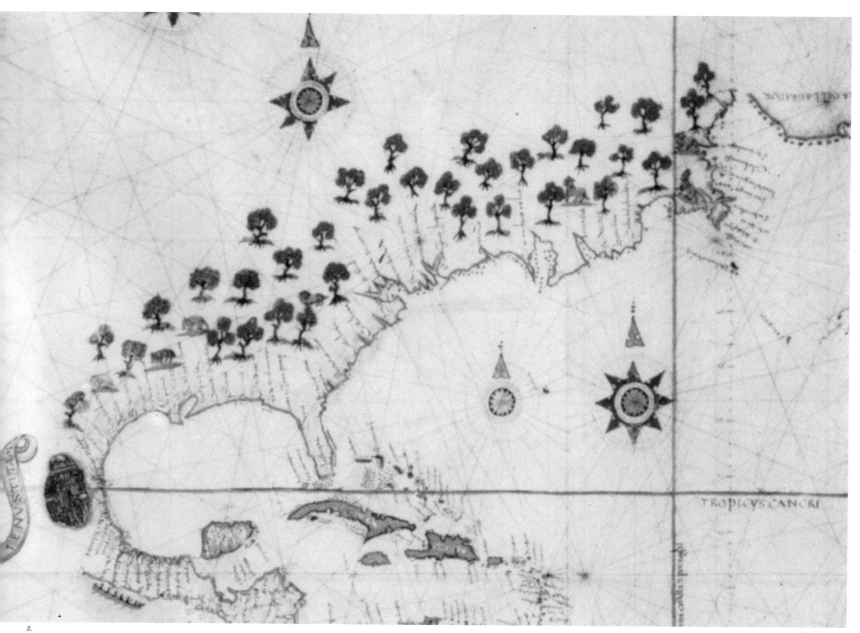

3.

America in 1524. In the course of that voyage he was the first European to enter and describe New York Bay and the Hudson River and to make contact with the Native Americans who had inhabited the region for some ten thousand years. When Verrazano arrived, the Indians residing in the area, which has since become New York, had settlements of bark- or grass-covered longhouses and were raising corn, beans, and squash. They had created an extensive network of footpaths that linked the immediate area. According to Algonquian lore, Broadway (Wiechquaekeck) was one of these trails used for trade.

1. Giovanni da Verrazano, drawn by G. Zocchi and engraved by F. Allegrini, 1767; PML. Verrazano arrived in New York Harbor in 1524, the year that Michelangelo began work on the Medici Library (Biblioteca Mediceo Laurenziana) in Florence.
2. Armaments for the warpath, from Samuel Champlain, Voyages et découvertes, *1620; LC. Champlain made drawings from observation, rather than secondhand descriptions, as was the case with most other depictions of Indians. In these drawings of Indians living north of New York City, there is a resemblance to Verrazano's description.*
3. East coast of North America and the Gulf of Mexico, from the Salviati world map, about 1525; BML.

VERRAZANO SIGHTS NEW YORK
"... we found a very agreeable situation located within two small prominent hills [entrance to New York Harbor], in the midst of which flowed to the sea a very great river [Hudson River], which was deep within the mouth; and from the sea to the hills of that [place] with the rising of the tides, which we found eight feet, any laden ship might have passed. . . . We were with the small boat, entering the said river to the land, which we found much populated. The people, almost like the others, clothed with the feathers of birds of various colors, came toward us joyfully, uttering very great exclamations of admiration. . . . [W]e were forced to return to the ship leaving said land. . . ."
GIOVANNI DA VERRAZANO, "CELLERE CODEX"

13

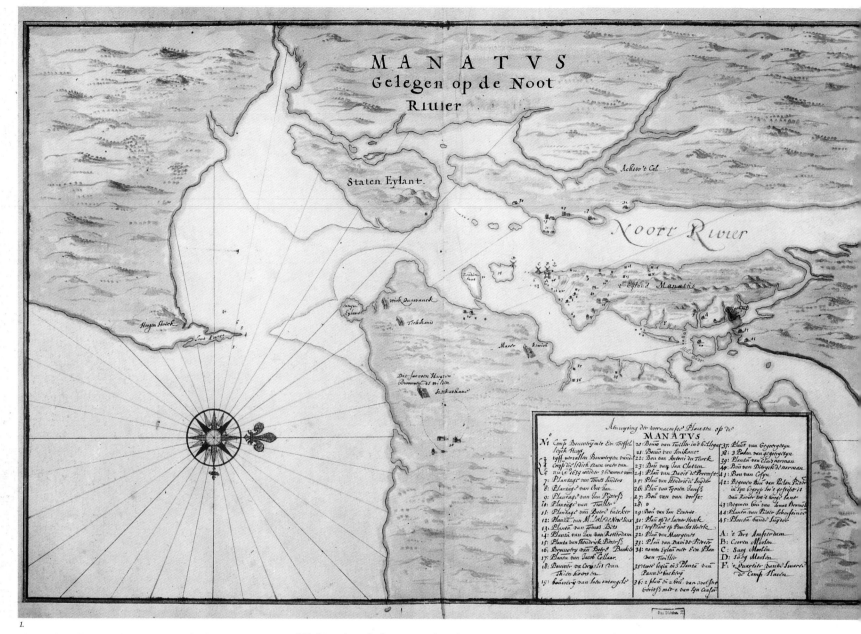

MANATVS
Gelegen op de Noot
Riuier

Staten Eylant.

Noort Rivier

1.

The Dutch Colony

Within the shifting sands of European battles for power, the 1607 Dutch defeat of the Spanish fleet at Gibraltar made the Dutch a more significant contender in the exploration of the North American continent. In 1609 Henry Hudson (a British explorer) entered into a contract with the Dutch East India Company to finance a voyage of discovery in which he was to seek a new route to the Indies along the northern coast of Russia and Siberia. Unable to make this passage because of ice, he headed south to the east coast of North America, and explored the region from New England to the Carolinas. He sailed into New York Harbor, anchored for thirteen days, and established contact with the Indians. Seeking the elusive passage to India, Hudson sailed up what the Dutch called the

North (Hudson) River; he later abandoned this quest. With an interest in the lucrative fur trade, the Dutch had established an irregular presence on Manhattan Island from 1614. In 1626 they negotiated a formal purchase of the island from the Indians, creating Fort Amsterdam, the first permanent European presence on the island in New York Harbor.

The colony was settled by about thirty families, mostly French-speaking Walloons; shortly thereafter Dutch, German, British, and Scandinavian immigrants began to arrive. The Dutch government exerted pressure on the West India Company to relax its monopolistic practices and encourage more settlers so that the colony might grow and prosper. Although Northern Europeans were the majority, African-Americans came as

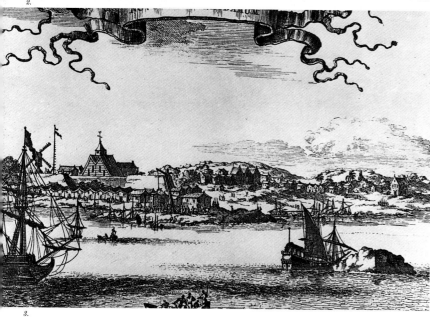

slaves in 1626; by 1644 the West India Company had granted freedom to some of them. In 1654 twenty-three Sephardic Jews came and in 1657 the first Quakers arrived. Until Dutch rule ended in 1664, at least one-half of the population was Dutch.

1. Manhattan lying on the North River, about 1670 (copy of a previous map made in 1639); LC. This map indicates an early pattern of segregation. African slaves were housed at Point F (opposite what is now Roosevelt Island) beyond the precincts of the other settlers. Indian longhouses were situated at a distance on Long Island (now Brooklyn).
2. Dutch merchant ships, 1647; MCNY.
3. View of New Amsterdam, 1650; MCNY.
4. Cornelius Steenwyck, a leading merchant who served as a burgomaster, about 1660; NYHS.

A DUTCH APPRAISAL OF THE INDIANS
"... the Wappenos.

"These tribes of savages all have a government. The men in general are rather tall, well proportioned in their limbs, and of an orange color, like the Brazilians; very inveterate against those whom they hate; cruel by nature, and so inclined to freedom that they cannot by any means be brought to work; they support themselves by hunting, and when the spring comes, by fishing. In April, May, and June, they follow the course of these [the fish], which they catch with a drag-net they themselves knit very neatly, of the wild hemp, from which the women and old men spin the thread."
LETTER OF ISAACK DE RASIERES TO SAMUEL BLOOMMAERT, 1628 (?)

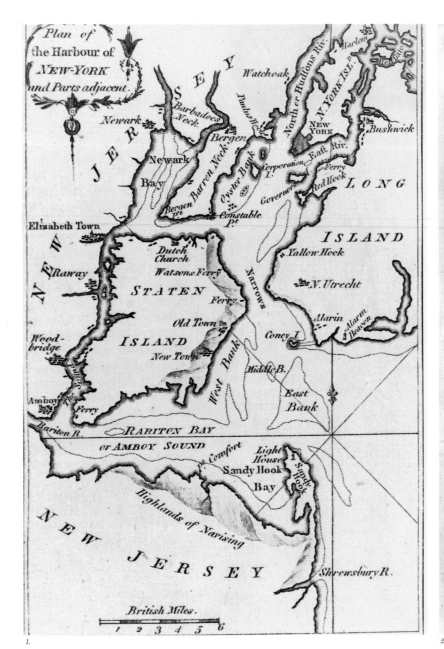

To the Honourable
RIP VAN DAM, Esqr.
PRESIDENT of His Majesty's Council for the PROVINCE of NEW YORK
This View of the New Dutch Church is most humbly
Dedicated by your Honours most Obedient Servt Wm Burgis

Becoming a British Colony

On September 8, 1664, the British captured the Dutch West India Company's colony of New Amsterdam and renamed it New York after King Charles II's brother, the Duke of York. Although English became the official language, many of the institutions, customs, and business practices instituted by the Dutch persisted.

The British conquest of Dutch New Amsterdam set a model that was to be repeated time and again in New York. The first group to arrive establishes social and cultural patterns. The new arrivals are compelled to adapt to those social and cultural patterns. In the process of adaptation the new arrivals contribute to a shared culture.

Although victors, the British remained a minority. As late as 1695 tax records indicate that the Dutch represented 58 percent of the population, the British were 29.5 percent, the French Huguenots 11 percent, and the Jews 1 percent. According to the 1698 census, of the 4,937 people living in New York County, 700 were African-Americans, while 296 of Brooklyn's 2,017 residents, were blacks. Religious diversity was evident. In 1678 Governor Edmund Andros said: "There are Religions of all sorts, one church of England, several Presbiterians & Independents, Quakers and Anabaptists of Several sects, some Jews but presbiterians & Independents most numerous & Substantiall."

3.

4.

1. *"Plan of the Harbour of New York and Parts adjacent,"* undated; SIHS.

2. *View of the New Dutch Church, drawn and possibly engraved by William Burgis, 1731; MMA. This Dutch church and Dutch names with adapted English spellings indicate the merging of these two cultures.*

3. *Reverend William Vesey, the first rector of Trinity Church; TC. A native of Massachusetts, Vessey was ordained deacon and priest by the bishop of London. He was inducted as rector on December 25, 1697, in the Dutch church since Trinity was not yet completed. He served the parish until 1746.*

4. *Mary Spratt Provoost Alexander, about 1750; MCNY. Her mother was Dutch, and her father Scottish. Her second husband was attorney James Alexander, a native of Scotland.*

"New York is built most of Brick and Stone, and covered with red and black Tile, and the Land being high, it gives at a distance a pleasing Aspect to the spectators. The inhabitants consist most of *English* and *Dutch*, and have a considerable Trade with the *Indians*, for *Bevers, Otter, Raccoon* skins, with other Furrs; As also for *Bear, Deer* and *Elke* skins; and are supplied with Venison and Fowl in the Winter, and Fish in the Summer by the *Indians*, which they buy at an easie rate; And having the Countrey roundabout them, they are continually furnished with all such provisions as needful for the life of man, not only by the *English* and *Dutch* . . . but . . . by the Adjacent Colonies."
DANIEL DENTON, *A BRIEF DESCRIPTION OF NEW-YORK: FORMERLY CALLED NEW-NETHERLANDS,* 1670

17

1.

2.

Two Patterns Emerge: Diversity and Intermarriage

The British ruled, but the society that they governed was not homogeneous. It was increasingly composed of diversified groups of people. Diversity was measured by both ethnicity and religious affiliation. In 1731, the New-York Gazette reported mortality statistics from a smallpox epidemic in terms of religious burials. A total of 475 deaths assigned to religious cemeteries was broken down in this way: Church of England, 229; Dutch Church, 212; French Church, 15; Presbyterians, 16, with Lutherans, Quakers, Baptists, and Jews each having only a few.

Although there continued to be a sense of ethnicity, intermarriage occurred and identities were merged. There were Dutch who married English and English who married Dutch. There were French and Scots who married both Dutch and English. On rare occasions a Jew would marry a Gentile, but this would generally be scorned by both groups.

3.

4.

1. Cadwallader Colden, portrait by John Wollaston, 1749–1752; MMA. Born in Scotland, a graduate of the University of Edinburgh, Colden was a colonial official, an author, and a scientist.

2. Edward Hyde in woman's attire, about 1705; NYHS. Hyde served as governor of the colonies of New York and New Jersey from 1702 to 1708. A label on the painting states: "Among other apish tricks, Lord Cornbury, the half-witted son of Henry Earl of Clarendon, is said to have held his state levees at New York, and received the principal Colonists dressed up in complete female court costume."

3. Anthony Duane, between 1725–1730; NYHS. Born in Galway, Ireland, Duane, after serving in the British navy, settled in New York City, where he had a successful career in commerce. He was a member of the Trinity Church vestry.

4. Augustus Jay, about 1725; NYHS. Born in La Rochelle, France, he was one of the city's most succcessful Huguenot merchants. He was married in the Dutch Reformed Church, then became elder of the French Church and later was a member of Trinity Church.

19

City of New-York, *ss.*

A LAW

For Regulating Negroes and Slaves in the Night Time.

BE It Ordained by the Mayor, Recorder, Aldermen and Affiftants of the City of New-York, convened in Common-Council, and it is hereby Ordained by the Authority of the fame, That from hence-forth no Negro, Mulatto or Indian Slave, above the Age of Fourteen Years, do prefume to be or appear in any of the Streets of this City, on the South-fide of the Frefh-Water, in the Night time, above an hour after Sun-fet; And that if any fuch Negro, Mulatto or Indian Slave or Slaves, as aforefaid, fhall be found in any of the Streets of this City, or in any other Place, on the South fide of the Frefh-Water, in the Night-time, above one hour after Sun-fet, without a Lanthorn and lighted Candle in it, fo as the light thereof may be plainly feen (and not in company with his, her or their Mafter or Miftrefs, or fome White Perfon or White Servant belonging to the Family whofe Slave he or fhe is, or in whofe Service he or fhe then are) That then and in fuch cafe it fhall and may be lawful for any of his Majefty's Subjects within the faid City to apprehend fuch Slave or Slaves, not having fuch Lanthorn and Candle, and forth-with carry him, her or them before the Mayor or Recorder, or any one of the Aldermen of the faid City (if at a feafonable hour) and if at an unfeafonable hour, to the Watch-houfe, there to be confined until the next Morning) who are hereby authorized, upon Proof of the Offence, to commit fuch Slave or Slaves to the common Goal, for fuch his, her or their Contempt, and there to remain until the Mafter, Miftrefs or Owner of every fuch Slave or Slaves, fhall pay to the Perfon or Perfons who apprehended and ~~committed~~ *convicted* every fuch Slave or Slaves, the Sum of *Four Shillings* current Money of *New-York*, for his, her or their pains and Trouble therein, with Reafonable Charges of Profecution.

And be it further Ordained by the Authority aforefaid, That every Slave or Slaves that fhall be convicted of the Offence aforefaid, before he, fhe or they be difcharged out of Cuftody, fhall be Whipped at the Publick Whipping-Poft (not exceeding *Forty Lashes*) if defired by the Mafter or Owner of fuch Slave or Slaves.

Provided always, and it is the intent hereof, That if two or more Slaves (Not exceeding the Number of Three) be together in any lawful Employ or Labour for the Service of their *Mafter* or Miftrefs (and not otherwife) and only one of them have and carry fuch Lanthorn with a lighted Candle therein, the other Slaves in fuch Compay not carrying a Lanthorn and lighted Candle, fhall not be conftrued and intended to be within the meaning and Penalty of this Law, any thing in this Law contained to the contrary hereof in any wife notwithftanding. *Dated at the City-Hall this Two and Twentieth Day of April, in the fourth year of His Majefty's Reign,* Annoq; Domini **1731.**

By Order of Common Council,

Will. Sharpas, *Cl.*

African Slaves and Freed Blacks

The first African-Americans arrived in New Amsterdam as slaves in 1626, two years after the colony had been established. In 1628 there were 14 blacks out of a total population of 270.

The slave trade was international. Some slaves came directly from Africa, others were picked up in Curaçao, and some were taken from foreign ships captured by Dutch privateers. Dutch, French, and Spanish ships delivered slave cargoes to New Amsterdam. In 1644 eleven slaves and their wives were given partial manumission. Although limited freedom offered advantages, they were required to make annual payments to the Dutch West India Company.

After the British gained control of New Amsterdam in 1664, the plight of slaves worsened. Most freed blacks were disenfranchised, and public assembly of more than three blacks or Native Americans was considered illegal. By 1698 there were approximately two thousand slaves in the New York metropolitan region. In the early eighteenth century there was a "slave market" on Wall Street where black and Native American slaves gathered to seek outside employment. It was "a place of meeting when their masters had no work for them."

There was resistance; there were revolts and runaways. A 1712 slave uprising left seven whites dead and nineteen blacks executed. The frequency of newspaper ads seeking runaways indicates that they were numerous. In 1781 the New York Manumission Society was formed to bring an end to slavery. Six years later the society opened an African free school to provide "for the

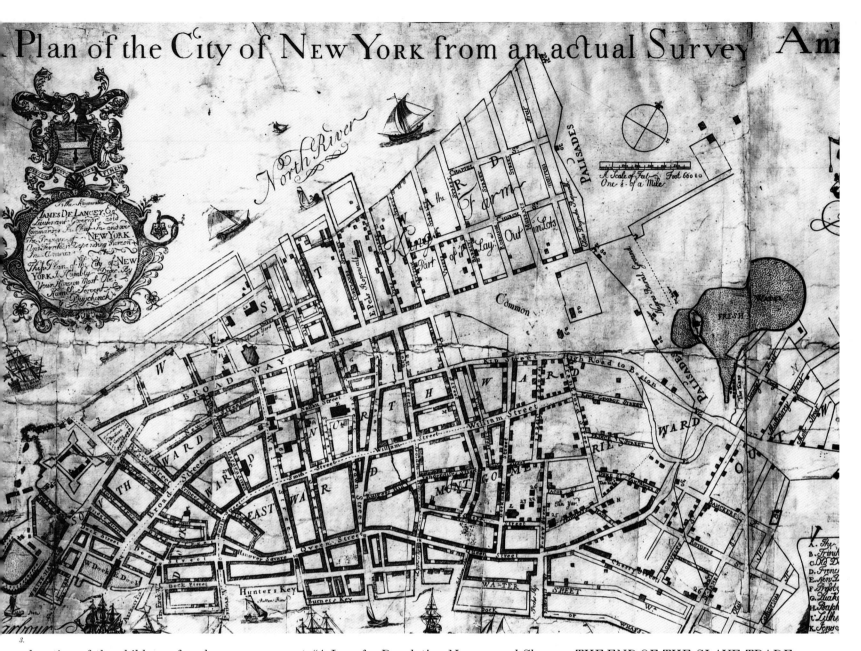

3.

education of the children of such persons as have been liberated from bondage, that they may hereafter become useful members of the community." By 1834 the society operated seven schools, which were transferred to the New York Public School Society in that year.

By 1790 there were 9,447 slaves and 3,573 free blacks in the six southern counties of New York. In 1799 the state legislature enacted the Gradual Manumission Act. A federal law ended the country's participation in the slave trade on January 1, 1808.

1. "A Law for Regulating Negroes and Slaves in the Night Time," 1731, NYPL.
2. Peter Williams, about 1810; NYHS. Born a slave, Williams became sexton of the John Street Methodist Church. He and his wife were given their freedom in 1796, after which he opened a tobacconist's shop on Liberty Street. He was one of the founders of Zion Church, a black Methodist congregation.
3. The Maerschalck or Duyckink Plan, 1755; NYHS. In the center of the right edge of this map can be seen a large irregular shape, "Fresh Water." Immediately to its south was the Negro burial ground. Nearly 390 of a possible 600 total burials were recently removed by archaeologists engaged by the African Burial Ground Project.

THE END OF THE SLAVE TRADE
"Fathers, brethen, and fellow citizens: At this auspicious moment I felicitate you on the abolition of the slave trade. This inhuman branch of commerce which, for some centuries past, has been carried on a considerable extent is, by the singular interposition of divine providence, this day extinguished, An event so important so pregnant with happy consequences, must be extremely consonant to every philanthropic heart.

"[T]his abominable traffic . . . has made, if not ourselves, our forefathers and kinsmen its unhappy victims and pronounced on them and their posterity, the sentence of perpetual slavery."
REVEREND PETER WILLIAMS, JR., AT THE AFRICAN CHURCH, JANUARY 1, 1808

21

Colonial Jews

Twenty-three Sephardic Jews arrived in New Amsterdam in 1654, establishing the first permanent Jewish settlement in North America. Since 1492, when the Inquisition expelled all Jews from Spain, Sephardic Jews had been wandering through the Mediterranean region, Western Europe, the Caribbean, and South America, seeking havens. Some had settled in the Dutch colony of Recife in Brazil. When the Portuguese overwhelmed the Dutch, Jews had to flee. Some arrived in New Amsterdam because the Dutch had been sympathetic to the flight of Jews from Spain. Although they were allowed to enter New Amsterdam, Governor Peter Stuyvesant protested their remaining. As a result of a petition by Jewish Dutch stockholders of the Dutch West India Company, Stuyvesant was com-

pelled to permit them to stay. Their acceptance in Dutch and British communities evolved slowly. In July 1655 they were given permission to purchase land for their own cemetery. In 1657 Asser Levy, after petition, was permitted to serve as a guard and admitted as a burgher. In 1690 they were permitted to worship in a special building on Beaver Street. By 1695 there were known to be 20 Jewish families. In 1730 the first Jewish synagogue building in America was opened on Mill Street. By 1750 there were an estimated 300 Jews; in 1790, they numbered between 1,300 and 1,500.

Books & Stationary,

FOR SALE BY

BENJAMIN GOMEZ,

No. 97, MAIDEN-LANE.

Among which are the following:

The PRACTICAL NAVIGATOR, and

SEAMAN's NEW DAILY ASSISTANT.

Lateſt London Edition.

*1. David and Phila Franks, about 1735;
AJHS. Phila, daughter of Abigail and David
Franks, shocked her parents by secretly mar-
rying a Gentile, Oliver Delancey.*

*2. Jacob Franks, about 1740; AJHS. Husband
of Abigail, Franks was one of New York's
wealthiest merchants.*

*3. Prayer book for the Jewish holidays, pub-
lished in New York in 1761; AJHS.*

*4. Bilhah Abigail Franks, about 1740; AJHS.
She was the wife of Jacob and the mother of
nine, including David and Phila.*

*5. Detail from an advertisement for Benjamin
Gomez, bookseller, 1791; AJHS. Gomez was
the first Jewish American bookseller; he
opened his shop in 1791.*

*6. New Game of the Jew (anti-Semitic board
game), eighteenth century; LC.*

HER DAUGHTER MARRIES A GENTILE

". . . I am now retired from town and would
from my self (if it were possiable to have
some peace of mind) from the severe afflic-
tion I am under on the conduct of that
unhappy girle [your sister Phila]. Good God,
wath a shock it was when they acquainted
me she had left the house and had bin married six months. I can hardly hold my pen
whilst I am a writing it. Itt's wath I never
could have imagined, especialy after wath I
heard her soe often say, that noe consideration in life should ever induce her to dis-
oblige such good parents.

"I had heard the report of her goeing to
be married to Oliver Delancey, but as such
reports had offten bin off either off your sisters [Phila and Richa], I gave noe heed to it
further than a generall caution of her con-

duct wich has allways bin unblemish'd, and
is soe still in the eye of the Christians whoe
allow she had disobliged us but has in noe
way bin dishonorable, being married to a
man of worth and character.

"My spirits was for some time so depresst
that it was a pain to me to speak or see any
one. I have over come it soe far as not to
make my concern soe conspicuous but I
shall never that serenity nor peace within I
have soe happyly had hittherto. My house
has been my prisson ever since. I had not
heart enough to goe near the street door. Its
a pain to me to think off goeing again to
town, and if your father's business would
permit him to live out of it I would never
goe near it again. I wish it was in my power
to leave this part of the world."

ABIGAIL FRANKS TO HER SON, JUNE 7, 1743

1.

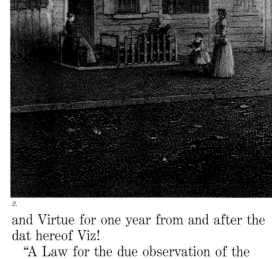

2.

The Year 1768

COMMON COUNCIL. DECEMBER 13, 1768

"[Aldermen Present:] Whitehead Hicks, Esq., Mayor, George Brewerton, Cornelius Roosevelt, Benjamin Blagg, Elias Des Brosses, Andrew Gotier, Abraham P. Lott. [Assistants Present:] Jacob Brewerton, Benjamin Huggit, Mathew Buyce, John Abeel, James Van Varick, Peter T. Curtenius, Huybert Van Wagenen.

"Be it ordained by the Mayor Aldermen & Commonalty of the City of New York, Convened in Common Council and it [is] hereby ordained by the Authority of the Same that the following Laws orders and ordinances of this Corporation be Renewed Established and published and that the Same do Continue and Remain in full force

and Virtue for one year from and after the dat hereof Viz!

"A Law for the due observation of the Lords day Called Sunday.

"A Law to prevent Strangers from being a Charge to this Corporation.

"A Law to appoint Sworn Surveyors of this City.

"A Law for Better preventing of Fires.

"A Law for marking of Bread.

"A Law prohibiting the Sale of Meal and flower by measure and for appointing proper places for the Sale of meal, flour, Corn & Grain.

"A law for Regulating negroes Mulattoes and other Slaves. . . .

"A Law for paving and Cleansing the Streets Lanes and Alleys within the City of

New York, and for preventing Nusances within the Same.

"A Law prohibiting Hawkers and Pedlers. . . .

"A Law to restrain and prohibit the Giving or Selling of Strong Liquors to any of the private Centinals of his majestys Garrison of the City of New York."

1. Map of New York, surveyed in the years 1766–1767; NYPL.
2. As seen in 1768, the south side of John Street between William and Nassau streets, painted by Joseph Smith in 1817; MCNY.

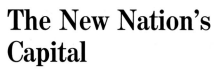

The New Nation's Capital

At the beginning of the revolutionary movement a large proportion of New York's elite was openly in support of the Sons of Liberty. The patriot party in New York was more aristocratic than in New England. During the Stamp Act period Livingstons and Delanceys were engaged in a heated contest to lead the struggle against British tyranny. Finding it difficult for himself to associate with more common people, James Delancey withdrew and formed his own Sons of Liberty. The radicals disdained the role of the Livingstons and Delanceys, saying that they had no right to call themselves Sons of Liberty. Of all the port cities, New York originally enforced the Nonimportation Agreement most rigorously. Later the wealthy merchants, suffering from an absence of trade, abandoned their boycott.

By 1775 some Americans were preparing for military action against the British oppressors while others were weighing the option of reconciling colonial liberty with British sovereignty. For a decade Americans sought to defend their rights by methods short of war. When fighting began at Lexington and Concord, the possibility of restraining the dispute between the mother country and the colonies evaporated. The radicals and the merchant elite abandoned their unity. Confrontation expanded; the American Revolution became a war of secession. When the British commander Sir William Howe moved his troops out of Boston in 1776, General George Washington prepared for a British invasion and moved his troops to New York City. Losing his first battles, Washington withdrew, and the

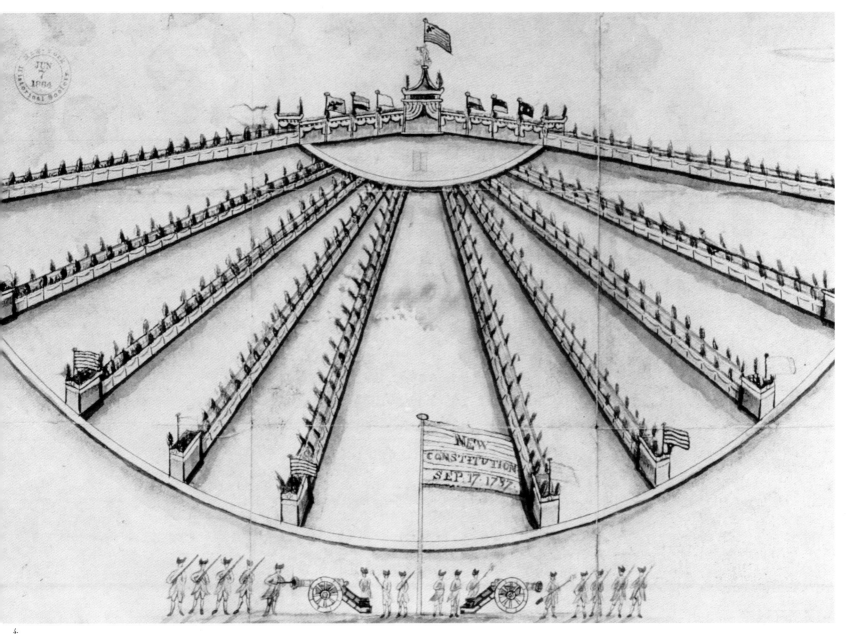

4.

British occupied New York City. The British retained control of New York from 1776 until Cornwallis's defeat in 1781. New York was the center of British authority in America. During the British occupation there were Tories who supported it and profited by it, and there were republicans who opposed it. Philadelphia was the seat of the Continental Congress and the birthplace of the Declaration of Independence, When fighting ended, a new federal government was formed. New York served as the new nation's capital in 1789 and 1790.

1. General George Washington taking the oath of office as first president of the United States, Federal Hall, Wall Street, 1789; MMA. John Adams was vice president, Thomas Jefferson was secretary of state, and Alexander Hamiliton was secretary of the treasury. This engraving by Amos Doolittle was issued in 1790.
2. Allegorical portait of General George Washington, depicted with Bowling Green, New York, in the background, 1783; MCNY.
3. Letter from George Washington to Jewish congregations, 1790; CMI. Having received congratulatory letters on his election as president from Jewish congregations in New York, Philadelphia, Charleston, and Richmond, Washington responded with this letter.
4. Federal banquet pavilion, 1788; NYHS.

Designed by Major Pierre Charles L'Enfant to accommodate more than five thousand people, this huge pavilion was erected near the present site of Broadway and Broome Street. The banquet was served in the afternoon of July 23, 1788 to all those who marched that day in the federal procession to indicate their support for the new Constitution.

27

1.

2.

Bankers, Brokers, Entrepreneurs, Lawyers, and Wall Street

During the course of its first two centuries the economic profile of New York shifted from trading post to port city. Under British rule, Boston, Charleston, Philadelphia, and New York were the principal colonial ports. Because of its isolation under British occupation during the Revolutionary War, the port of New York experienced some lean years when the war ended, while the ports of Boston and Philadelphia, which had been occupied sporadically, prospered. The wars in Europe at the end of the eighteenth and beginning of the nineteenth centuries created a boom period for all American ports. By 1797 New York had replaced Philadelphia as the leader in import-export tonnage.

In 1784 two events affected the future of the city. On February 22 the *Empress of China* sailed from New York to Canton, a

precursor of clipper ship trade, which arrived years later. On June 9, 1784, the Bank of New York was established, initiating an era of commercial banking that became a mainstay of the city's economy. In 1798 the Bank of New York opened its doors at William and Wall streets. In 1799 the Manhattan Company was established. Over the next two decades more banks began operations. At this time commercial banks performed a number of functions. They could receive deposits, lend capital, and facilitate trades between businesses through the use of discounted notes. Only chartered commercial banks could issue bank notes, which served as currency during the first half of the nineteenth century.

At the end of the Revolutionary War the economy of the United States was based

3.

primarily on agriculture. The cessation of hostilities provided the opportunity for westward expansion. The country was experiencing economic growth. During the 1790s banks, insurance companies, road construction companies, and mining companies were formed. In 1792 the New York Stock Exchange was founded; it created a formal mechanism for trading securities in which members agreed to trade with each other at minimum commission rates.

1. *Alexander Hamilton, after 1804; portrait by John Trumbull, NYHS. Hamilton could be described as one of the first of a long line of immigrant entrepreneurs who came to New York City from modest circumstances and became wealthy and eventually powerful in both business and politics. Born in Nevis, British West Indies, he studied at King's College (later Columbia College), married Elizabeth Schuyler, was a delegate to the Continental Congress, and served as the nation's first secretary of the treasury. From 1783 to 1790 he lived on Wall Street. On July 11, 1804, he lost his life in a duel with Aaron Burr.*
2. *Robert R. Livingston, Jr., 1804; portrait by John Vanderlyn, NYHS. A member of one of New York's most influential families, Livingston had a very distinguished career.*

He was a law partner of John Jay, recorder of the City of New York, and a delegate to the Continental Congress. As chief judge of the Court of Chancery of New York State he administered the presidential oath to George Washington. As Jefferson's minister to France he was involved in negotiations leading to the Louisiana Purchase, and he was a supporter of Robert Fulton's steamboat enterprises.
3. *Wall Street, 1780; NYHS. Depicted are the Bank of New York at 32 Wall Street, New York Insurance Company at 34 Wall Street, and Bank of United States branch, at 48 Wall Street.*

1.

2.

Some Prominent People: Clergyman, Mayor, Inventor and his Wife

1. John Christopher Kunze, 1818 (completed after his death, in 1807); portrait by John Wesley Jarvis, NYHS. A Lutheran clergyman and professor of Oriental languages at Columbia College, Kunze came to America from Saxony in 1770. He first served Lutheran churches in Philadelphia, then, in 1784, became minister of the Evangelical Lutheran Church on Frankfort Street. He was a scholar, classicist, and collector of coins and medals.

2. Richard Varick, undated; portrait by John Trumbull, MCNY. Born in Hackensack, New Jersey, Varick moved to New York in 1775. As a member of the Continental army he was an aide-de-camp to Benedict Arnold and later became George Washington's secretary. After holding city and state offices, in 1789, he was

appointed mayor of New York by Governor De Witt Clinton and served until 1801.

3. Robert Fulton, about 1806; portrait by or after Elizabeth Emmett, NYHS. Artist and inventor, Fulton was born in Lancaster County, Pennsylvania. In 1782 he began painting portraits in Philadelphia and four years later went to London to study with Benjamin West, then president of the Royal Academy. Becoming interested in mechanics and engineering, Fulton spent nine years (1787–1806) in Paris, where he designed Nautilus, *an underwater boat that was a prototype of the submarine. In Paris he met Robert R. Livingston, Jr., then the U.S. minister to France, who agreed to finance Fulton's experiments in steamboat technology and contracted with him to construct a steamboat*

3.

4.

to operate between New York and Albany.
After returning to America in December
1806, Fulton built the North River Steamboat (later called the Clermont). Powered
with a Watt steam engine, it began successful
passenger steamship service on August 17,
1807. Fulton is often called the inventor of the
steamboat; this was not the case. In France a
Watt engine had been installed on a boat as
early as 1776 and by 1783 there was a 150-
foot boat navigating the Saône River. In the
United States John Fitch had offered regular
passenger service on the Delaware River
between Philadelphia and up river towns in
the 1780s.

4. Harriet Livingston Fulton, portrait by
Robert Fulton, between 1810–1815; NYHS.
The daughter of Walter and Cornelia

(Schuyler) Livingston of Teviotdale, Livingston Manor, New Jersey. She was the niece of
Robert R. Livingston, Jr.

1.

2.

A City of Contrasts

In 1790 New York City's population totaled 33,131. By 1800 it had nearly doubled, reaching 60,489, and by 1810 it had increased another 50 percent, to 96,373. Between 1816 and 1825 it soared by 70 percent to 166,086. The great majority of new residents were New Englanders. In the midst of this cycle of ascending growth, there was a two-year plateau caused by the War of 1812 with Great Britain. The British set up a blockade off Sandy Hook, resulting in a standstill of foreign commerce and coastwise shipping. The fear that the British would attack the city never materialized. When news of the signing of the peace treaty in Ghent reached New York on February 11, 1815, there was jubilation with torchlight parades.

The end of the war assured New Yorkers of the city's resurgence as a dynamic center of foreign and domestic commerce. Immediately after the war British ships descended on the city, dumping their country's manufactured goods. Although New Yorkers assumed that the dumping would damage New York's economy, its effect was to the contrary; it stimulated growth. With a vibrant economy and growing population, New York was becoming more urban and more sophisticated. European culture was imported and presented in local theaters. As a consequence of the Revolution, some French dancers settled in the city. Lorenzo Da Ponte, Mozart's librettist for *The Marriage of Figaro, Don Giovanni,* and *Così Fan Tutte,* moved to the city in 1805. He was appointed the first professor of Italian at

Columbia College in 1830. Through his efforts, the first Italian opera companies were brought to this country.

At the same time that culture flourished, female prostitution could be found around the corner. The police office issued this notice in January 1813: "The Landlords, Tenants, and Occupiers of all houses of ill fame, situated in and about the neighborhood of East George-street, in the Seventh Ward, are hereby notified, that all houses of the above description, found west of Rutgers-street from and after the first day of May next, will become the particular objects of the vigilance of the Police, until they are suppressed."

PIGS IN THE STREETS

". . . The Yorkers look upon their City-Hall as a noble structure. . . . This building swells the Americans with pride, but by any Englishman it is little noticed; and if it stood in any of our inferior squares in London, it would be unknown, except to the person to whom it might accidentally belong. This little grass-plat which stands before it, which is called *the park*, is in the form of a triangle, fenced on all sides by a wooden paling. Hogs run about the streets of New-York in immense numbers—more numerous than children do in the country villages of England. This is an old established nuisance, of which thousands constantly complain, but to no purpose."
JOHN WILSON, STATEMENT OF NEW YORK, 1819

1. Interior of the Park Theatre, 1822; NYHS. The Park Theatre stood on Park Row directly opposite City Hall; it presented some of the most accomplished actors from England and America's most talented performers.
2. Broadway and City Hall, 1819; NYHS. Axel Klinckowstrom, the artist who depicted this scene, described it: "About a third of the length of the street [Broadway] from the Battery you come across a large 3-cornered place, which is shaded by beautiful trees. Here is the City Hall. It is built in a light and very pretty style. As I have made a correct drawing of this place and of Broadway and Chatham [Street] you will get a good idea of this part of New York, which really is attractive."

During the first half of the nineteenth century, territorial expansion became the American imperative. When the Revolutionary War ended in 1783, the United States consisted of a group of eastern seaboard colonies with a limited hinterland. By the middle of the next century, the area from the Atlantic to the Pacific Ocean, comprising the forty-eight states, was administered by the United States government. Areas that had been controlled by Native Americans, France, Mexico, and Spain were purchased or conquered and incorporated into American territory.

Between 1820 and 1880, the population of the United States increased by thirty million, nine million of whom were immigrants from Northern and Western Europe. In 1808, the United States Congress prohibited further importation of slaves. The New York State Legislature emancipated all slaves and eliminated the last vestiges of slavery in 1827. Union victory in the Civil War resolved the conflict between the contrasting economic systems of free-labor capitalism in the North and plantation slavery in the South. Post–Civil War industrial and agricultural expansion stimulated the American economy. By the 1880s networks of railroads linking the frontier with the eastern seaboard had been built. In less than a century, the American republic had been transformed from a struggling former colony into one of the world's major economic powers. New York City was an agent in this process of national transformation as well as a beneficiary of its consequences.

First and foremost, New York was a seaport. By 1797, it had surpassed both Boston and Philadelphia as the nation's leading port. New York maintained its dominance by formulating a strategy for bringing commerce to its wharves. Without producing many of the articles of commerce itself, New York became a center in which goods of every sort from every place were exchanged. Commerce dominated and many New Yorkers became rich from the profits, commissions, freights, and related services resulting from this volume of business activity.

It would be difficult to describe New York as a frontier town; however, the spirit of the frontier, with its fixation on growth and its appetite for exploitation of land, resources, and people, pervaded New York as much as it did the country elsewhere. Economic and physical growth were deemed to be virtues. Manhattan grew steadily northward, swallowing farms and estates that had shanty towns dotting their fringes. This frontier spirit is reflected in the name given to the luxury apartment building at 1 West 72nd Street; it was called the Dakota because of its location in the largely unbuilt Upper West Side and its remoteness from prime residential areas. A metropolitan region defined by a network of ferry boats emerged with Manhattan at its center, integrating parts of Brooklyn, Staten Island, the Bronx, Long Island, and New Jersey.

The seaport created a transportation nexus. DeWitt Clinton's dedication to the construction of the Erie Canal made it a reality. In 1825, the Erie Canal became New York City's direct link to the expanding Western frontier. Manufactured goods and people (mostly immigrants) moved westward, while agricultural products moved eastward. Soon after the canal was completed, railways were built along parallel routes.

Economic and physical growth require people. Between 1820 and 1880, New York City's population grew tenfold to 1,206,299, while Brooklyn's population grew sevenfold between 1845 and 1880 to 566,663. This growth can be attributed to several factors. In a period in which large families were common, there was a natural increase in population. A considerable number of people moved to New York from upstate and New England. Most significant was the dramatic influx of immigrants from Northern and Western Europe—with the largest number coming from Ireland and Germany. While the United States was experiencing territorial expansion and economic growth in the nineteenth century, Western Europe was in the midst of enormous economic, social, and physical dislocations wrought by the Industrial Revolution. These conditions provided a stimulus for Germans to emigrate. Ireland was suffering from the Great Famine and British oppression. Between 1845 and 1850, more than a million Irish died and more than another million emigrated, principally to the United States.

New York emerged as the principal port of entry for these emigrants with Boston, Philadelphia, Baltimore, and New Orleans accounting for the rest. In 1840, New York accommodated two-thirds of the 92,000 immigrants arriving in the United States. In 1860, New York continued to retain its cen-

Chapter Two
Frontier City: 1825–1880
The Irish and Germans
Leave Their Mark

trality; another two-thirds of the total of 131,000 came through New York. Although many of the new immigrants moved to other parts of the country, a considerable number remained in New York.

Since the Walloons established the Dutch West India Company colony in the early seventeenth century, New York had been a city of varied ethnic composition. However, few of these groups had attempted to define their ethnicity with a territory of their own. African-Americans were the exception; they had been segregated since their arrival in 1626. When the huge influx of Irish and Germans was added to the texture of New York's population, they created a pattern that has been repeated by every ethnic group coming to New York since that time. They created their own "immigrant ethnic" neighborhoods. The Irish moved into the Sixth Ward, bounded by Broadway on the west, Chatham Street on the south, Canal Street on the north, and the Bowery on the east. Know as "Little Ireland," the Sixth Ward included the notorious Five Points area. By 1855, the Irish accounted for forty-two percent of its residents.

The Germans created *Kleindeutschland* (Little Germany). Located on Manhattan's Lower East Side, it was bounded by Division Street on the south, Mott Street and the Bowery on the west, Fourteenth Street to the north, and the river on the east. Following the Revolution of 1848, German emigration accelerated. *Kleindeutschland* contained four times as many German immigrants in 1855 as it had ten years earlier. Although English had been

accepted as the common tongue by other immigrants, the Germans were the first large immigrant group who preferred to retain their native language. They attempted to maintain their own culture by establishing German-language newspapers, conducting their religious services in German, and creating their own food stores and restaurants. The German immigrant community was predominantly Protestant and Catholic; it contained a considerable number of Jews.

Most Irish and German immigrants lived in tenements. The existing housing stock could hardly accommodate the huge influx of new people. Some dwellings were converted into apartments and rooming houses. Newly constructed tenements offered miserable living conditions; they were crowded, lacked plumbing, and provided limited ventilation. The next wave of immigrants, Italians and Jews, inherited them.

In the fifty-five years between 1825 and 1880, much of New York's enduring character was formulated. Unquestionably America's premier city in size of population and magnitude of commerce, New Yorkers developed a sense of hauteur, similar to the post-Revolutionary Parisian bourgeoisie. Both Parisians and New Yorkers recognized the importance of their cities and identified with it.

Unlike major European cities of the time, with which New Yorkers often made a comparison, New York was a city of immigrants. In 1851, an observer wrote: "The city of New York is composed of inhabitants from all of the countries of Christendom."

The streets were noisy, crowded, and dirty.

In 1852, the *New York Daily Tribune* said of Broadway, "The more noise, the more confusion, the greater the crowd, the better the lookers on and the crowders seem to like it."

A city of stark contrasts, there were the very rich and the very poor. There were people living in mansions and people living in tenements; there were beggars, rag pickers, and thieves. Gangs controlled blocks of Lower Manhattan and honest, hard-working families lived around the corner.

Real estate speculators operated downtown where they initiated the tear down/build up cycle and uptown (above Forty-second Street) where they transformed farms and estates into apartments and mansions. There were tales of escalating values. In ten years, a house could be sold for ten times its purchase price.

Most of all, New York was seen as the city of opportunity. In the 1820s, Samuel F. B. Morse selected New York over Boston or Philadelphia because "it will be advantageous to me to be identified among her citizens as a painter." German immigrant John Jacob Astor became one of the world's richest men. Cornelius Vanderbilt of Staten Island built a railroad empire. Rags-to-riches stories abounded. The old rich whose fortunes were founded in colonial times described these successful entrepreneuers as "nouveaus."

p. 36: Knickerbocker Stage Line Omnibus, about 1850; painting by W. Seaman, NYHS. Below: Elevated locomotive, 1878; OYL. Preceding pages: Panoramic view of New York City, pen and ink by Edward Burckhardt, 1842–1845; NYHS.

1.

The Nation's Leading Port

In 1797 New York displaced Philadelphia as the nation's leading port. With completion of the Erie Canal in 1825, New York's position was guaranteed. First advocated in 1810 by then Mayor and later Governor De Witt Clinton, the canal was constructed between 1817 and 1825. As the canal's principal proponent Clinton managed to get the state legislature, by a margin of one vote, to appropriate the funds to build the canal. The labor force was a mixture of native-born Americans and European immigrants. Recruiters, offering wages of eighty cents a day, were sent to New York City to meet ships arriving from Ireland. Irish laborers, who began to arrive upstate in 1818, made up about a quarter of the work force.

With 123,706 residents in 1820 New York was the nation's largest city. While other ports handled exports, New York was dominant in distributing imports from Europe, China, and Latin America. Before the canal's completion, it cost $125 a ton to move freight from Albany to Buffalo. When the canal opened, the cost dropped to $5 per ton. The Erie Canal consolidated New York's economic lead, becoming the symbol of its national and international prominence. In 1824 Governor Clinton had predicted the canal's impact: "[The] City will in the course of time become the Granary of the western world, the emporium of commerce, the seat of manufacture, the focus of great moneyed operations, and the concentrating point of vast, disposable and accumulating capital which will stimulate, enliven, extend, reward the exertions of human labor and ingenuity."

On October 26, 1825, festivities to cele-

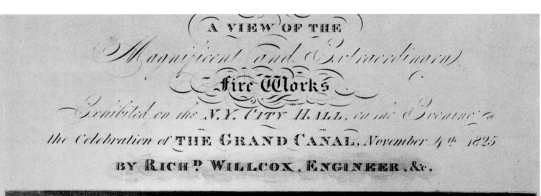

A VIEW OF THE

Magnificent and Extraordinary

Fire Works

Exhibited on the N.Y. CITY HALL, on the Evening of the Celebration of THE GRAND CANAL, November 4th 1825

BY RICHD. WILLCOX, ENGINEER, &c.

EXPLANATION.

The City Hall was illuminated with 1,542 wax candles, 454 lamps, and 310 variegated lamps; total 2,306. — To eclipse this great effusion of light was not within the powers of ordinary Fire works. Hence extraordinary means were employed, which consisted of 13 compounded Gerbs, each containing 58 lbs. of brilliant Chinese and Diamond fires, which changed alternately. These fires were supported by a back-ground of Spur Fire, which projected 1500 Brilliant Stars, intersecting each other in fanciful directions. During the evening were projected 320 4lb. Rockets; 30 9lb. and 24 20lb. Rockets; total 374; with a great variety of minor amusing pieces. The general bursts of simultaneous applause from a great concourse of citizens afford the best panegyric on the decided superiority of these Fire Works, both as to Extraordinary Grandeur and Brilliant Display.

brate completion of the canal commenced in Buffalo with Clinton leading the parade. Celebrations were held in canal towns along the way. The ceremonies were completed in New York City's harbor with a "Wedding of the Waters," in which waters from the world's great rivers were poured into the Atlantic Ocean. A parade said to be five miles long reached the Battery to welcome Clinton as he stepped ashore.

1. New York from Brooklyn Heights, 1837; NYPL.

2. Broadside commemorating Erie Canal completion ceremonies in New York City, 1825; NYHS. There were fireworks, and City Hall was illuminated with "1,542 wax candles, 454 lamps and 310 variegated lamps."

1.

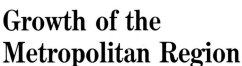

2.

Growth of the Metropolitan Region

New York's great natural harbor offered an advantage while the geographical division of its immediate region by wide rivers and large bodies of water was a disadvantage. Robert Fulton's steamboats contributed to the unification of the region. Manhattan's insular position made ferry service vital to its growth. In 1811 John Stevens began operating the *Juliana*, the world's first steam ferryboat, between Hoboken, New Jersey, and New York. By 1815 Fulton was operating the steam ferries *York and Jersey* between Manhattan and Jersey City and the *Nassau* on the East River between Brooklyn and Manhattan. Although the ferries were primarily for passengers, steam power contributed to moving freight throughout the metropolitan region.

New York became a center of steamboat construction. The hulls were built in area shipyards, and the engines and boilers in local ironworks. Around this industry grew a core of marine engineers and skilled mechanics. The Brooklyn Navy Yard began as a U.S. government entity in 1801. Utilizing this pool of talent, it expanded its operations to become a large industrial complex.

In 1790 the population of Kings County was 4,495. By 1830 it had reached 20,535, of whom 15,394 lived in Brooklyn. Within Kings County there were 1,479 slaves in 1800 and 879 in 1820. In 1834 Brooklyn became a city within Kings County. At this time Brooklyn grew more rapidly than the other towns in Kings County because its growth was tied to New York's rapid expansion.

The Bronx, which was primarily agricultural, growing wheat and raising livestock, saw its population rise from 1,755 in 1800 to 3,023 in 1830.

Between 1800 and 1830 the population of Queens, another area of farms and agricultural villages, rose from 5,791 to 7,806. Queens's access to urban markets was improved by the construction of six turnpikes between 1801 and 1826, with two running end to end between Flushing and Brooklyn through Newtown and two more from Jamaica to Brooklyn.

Staten Island's economy was primarily agriculture and fishing. When ferries linking it to New York were established, its growth accelerated.

1. Map of New York and its vicinity, 1835; MCNY.
2. View of South Street from Maiden Lane, about 1828; MMA. New York was a thriving port, and South Street was the center of its shipping industry. A few blocks away on Wall Street were banks and brokerage houses. In 1825, the year of the Erie Canal's opening, about five hundred new businesses began operations in this area.
3. Brooklyn Navy Yard, about 1850; QBPL.
4. Brooklyn as seen from the foot of Wall Street, 1853; QBPL.

"On Sunday last commenced running the new and beautiful steamboat Nassau, as a ferry boat between New York and Brooklyn. This noble boat passed the expectations of the public in the rapidity of her movements. Her trips varied from five to twelve minutes, according to tide and weather. The inhabitants of Long Island, particularly, will find this a most interesting improvement as the ferries heretofore, however well conducted, have been inconvenient, and to many a subject of dread. Carriages and wagons, however crowded, pass on and off the boat with the same facility as in passing a bridge. There is a spacious room below where passengers may secure from the weather."
LONG ISLAND STAR, MAY 11, 1814

1.

2.

3.

The Irish and the Germans Arrive

In the post-Revolutionary War period, New York City's population quadrupled in a thirty-year period from 33,131 in 1790 to 123,706 in 1820. The most important new group arriving in New York was New Englanders, not Europeans. However, this soon changed.

In 1820, 10,000 foreigners (immigrants and travelers) were reported to have arrived in the United States. Of that number, 3,000 came through New York. By 1828 there were 19,000 arriving in New York. In 1842 the number was 110,000, and in 1845 it was 119,000. Although there had been an Irish presence in New York for more than a century, in 1845 it was estimated to be 70,000, the most numerous of any ethnic group residing in the city.

For many Irish, emigration was seen as

the only solution to their situation. Suffering from British oppression, primarily agricultural and dependent on one crop, potatoes, Ireland's population was increasing while its farming deteriorated. Between 1800 and 1845, Ireland's population doubled. Disaster struck between 1845 and 1850, the period of the Great Famine; more than a million perished and more than another million fled, mostly to the United States.

The German situation was different. The Germans came from a fragmented region of thirty-nine states and free cities making up the German Confederation. Following the Napoleonic Wars, there was a burst of emigration from some regions of the German Confederation. In succeeding years there was a slow but steady flow of German emigrants to the United States. By the 1830s

4.

5.

6.

the number had increased; in the 1840s it was a tidal wave, caused by the potato blight and dislocations resulting from industrialization. The failure of the Revolution of 1848 drove many liberal and radical German intellectuals, along with their peasant and artisan compatriots, into exile. In 1850 there were 56,140 German-born Americans in New York City.

1. Tapscott's Emigration and Foreign Exchange, broadside, 1859; NYHS. Liverpool was the principal port of debarkation for British and Irish emigrants.
2. Apprentice indenture for Patrick Fogarty to become a rigger, 1807; MCNY. Indenture committed an individual to work as an apprentice for a specified period of time.
3. The Bay and Harbor of New York, *1855; painting by Samuel B. Waugh, MCNY. Irish immigrants are seen arriving at the Battery.*
4. Registering German immigrants at Castle Garden, about 1870; NYHS.
5. German emigrants expressing wonder at the size of a building on the corner of Cedar Street, 1871; MCNY.
6. Arriving at Castle Garden, 1879; NYHS.

"The German immigrants seem altogether to be those who give the least trouble in the [Castle] Garden. They are willing, obey instructions, and try to help each other along. If one of their number is short a couple of dollars in the purchase of a railway ticket, it is seldom that he can not raise that by the assistance and cooperation of a few countrymen. The Irish are a little more troublesome from their innumerable and repeated questions; but the most troublesome and patience-exhausting fellow-creatures are undoubtedly the Swedes. They are an excellent class of people, and form excellent and most desirable citizens, but cause a great deal of trouble on their arrival."
HARPER'S NEW MONTHLY MAGAZINE, 1871

43

The Immigrant
Experience

The immigrant experience—the trauma of arriving in a foreign country, not knowing its language or customs, being processed by hostile bureaucrats and being preyed upon by people of their own ethnic background who stood ready to swindle them of their savings—is common to most American families no matter when they or their ancestors arrived in this country. During the seventeenth and eighteenth centuries, there was no central port of arrival. Boston, Philadelphia, New York, New Orleans, Baltimore and Charleston were ports for European immigrants. African-Americans, who arrived in large numbers, came through ports with slave markets.

As one of the consequences of the opening of the Erie Canal in 1825, New York City became the principal port of entry for immi-grants, many of whom settled in New York. Others made their way west, first by canal-boat and later by railroad. Of New York City's 202,589 residents in 1830, 17,773 were foreign-born. With more immigrants arriv-ing, the need for a central immigration pro-cessing center became apparent. In 1855 Castle Garden, formerly Castle Clinton, was adapted for that purpose.

Built as a fort at the Battery between 1808 and 1811 to protect New York from possible British invaders, it was given to the city in 1823 and converted into Castle Garden, which became a public space used for hosting large celebrations and present-ing theatrical events. Castle Garden provid-ed a variety of services for new immigrants: medical care, currency exchange, informa-tion about housing, employment, and travel

44

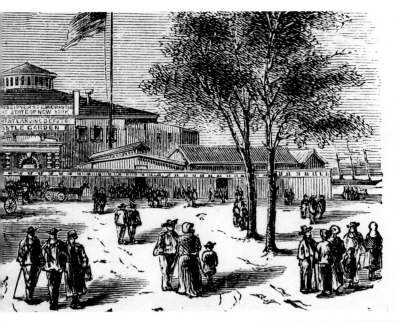

QUALIFICATIONS FOR
Naturalization.

FIRST.

Any Alien may be admitted a citizen on the following conditions:

First—By making in any court of record a declaration of his intention to become a citizen, and which must be made at least *three* years before his admission as a citizen.

Second—In addition to the declaration, he must have resided in the United States *five* years at least, before his admission, and within the State or Territory, where he makes his application, he must reside at least one year before making such application. His residence and good character must be proved, by two witnesses, citizens of the United States, *and in no case can the oath of the applicant be admitted to prove his residence.*
[Act of April 14, 1802.]

SECOND.

An alien under the age of twenty-one, who resided in the United States *three* years next preceding his coming of age, and shall have continued to reside therein, may be admitted a citizen on coming of age, after he shall have resided *five* years in the United States, including the *three* years of his minority, on proof of such residence, and that for the last *three* years it was his bona fide intention to become a citizen.
[Act of May 26, 1824.]

THIRD.

The children of persons naturalized, being under the age of 21 at the time of naturalization of their parents, and dwelling in the United States at the time of such naturalization, shall be considered citizens; and the children of citizens of the United States, though born out of the jurisdiction of the United States, shall also be considered citizens.
[Act of April 14, 1802.]

FOURTH.

If after an alien has declared his intention to become a citizen under the act of April 14, 1802, he die, his children shall be deemed citizens, notwithstanding their parent may not have been actually naturalized.
[Act of March 26, 1804.]

FIFTH.

All aliens arriving in the United States since Feb. 17, 1815, must have had a continued residence therein, for *five* years next preceding their admission as citizens, "*without being at any time during said five years out of the territory of the United States.*"
[Act of March 3d, 1813, Sec. 12.]

From the provisions of the act of April 14, 1802, requiring a previous declaration of intention, the following exceptions have been made, by which the Declaration of Intention is not required:

First—An alien who resided within the limits and jurisdiction of the United States before January 29, 1795, may be admitted a citizen on proof of residence of two years in the United States, and one year at least in the State where he applied for admission.

Second—Any alien who has resided within the limits and jurisdiction of the United States, between January 29, 1795, and June 18, 1798, may within two years from April 14, 1802, be admitted a citizen on proof of residence of two years within the United States.
[Act of April 14, 1802.]

Third—Any alien who has resided in the United States between June 18, 1798, and April 14, 1802, and continuing so to reside, may become a citizen on proof of a residence of two years.
[Act of March 26, 1816.]

Fourth—Any alien who resided in the United States between April 14, 1802, and June 18, 1812, and who has continued to reside within the same, may be admitted a citizen, provided he has resided within the limits of the United States before June 18, 1812, and who has continued to reside within the same, and his residence within the limits and under the jurisdiction of the United States for at least five years immediately preceding his application shall be proved by two witnesses, citizens of the United States, and also his places of residence during that time.
[Act of May 24, 1828.]

RESIDENCE.

In the case of Roosevelt vs. Kellogg, 20 Johnson's Reports, p. 210, the Court say, "A *resident* is synonimous with an *inhabitant*, one that resides in a place."

In the case of Fitzgerald, 2 Caime's Reports, p. 319, it was held that a subject of Great Britain, who had been several years trading in this country, was a non-resident here, the "intention of returning having never been laid aside."

In the case of Wrigley, 8 Wendell's Reports, page 134, the Court of Errors held that a man, who came to New York in 1821, and remained in business here till 1828 as a commission merchant, and then went to England, but returned and applied to our Courts here for a discharge under the Insolvent Act of this State, alleging that he was an inhabitant of this State, was *not an inhabitant* of this State.

James F. Wright, Printer, 74 Cedar st., N. Y.

---

to other parts of the country. In the absence of a Federal immigration service, it was operated by New York State. Between 1855 and 1889, more than 8,000,000 immigrants, primarily Irish, German, British and Scandanavian, were processed there.

Prior to the passage of the first federal naturalization law in 1790, the process of becoming a citizen was administered by individual states. That law stipulated that an applicant had to be a "free white person" who had resided for two years "within the limits and under the jurisdiction of the United States." A uniform national rule for acquiring citizenship existed, but the states were left free to fix the political and civil rights of immigrants until enactment of the Fourteenth Amendment in 1868.

1. Immigrants greeted by friends on arriving at Castle Garden, 1871; MCNY.
2. Immigrants leaving Castle Garden, 1871; MCNY.
3. Interior of Castle Garden immigration station, 1871; MCNY.
4. Exchange broker's office at Castle Garden, 1871; MCNY.
5. "Qualifications for Naturalization," broadside, 1828; NYHS.

"The steamer *Holland*, from Liverpool, had just arrived, and the steerage passengers were being landed. It was a motley, interesting throng. Slowly, one by one, the new-comers passed the two officers whose duty it was to register every immigrant's name, birthplace, and destination in large folios—a work that is often rather more difficult than it would first appear to be. In the first place, the officer in charge must be able to speak and understand nearly every language under the sun. This, however, can be learned and mastered; but then arises a second difficulty—the remarkable want of intelligence and the . . . misapprehension shown by some of the passengers.
HARPER'S NEW MONTHLY MAGAZINE, 1871

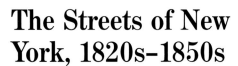

The Streets of New York, 1820s–1850s

"The city of New York is composed of inhabitants from all the countries of Christendom. Beyond a doubt a very large majority, perhaps nine-tenths, are natives of the United States, but it is not probable that one-third who live here first saw the light of day on the island of Manhattan. It is computed that one in three are natives of New England, or are descendants of those who have emigrated from that portion of the country. To these must be added the successors of the Dutch, the English, the French, the Scotch and the Irish, and not a few who came in their proper persons from countries occupied by these several nations. . . . it is exceedingly difficult to extract anything like a definite general character."

JAMES FENIMORE COOPER, *NATIONS OF THE AMERICANS*, 1827–1828

"The lower part of the city has a few narrow zig-zag cow-path streets, imitating somewhat our sister city to the East. But they are less crooked, and fewer of them. The upper part of the town is well laid out, all the streets being straight, running in parallel lines, and at right angles to those they cross. . . .

"Below 34th-street, we have 200 miles of paved streets, and this district embraces the most of the *paved* streets in town. The whole number of streets laid out, many of which are unopened, amount to 400, the aggregate length of which is about 500 miles. The streets are generally paved with round cobble stone, at an expense of fifty cents per square yard.

"*Wooden* pavements have been tried, by setting blocks about ten inches square, on

the ends. But they soon wear out and rot, and are laid aside. Any man who can invent such a method of paving as to preserve a smooth, unbroken, durable surface at *low price* will be sure of reaping a rich reward. . . .

"Neither would we have our pavements rough enough to lead the traveller to suppose, as he rides along in his sulky, that by some means or other he has got one wheel on top of the 'Blue Ridge,' and the other wheel on the crest of the 'Allegheny Mountains.'"

JOEL H. ROSS, *WHAT I SAW IN NEW YORK, OR A BIRD'S EYE VIEW OF CITY LIFE*, 1851

1. *Number 7 1/2 Bowery, about 1837–1839, NYHS.*
2. *The Times, 1837; NYHS. As a political cartoon this colored lithograph represents some buildings existing in New York at the time and provides a caricature of street life.*
3. *The Milkman, about 1840–1844; watercolor by Nicolino Calyo, MCNY.*
4. *The Ice Cart, about 1840; watercolor by Nicolino Calyo, MCNY.*
5. *Steamboat wharf, Battery Place, about 1831; NYHS.*
6. *The Cab, about 1840; watercolor by Nicolino Calyo, MCNY.*
7. *The Oyster Stand, about 1840–1844; watercolor by Nicolino Calyo, MCNY.*

City of Commerce and Industry

"The prosperity of New-York has always depended upon its commerce. It has indeed other sources of prosperity, in its manufactures, its buildings giving constant occupation to a great number of artisans and laborers, its schools, its public institutions and private residences; but these are only incidental, while commerce is the source of life and activity to the whole. This commerce is both foreign and domestic; penetrating by the latter to every village and neighborhood in the whole country, and reaching by the former to every portion of the habitable world. The commerce of western Europe and America has increased very greatly during the past half-century, and is still advancing with even accelerated rapidity. It is constantly opening new fields for its own enterprises as well as greatly enlarging those already occupied. Its facilities have almost immeasurably increased by the use of steam in navigation and on railroads. The most remote regions of the earth are now . . . accessible . . . with less difficulty than fifty years ago. . . . As a result of this facility of traveling and transportation, the business of commerce is concentrating at certain great central points. Merchants are eminently gregarious . . . as the facilities of passing from place to place are increased, they congregate in a common mart of trade."

A HISTORICAL SKETCH OF THE RISE AND PROGRESS OF THE METROPOLITAN CITY OF AMERICA, 1853

THE BLIND MUSICIAN

"You meet him in your walks when the cool shadows of morning stretch far over the pavement, pausing beneath some window which an early housekeeper has thrown open to receive the fresh air. Rosy and good-humoured, as people who rise early generally are, she receives the blind man's matin with a complacent smile, and throws him a few cents as she gives the last flourish of her dusting-cloth upon the window-sill. You meet him at noon-day; he has taken his place upon the crowded sidewalk, and undismayed by the rude jostle around him, the dust from rattling carts, or the rays of the August sun, which beats upon his head, the blind musician still pours forth his humble offering; while the little girl by his side watches unobtrusively the venetian blinds opposite, hoping each moment that some charitable hand will unclose them. You meet him at evening; the toils of our busy city are over. The merchant has left his warerooms, the tradesman his counter, and the streets are swarming with the various persons in their employ, who now released from their duties, come forth to breathe the air, and catch a share of vivacity from the gay promenaders about them."
NEW YORK MIRROR, AUGUST 12, 1837

1. Catherine Market, 1850; OYL.
2. Interior of the New York Post Office, 1844; NYHS.
3. The Life of a Fireman, 1854; NYHS.
4. Public room, Merchants Exchange, about 1830; NYHS.
5. Workers at the Brooklyn Navy Yard, 1861; QBPL.
6. J.& R. Fisher's Bloomingdale Flint Glass Works, 1837; painting by B.Whittle, NYHS.
7. Workers at the Brooklyn Navy Yard, 1861; QBPL.
8. The Blind Musician, 1837; MCNY.

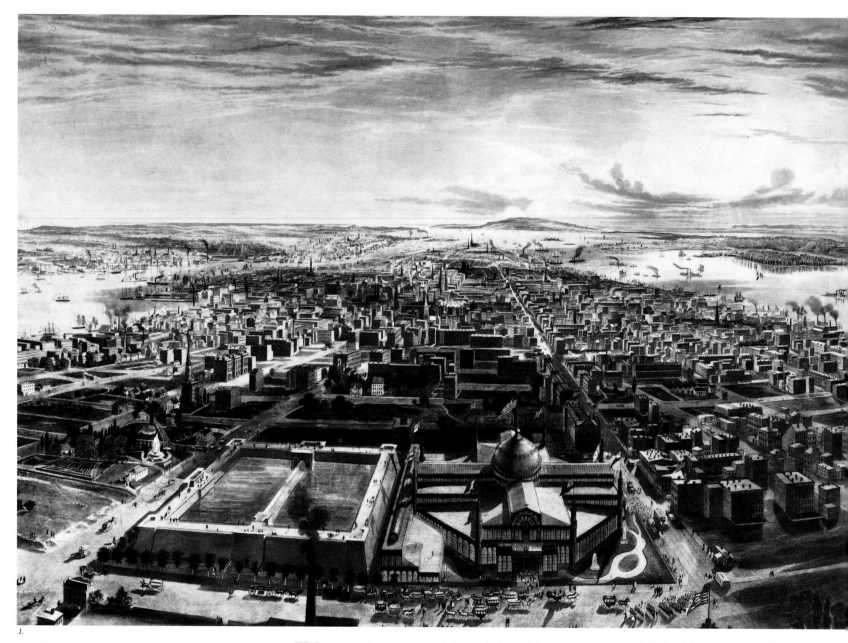

1.

Expanding Metropolis

With a growing commercial and industrial base and a population explosion fueled by the arrival of new immigrants, the city spread to the north in an irregular pattern across the width of Manhattan from the Battery to the Harlem River. What had been agricultural became urban. With a clear anticipation of considerable future growth, the 1811 street plan established the rectangular grid covering most of Manhattan. By 1806 Grand Street was a northern boundary of the developed area; by 1817 the boundary had moved to Houston Street, and by 1836 it had reached Fourteenth Street. By 1855 Forty-second Street was the northern perimeter.

The built-up areas consisted of two- to four-story buildings that abutted one another. They were a mix of individual residences, tenements, loft buildings that housed commercial and light industrial firms, and churches, whose spires were the skyline's most prominent feature. In the developed areas many of the streets were paved. In the undeveloped area they were not. The undeveloped areas were generally sizable estates or farms with detached houses, gardens, fields under cultivation, and adjacent woodlands. In some of these undeveloped areas, immigrants had erected shacks. Horse-drawn streetcars and carriages were the principal modes of transportation until the elevated railways began operating in the late 1860s.

Living conditions in the mid-nineteenth century, as endured by Irish and German immigrants, became a pattern that was repeated toward the end of the century by

Italian and Jewish immigrants. Exploited by landlords who charged exorbitant rents, cramped in minuscule apartments, lacking ventilation or daylight, and without indoor plumbing, they lived under miserable conditions that incubated disease. The buildings they occupied were a mix of homes that had been converted into boardinghouses and apartments and new tenement buildings constructed specifically for working-class people. At this time most of the Irish and German immigrants lived in what today is called the Lower East Side.

Although Manhattan provided the economic engine that drove the economy of the region, growth and development were apparent in other areas. The region was interconnected by railroad trains and ferryboats. Brooklyn was clearly the largest and most developed. Sizable sections of Brooklyn echoed the physical development of Manhattan. For those who wanted to escape the tempo and congestion of city life, Daniel Curry predicted in 1852: "Fifty years hence a city of cottages with gardens and villas with parks and pleasure ground, and clusters of dwellings among cultivated fields and miniature groves will cover a circular area of fifty miles diameter, centering at the present site of City Hall."

1. *The view south from the Latting Observatory on Forty-second Street, 1855; NYPL. In the foreground are the Croton Aqueduct and the Crystal Palace Exposition, patterned after London's, to present the latest industrial technologies and consumer goods. Inaugurated in 1842, the Croton Aqueduct provided the city's first reliable public water supply. It was piped from the Croton Dam, forty-one miles to the north.*
2. *Remsen Street, Brooklyn, 1867; QBPL.*
3. *Entrance to Green-Wood Cemetery, Brooklyn, 1852; QBPL.*
4. *Residence of John Whelp, Mariner's Harbor, Staten Island, about 1830–1840; painting by John La Farge, NYHS.*
5. *Jamaica Village, Long Island, 1844; QBPL.*

1. Anthony J. Bleecker, Auctioneer.
AUCTION SALE OF
225 HARLEM LOTS,
BETWEEN 2ND. Avenue & East River, and between 108 & 113 Sts.
A.J.BLEECKER & CO.
WILL SELL AT AUCTION, ON
FRIDAY, APRIL 24th., 1857, at 12 M.,
At the Merchants' Exchange, New York,
THE ABOVE 225 LOTS, BEING THE FAMILY MANSION AND GROUNDS OF
George Bradish, Esq., Dec'd.

2. **41 VALUABLE LOTS**
Comprising the Entire Block
BOUNDED BY
BLEECKER, FOURTH, CHARLES & PERRY STS.
ADRIAN H. MULLER, P. R. WILKINS & CO.
WILL SELL AT AUCTION,
On THURSDAY, May 25, 1865,
AT TWELVE O'CLOCK,
At the Exchange Salesroom, 111 Broadway,
By order of the Executor of Abraham Van Ness, dec'd, the following described property, viz:
The entire Block of Ground bounded by Bleecker, Fourth, Charles and Perry Streets, containing about 41 Lots, as per diagram above. The Buildings, consisting of a two-story Frame Dwelling, 51 ft. 10½ ins. by 33 ft.

3. **Real Estate**
FOR SALE
THE FOLLOWING VALUABLE
Real Estate,
WILL BE SOLD
At PUBLIC AUCTION,
At the Merchants' Exchange, on the 13th day of February, inst.
at 12 o'clock, noon,
BY JOHN HONE & SONS.
MAP OF LOTS, BELONGING TO THE ESTATE OF THE LATE T. A. EMMET.
E. Conrad, Printer, 11 Frankfort street, New York.

Real Estate Brokers and Developers

As lower Manhattan became increasingly more congested, noisy, and unhealthy, those who could afford to move out did; those who could not stayed. The real estate market prospered, and developers created new complexes of buildings. There was a clear understanding of the geographical limits of Manhattan. In 1847 it was estimated that there were 168,000 potential building lots on the island and that 148,000 would be occupied by 1883 with an average density of 10 persons per acre. This followed to a conclusion; it was further estimated that the population of Manhattan would be about 1.5 million by 1883.

Although there were numerous pockets of undeveloped land in lower Manhattan, there was a decisive movement to the north. It was in the upper part of the island that lots were sold for individual family dwellings and that developers purchased contiguous lots in order to build groups of similar houses. The terrain of Manhattan was reconfigured; hills, ponds, and streams were eliminated and replaced with buildings and streets.

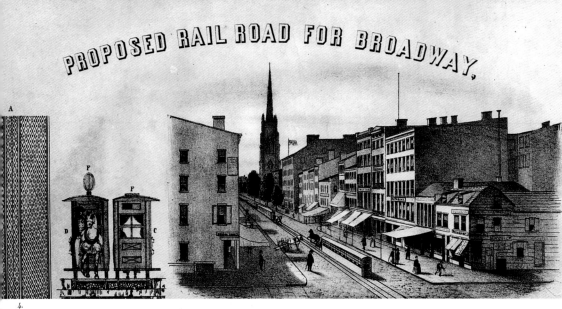

PROPOSED RAIL ROAD FOR BROADWAY,

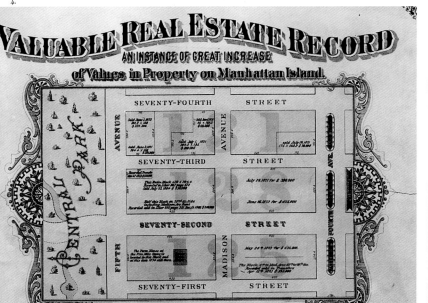

VALUABLE REAL ESTATE RECORD

AN INSTANCE OF GREAT INCREASE

of Values in Property on Manhattan Island

"Many capitalists have made their fortunes by successful operations in real estate. This must not be classed with speculations in bonds or stocks. Of course, one may be cheated in buying real estate as well as in any other purchase; but as a general rule, he who invests his money in houses or lands, gets the full value of it. The rapid growth of the city has increased the value of property in the upper sections at an amazing rate, and has made the fortune of everyone who held land in those sections. The Astors, A. T. Stewart, Clafin, Vanderbilt, Drew, and hundreds of others who were wise enough to foresee and believe in the future of New York, have made handsome fortunes on the investments made by them a few years ago.

"In 1860 a gentleman purchased a handsome house in a fashionable neighborhood. It was a corner house, and fronted on Fifth Avenue. He paid fifty thousand dollars for it. He spent twenty-five thousand more in furnishing and fitting up. His friends shook their heads at his extravagance. Since then he has resided in the house, and each year his property has increased in value. A few months ago he was offered nearly three hundred thousand dollars for the house and furniture, and refused it, declaring his belief, that in ten years more the property will be worth over half a million."

EDWARD WINSLOW MARTIN, *THE SECRETS OF THE GREAT CITY*, 1868

1. Harlem real estate, broadside, 1857; MCNY.
2. Manhattan real estate, broadside, 1865; MCNY.
3. Manhattan real estate, broadside, 1827; MCNY. This auction was to dispose of the property belonging to Thomas Addis Emmet, a distinguished Irish-born Protestant lawyer.
4. "Proposed Rail Road for Broadway," 1848; MCNY.
5. Manhattan real estate, broadside, 1876; MCNY.
6. Broadway between Howard and Grand streets, 1840; OYL.
7. Prospectus for a block of houses, Manhattan, 1845–1850; OYL. A typical developer project with eleven houses for sale. The developer bought the land and hired the architect, Alexander Jackson Davis.

1.

Public and Private Schools

When New York was first a Dutch colony and later a British colony, education was private and provided by tutors and church schools. Following the American Revolution, there was enthusiasm for public education. Most middle-class children went to school, but poor and immigrant children often did not. In 1805 civic leaders created the Public School Society to encourage universal free education. They created a number of schools that eventually served as the foundation for Manhattan's public school system when it was established in 1842. The children of the well-to-do either had tutors or went to one of the numerous private schools.

"I am ten years old to-day, and I am going to begin to keep a diary. My sister says it is a good plan, and when I am old, and in a remembering mood, I can take out my diary and read about what I did when I was a little girl. . . .

"I love my music lessons, I began them when I was seven years old. Our piano is in the middle room between the parlor and dining-room, and my teacher shuts the sliding doors, and Ellen peeked through the crack to see what I was doing, but she was only six years old.

"My teacher is very fond of me. Last year my sister let me play at a big musical party she had, and I played a tune from 'La Fille du Regiment,' with variations. It took me a good while to learn it, and the people all liked it and said it must be very hard. My

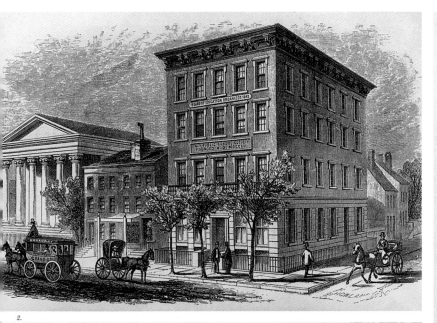

GARDEN FRONT, LIVINGSTON STREET.

PACKER COLLEGIATE INSTITUTE,

BROOKLYN HEIGHTS, L. I.

This Institution claims to give to females all the advantages for thorough and complete education that are enjoyed by the other sex in our best appointed Colleges.

It is liberally endowed, and is under the patronage of the State.

Its location, in the city of Brooklyn, opposite New York, enables it to command all the educational resources of the metropolis; while no country village is more quiet, beautiful, or healthy.

THE COURSE OF INSTRUCTION

Is under the direction of A. Crittenden, A.M., who has devoted his whole life to female education. He is assisted by twenty-four professors and teachers; and the course of instruction embraces the modern languages, with Latin, the various branches of Literature, History, Mathematics, Chemistry, Natural, Moral, and Intellectual Philosophy, Music, Drawing, Painting, &c. &c.

THE LABORATORY

Is a model of its kind, and furnished with every necessary article of apparatus.

THE OBSERVATORY

Has an excellent achromatic telescope of six inches object glass. It is equatorially mounted, moved by clockwork, &c.

THE CABINETS

Are amply provided with minerals, shells, &c. One or two articles of apparatus particularly arrest the attention of the observer,—one of Ross's Compound Microscopes, which magnifies 1800 diameters, also Barlow's large Planetarium, eleven feet in diameter.

The accommodations for pupils from abroad are intended to afford all the comforts of home, and to secure for them social, intellectual, and moral culture.

746

mother had all my pieces bound in a book and my name put on the cover.

"I love music first, and then my arithmetic. Sometimes our class has to stand up and do sums in our heads. Our teacher rattles off like this, as fast as ever she can, 'Twice six, less one, multiply by two, add eight, divide by three. How much?' I love to do that.

"I have a friend who comes to school with me, named Mary L. She lives on Ninth Street, between Broadway and the Bowery. She and I began our lessons together and sat on a bench that had a little cupboard underneath for our books. She has a nurse named Sarah. Sometimes Ellen and I go there and have tea in her nursery. She has a lot of brothers and they tease us. One time we went, and my mother told us to be polite

and not to take preserves and cake but once. But we did, for we had raspberry jam, and we took it six times, but the plates were dolls' plates, and of course my mother meant tea plates."

CATHERINE ELIZABETH HAVENS, *A LITTLE GIRL IN OLD NEW YORK*, 1849–1850

1. First Infant School in Green Street, *about 1825; MCNY. The children are marching and reciting aloud, "Twice twos, Fours," etc.*
2. Board of Education building, *about 1850; OYL.*
3. "Interior of Somerindyke House in which Louis Philippe (late king of the French) taught school," *1863; OYL.*
4. Packer Collegiate Institute advertisement, *about 1850; QBPL. Founded in 1814 as a female academy, it is the oldest private school in Brooklyn.*

55

1.

German Jews Outnumber Sephardic Jews

The American Jewish community was established in 1654, when 23 Sephardic Jews who had been living in the Dutch colony of Recife, Brazil, were given refuge in New Amsterdam. Governor Peter Stuyvesant accepted them reluctantly because Sephardic Jewish stockholders of the Dutch West India Company interceded. In 1690 the British granted the community of 100 Jews permission to worship in a building on Beaver Street. By 1730 the first synagogue building in America had been erected on Mill Street. Ten years later the British Parliament authorized Jews to become naturalized citizens after seven years of residence. By 1789, when there were between 1,300 and 1,500 Jews residing in New York, Reverend Gershom Mendes Seixas of Congregation Shearith Israel, along with

representatives of other religious groups, participated in the inauguration of President George Washington. When the New York Stock Exchange was founded in 1792, Benjamin Seixas and Ezekiel Hart were among its first members. By 1820 the majority of New York's Jews were Ashkenazim (Jews from Eastern and Western Europe). Finding the Sephardic ritual no longer acceptable, in 1825 some German Jewish members of Congregation Shearith Israel, the Sephardic synagogue, seceded to form their own synagogue, Congregation B'nai Jeshurun, setting a pattern followed by other German Jews.

5608 – 1848

FRESH TEAS.

CHOICE GROCERIES FOR PASSOVER,
פסח
AT D. BEHRMAN'S NEW STORE,
172 BOWERY
Opposite Delancy Street, NEW-YORK

Which will be Superintended by L.M. RITTERBAND.

The subscriber begs to inform you, that he has made the necessary arrangements for the ensuing holydays, and will keep a full assortment of Groceries, also, every other article suitable for the occasion ; and guarantees the same to be of the most superior quality, and at the lowest market prices, delivered free of expense to any part of the city. The goods will be ready for sale on the 3d of April, to which the subscriber respectfully solicits your custom.

D. BEHRMAN,
172 BOWERY, Opposite Delancy Street.

Orders received immediately if required

הגדה של פסח In Hebrew and English For Sale.

Groferies für פסח.

Der Unterzeichnete eröffnet am 3ten April seine Niederlage von Groferies, von befter Qualität für die zukünftigen Feiertage פסח, unter der Auffsicht von L. M. Ritterbänd.

Es wird alles zum billigsten Preise verkauft und kostenfrei zu irgend einem Theil der Stadt gesandt.

D. Behrman,
172 Bowery, gegenüber Delancy Street.

Orders werden jetzt angenommen wen man es verlangt.

JACKSON, Cheap Printer, 190 Houston Street, and 203 Bowery.

ENCOURAGING GERMAN JEWS TO EMIGRATE

"The wealth and enterprize of the Jews would be a great auxiliary to the commercial and manufacturing, if not agricultural, interests of the United States. A new generation, born in more enlightened times and having the benefit of education, would be free from those errors generally imputed to the Jews, and participating in the blessings of liberty, would have every inducement to become valuable members of society.—That toleration and mildness upon which the Christian religion is founded, will lend its influence to the neglected children of Israel, who, in the United States, can find a home undisturbed—land which they dare call their own—laws which they will assist in making—magistrates of which they may be of the number—protection, freedom, and as they comport themselves respect and consideration. We shall not be surprised if the views which shall be spread before them should lead to valuable emigration of these people; and when they perceive one of their brethren honored with the highest executive office of the metropolis of the Union, and exercising a jurisdiction over Christians with Christian justice, they will be satisfied of the practical utility of those institutions which proclaim equal freedom and privileges to all."

NEW YORK COMMERCIAL ADVERTISER, OCTOBER 18, 1822

1. Preparing and baking matzos, 1855; LC. Traditionally Jews baked matzos themselves, but two hundred years after the Jews arrived in New York, making matzos became a factory process, and distribution was a commercial enterprise. The ever-present rabbi can be seen to the left.

2. Congregation Rodeph Shalom Synagogue, Clinton Street, 1853; LC. One of the first German Jewish congregations.

3. Advertisement for Passover groceries, 1848; LC. Certain types of food are prohibited from use during Passover; stores serving a Jewish clientele made a special effort to stock the goods that Jews required for this holiday.

FREEDOM'S JOURNAL.

" RIGHTEOUSNESS EXALTETH A NATION." .

CORNISH & RUSSWURM, Editors & Proprietors.   NEW-YORK, FRIDAY, MARCH 16, 1827.   VOL. I. NO. 1.

Finally, Slavery Ends in New York City

Slavery did not end in one dramatic act. The Gradual Manumission Act passed in 1799 by the New York State Legislature stated that every male child born a slave after July 4, 1799, would be free after twenty-eight years of service to the owner of his mother, and every female child after twenty-five years. Manumission, the freeing of slaves, occured intermitently. In 1827, the State Legislature passed another act which emancipated all slaves who had not been manumitted previously and abolished slavery in the state.

Also in 1827, the first African-American newspaper in this country, *Freedom's Journal*, appeared in New York. The 1830 census recorded 14,083 free Blacks living in New York City.

"In presenting our first number to our Patrons, we feel all the diffidence of persons entering upon a new and untried line of business. . . . [W]e believe, that a paper devoted to the dissemination of useful knowledge among our brethren, and to their moral and religious improvement, must meet with the cordial approbation of every friend to humanity. . . .

"We wish to plead our own cause. Too long have others spoken for us. Too long has the publick been deceived by misrepresentations, in things which concern us dearly, though in the estimation of some mere trifles; for though there are many in society who exercise towards us benevolent feelings, still (with sorrow we confess it) there are others who make it their business to

By Jacob Radcliff Mayor, and Richard Riker Recorder, of the City of New-York,

It is hereby Certified, That pursuant to the statute in such case made and provided, we have this day examined *one* certain *male* Negro Slave named *George* the property of *John Delany* which slave *is* about to be manumitted, and *he* appearing to us to be under forty-five years of age, and of sufficient ability to provide *for himself* we have granted this Certificate, this *twenty-fourth* day of *April* in the year of our Lord, one thousand eight hundred and *seventeen*

Jacob Radcliff

R Riker

Register's Office Lib Nº 2 of Manumissions page 62

W S Slocum Register

4.

5.

6.

enlarge upon the least trifle, which tends to the discredit of any person of colour; and pronounce anathemas and denounce our whole body for the misconduct of this guilty one. . . .

"Education being an object of the highest importance to the welfare of society, we shall endeavour to present just and adequate views of it, and to urge upon our brethren the necessity and expediency of training their children, while young, to habits of industry, and thus forming them for becoming useful members of society. It is surely time that we should awake from this lethargy of years, and make a concentrated effort for the education of our youth. We form a spoke in the human wheel, and it is necessary that we should understand our

pendence on the different parts, and theirs on us, in order to perform our part with propriety. . . .

"Our vices and our degradation are ever arrayed against us, but our virtues are passed by unnoticed. And what is still more lamentable, our friends, to whom we concede all the principles of humanity and religion, from these very causes seem to have fallen into the current of popular feeling and are imperceptibly floating on the stream—actually living in the practice of prejudice, while they abjure it in theory, and feel it not in their hearts."
FREEDOM'S JOURNAL, MARCH 16, 1827

1. Masthead, 1827; NYPL/SC.
2. John B. Russwurm, undated; NYPL/SC. With Samuel Cornish, Russwurm founded Freedom's Journal in 1827.
3. Reverend Samuel Cornish, undated; NYPL/SC. Cofounder of Freedom's Journal, he was pastor of the first African Presbyterian Church (later Shiloh) in New York.
4. Manumission certificate for a slave named George, 1817; OYL.
5. Juliette Noel Toussaint, about 1825; miniature by Antonio Meucci, NYHS. Her husband, Pierre, purchased her freedom.
6. Pierre Toussaint, about 1825; miniature by Antonio Meucci, NYHS. Born a slave, freed in 1807, Toussaint was a fashionable hairdresser with patronage among wealthy women.

1.

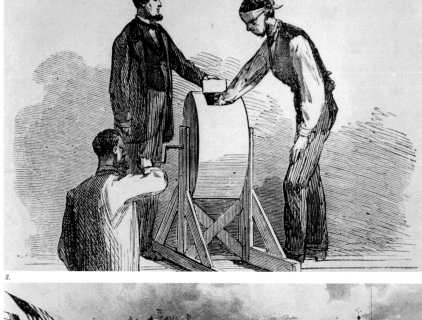

3.

2.

4.

Civil War and Draft Riots

When French observer Alexis de Tocqueville wrote in *Democracy in America* in 1835, "If ever America undergoes great revolutions, they will be brought about by the presence of the black race on the soil of the United States; that is to say, they will owe their origin, not to the equality, but to the inequality of condition," he anticipated the outbreak of the Civil War.

In response to President Lincoln's 1861 call for volunteers, immigrants demonstrated their patriotism by joining New York regiments. The Germans and the Irish were prominent in forming companies and promoting recruitment. Initial enthusiasm turned into discontent. The Conscription Act of 1863 made it possible to avoid going to war by paying a fee of three hundred dollars; this provoked resentment among the poor, who saw it as favoritism toward the rich. Irish immigrants feared that freed slaves would take their jobs. Together the Emancipation Proclamation and the Conscription Act served as the fuse to ignite some of the darkest days in New York City's history, the Civil War draft riots. During the week of July 11, 1863, the city was in chaos. Mobs assaulted and killed blacks; they burned black institutions; they sacked the homes of antislavery advocates and participated in an orgy of robbery and pillage. The police and a small military contingent vainly sought to control the situation. Approximately 105 died, of whom at least 11 were black. Order was restored by five regiments of the Union Army, rushed north from the battlefield at Gettysburg, Pennsylvania.

1. *Recruiting poster, 1861; QBPL.*
2. *"The Wheel for the Draw of the Names," 1863; MCNY.*
3. *Departure of the Sixty-ninth (Irish) Regiment from St. Patrick's Cathedral, Prince and Mott streets, 1861; MCNY.*
4. *Departure of the Seventh Regiment, 1861; MCNY.*
5. *Military firing on rioters, 1863; MCNY.*
6. *"Hanging a Negro in Clarkson Street and Burning His Body," 1863; MCNY.*
7. *"Cruelty Inflicted on a Negro boy, near Orphan Asylum," 1863; MCNY.*
8. *"The Brutal Murder of Colonel O'Brien," 1863; MCNY.*

LYNCHING OF WILLIAM JONES
"A crowd of rioters in Clarkson Street in pursuit of a negro, who in self-defence had fired upon some rowdies, met an inoffensive colored man returning from a bakery with a loaf of bread under his arm. They instantly set upon him after nearly killing him, hung him to a lamp post. His body was left suspended for several hours. A fire was made underneath him and he was literally roasted as he hung, the crowd reveling in their demonic act."
THE DRAFT RIOTS IN NEW YORK, JULY 1863, THE METROPOLITAN POLICE: THEIR SERVICES DURING THE RIOT WEEK, THEIR HONORABLE RECORD

COLORED ORPHAN ASYLUM BURNED
"About 4 o'clock on the afternoon of July 13, a mob of some three thousand attacked the Asylum for Colored Orphans on Fifth Avenue—(extended from 43rd to 44th St.)— In an hour and a half only a small portion of the walls remained. After their escape from the building, the orphans were hurried in mournful procession to the Twelfth Precinct . . . where they were sheltered and provided for until their removal to Blackwell's Island. Except for the clothes they wore, not an article was saved for them. The loss to the Society in building, furniture and clothing was estimated at $80,000."
THE DRAFT RIOTS IN NEW YORK, JULY 1863, THE METROPOLITAN POLICE: THEIR SERVICES DURING THE RIOT WEEK, THEIR HONORABLE RECORD

THE NEW YORK HERALD.

OUR LOSS.

The Great National Calamity.

DEATH

OF THE

PRESIDENT.

Sad Details of the Terrible Event.

The Last Moments of the President.

SCENE AT THE DEATH BED.

The Life and Services of Mr. Lincoln.

IDENTIFICATION OF THE MURDERER.

John Wilkes Booth the Assassin.

1.

Lincoln's Funeral and After the War

3.

4.

On the evening of April 14, 1865, while President Lincoln was attending a performance at Ford's Theater in Washington, he was shot and gravely wounded by actor John Wilkes Booth. Shortly after Lincoln's death the Confederacy capitulated. It was a costly war for both sides. There was a total of 359,528 Union dead, among them many New Yorkers, whose bodies were buried in local cemeteries.

On February 26, 1869, Congress proposed the Fifteenth Amendment, forbidding any state from depriving a male citizen of his vote because of race, color, or previous condition of servitude. After approval by individual states, it was proclaimed on March 30, 1870.

1. Announcing Lincoln's death, April 16, 1865, New York Herald; QBPL.
2. Funeral procession on Broadway, April 25, 1865; MCNY.
3. Removing the body from City Hall and placing it in the funeral car, April 25, 1865; OYL.
4. Citizens viewing the body, City Hall, April 25, 1865; OYL.
5. African-Americans parading on Fifth Avenue to commemorate adoption of the Fifteenth Amendment, 1870; OYL.
6. Visiting the graves of the war dead, Cypress Hill Cemetery, 1868; OYL.
7. Sioux Chief Red Cloud in the Great Hall, Cooper Union, describing the wrongs done to his people, 1870; NYHS.

5.

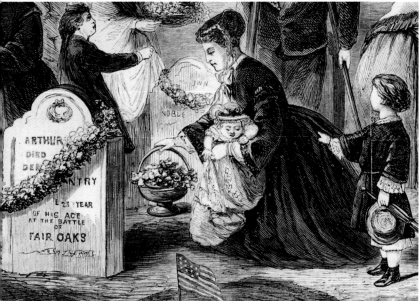

6.

7.

NEW YORK MOURNS

"The scene from the balcony at this moment was one never to be forgotten. Far off and near waved mournfully in the bright, balmy air, the draped colors of a sorrow-stricken nation. From every possible point of exhibition were flung to the view of scores of thousands, clean against the blue horizon, the red, white and blue emblem of liberty, sabled with the sombre tone of mourning.... From distant batteries the cannon belched at each minute a thunder tone of woe. From all the steeples came forth the wailing of bells, while from the spire of old Trinity floated upon the breeze the tuneful chimings of 'Old Hundred.'"

NEW YORK TIMES, APRIL 25, 1865

THE EMANCIPATION PROCLAMATION AND VOTING RIGHTS FOR BLACK WOMEN

"... Now colored men have a right to vote; and what I want is to have colored women have the right to vote. There ought to be equal rights more than ever, since colored people have got their freedom.

"I know that it is hard for men to give up entirely. They must run in the old track. I was amused how men speak up for one another. They cannot bear that a woman should say anything about the man, but they will stand here and take up the time in man's cause. But we are going, tremble or no tremble. Men are trying to help us. I know that all—the spirit they have got; and they cannot help us much until some of the spirit is taken out of them that belongs among the women. Men have got their rights, and women has not got their rights. That is the trouble. When woman gets her rights man will be right. How beautiful that will be. Then it will be peace on earth and good will to men. But it cannot be until it be right.... The great fight was to keep the rights of the poor colored people. That made a great battle. And now I hope that this will be the last battle that will be in the world. Let us finish up so that there will be no more fighting. I have faith in God and there is truth in humanity. Be strong women! Blush not! Tremble not!... I am going round to lecture on human rights. I will shake every place I go to."

SOJOURNER TRUTH, SPEECH AT AMERICAN EQUAL RIGHTS ASSOCIATION, MAY 9, 1867

CASE MAKING BUILDING AND DRYING KILNS.

FOUNDRY, METAL WORKS AND SAW MILL.

1.

Birth of an Industrial Era

The 1853 Crystal Palace Exposition, on Forty-second Street at Sixth Avenue behind the Croton Aqueduct, introduced New Yorkers to the new era of consumer goods and industrial technologies. A transformation was evident. Craftsmen were being replaced by skilled mechanics, individual workers by wage earners, and merchant princes were beginning to share their exalted position with the new lords of industry. Some industries like clothing manufacturing and printing had no difficulty remaining in crowded and congested Manhattan; however, new industries requiring more space located in undeveloped areas of Astoria, College Point, Greenpoint, and Williamsburg.

The Steinway & Sons piano factory in Astoria represented the new American phenomenon, the factory town. Occupying a tract of four hundred acres, William Steinway built a complex that included buildings with such varied functions as drying kilns, casemaking, metalworking, and a foundry. There was the owner's mansion, a church, a library, a kindergarten, and a trolley line.

In College Point, Conrad Poppenhusen built the India Rubber Comb Company complex, which consisted of factory buildings, workers' housing, and the owner's mansion. The Havemeyers built a huge sugar refinery in Williamsburg, and the Standard Oil Company built a refinery in Greenpoint. In 1875, fifty oil refineries lined the Greenpoint, Newtown Creek, and Williamsburg waterfronts.

New York's industrial base was not concentrated in a few industries. As a consequence of this industrial expansion, two new

2.

4.

3.

5.

social classes emerged: industrialists, the owners and managers of these new enterprises, and an industrial working class. Factory owners and factory workers became partners in a new social and economic dynamic: confrontation between organized labor and industrial management.

1. "Steinway & Sons Pianoforte Factory, Foundry, Metal Works and Lumber Yard," about 1875; QBPL.

2. The New York Times *printing plant, Manhattan; 1859.*

3. South Brooklyn steam engine works, 1873; QBPL. Workers are seen casting twenty-four-ton plates that are to serve as anchors for the cables of the Brooklyn Bridge.

4. Levinger's brewery, College Point, 1873; PI.

5. Babcock and Wilcox boilers at the Standard Oil Company's refinery, Greenpoint, 1880; QBPL. In 1874 Charles Pratt went into partnership with John D. Rockefeller, head of Standard Oil. Together they purchased a number of Brooklyn oil refineries.

65

The Nation's Financial Capital

Aside from the social and humanitarian issues involved, the Union victory over the Confederacy could be viewed as the triumph of industrialization over agriculture. The economy of the North was built on a foundation of commerce and industry. The economy of the South was based on slavery. With this issue resolved, industrialization, urbanization, and geographical expansion were in the ascendancy. As new territories opened in the West, railroads were built. New towns and cities were built along the railroad lines. Resident Americans and immigrants settled lands formerly occupied by Native Americans. Agriculture was mechanized, and new crop strains were developed. America became the world's leading agricultural producer and was on the verge of becoming the world's leading industrial power. Factory

production was rising at the rate of 300 percent. The American economy was growing at the rate of 1.6 percent per capita annually.

New York, a center for investment and financial management, was the direct beneficiary of this incredible growth. The American Bankers Association, formed in 1876, made its headquarters in New York. In the same year fifteen banks could be counted on Wall Street, and fifty-five others throughout Manhattan. Because the city's banks served a network of local and regional banks, it was called the clearinghouse of the world.

The New York Stock Exchange was both an agent and a participant in this period of economic growth. Under the call system, members made "trades" or "bids and offers" as the president read the list of securities

from a podium. As trading volume increased, the Stock Exchange responded. The call system was abandoned in 1871 and was replaced by continuous trading; there was simultaneous trading in all stocks on a large, open trading floor with trading posts, specific locations on the trading floor where particular stocks were traded. This led to the development of the specialist system.

THE GOLD ROOM

". . . The members of the Board are always too much excited to sit, and seats are only in the way. . . . During the sessions of the Board, it is filled with an excited, yelling crowd rushing about wildly, and, to a stranger, without any apparent aim. The men stamp, yell, shake their arms, heads, and bodies violently, and almost trample each other to death in the violent struggle. Men, who in private life excite the admiration of their friends and acquaintances by the repose and dignity of their manner, have lost the self possession entirely, and are more like maniacs than sensible beings."
EDWARD WINSLOW MARTIN, *THE SECRETS OF A GREAT CITY*, 1868

1. *"Black Friday," September 24, 1869; NYHS. A financial panic engineered by Jay Gould and "Jubilee Jim" Fisk caused the price of gold to plummet.*
2. *New York Stock Exchange trading floor, 1871; NYSE.*
3. *Bank clerks and messengers at New York Clearing House, 1875; NYHS. Checks, drafts and bills are presented for clearance—exchange of funds.*
4. *Bulls and Bears cartoon, 1864; NYSE.*
5. *Counting gold in the U. S. Subtreasury, 1859; NYHS.*

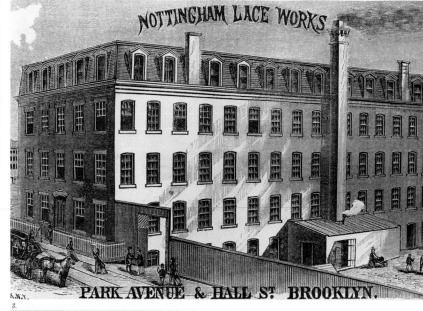

Ways of Working

In the post–Civil War period, manufactured goods were produced by two different systems: artisan production, in which an individual worker fashioned a completed product, and factory production, in which tasks were divided among a number of workers who contributed to a finished product. Traditional industries such as woodworking employed artisan production while those involved in metalworking, shipbuilding, sugar refining, and clothing manufacturing moved toward the factory system. For industrial workers, there were no age or sex differentials; adults and children worked. Not everyone worked in factories; others worked in commercial establishments and some, like newsboys, worked on the street.

CHILD LABORERS
"One of the most touching facts to any one examining the lower strata of New York is the great number of young children toiling in factories and shops. With the children of the fortunate classes there are certain years of childhood which every parent feels ought to be freed from the burdens and responsibilities of life. The 'struggle for existence,' the labor of money-making, the toil for support, and all the cares and anxieties therewith, will come soon enough. . . .

"The tobacco factories contain fully 10,000 children, of whom 5,000 at least are under fifteen years. The youngest child we saw employed in them was four years of age."
HARPER'S NEW MONTHLY MAGAZINE, AUGUST 1873

WAITING FOR THE PAPERS.

NEWSBOYS' LODGING HOUSE

"This is now situated in Park Place, near Broadway. . . . The boys pay five cents for supper, and five cents for bed. . . . Supper is served for them between six and seven o'clock. . . . The boys then adjourn to the lecture-room. . . . The sitting generally terminates about nine o'clock, with the recitation of the Lord's Prayer and the singing of the Doxology. The singing is marked with force, rather than great accuracy; it sometimes partakes very much of the character of a bawl. . . . After these exercises, the tired ones go to bed, the lively blades to the gymnasium, the philosophic apply themselves to draughts and dominoes."

EDWARD WINSLOW MARTIN, *THE SECRETS OF A GREAT CITY*, 1868

BEGGARS

"After living in New York for a few months, you cannot resist the conclusion that it is a City of Beggars. You meet them at every step, and they follow you into your residence and place of business. A few you know to be genuine, and you give them gladly, but cannot resist the conviction that the majority of those who accost you are simply impostors, as indeed they are. Begging is not allowed on the street-cars, in the stages, the ferry-boats, or at any place of amusement, but there is no law against the practice of it on the street. Broadway is the favorite resort of this class, as it is the principal promenade of the city people. . . ."

EDWARD WINSLOW MARTIN, *THE SECRETS OF A GREAT CITY*, 1868

1. *Gold leaf workers*, 1873; NYHS.
2. *Twine makers*, 1873; NYHS.
3. *Lace factory*, about 1865; QBPL.
4. *Sewing room of the A. T. Stewart department store*, 1875; LC.
5. *Newsboys bathing*, 1867; LC.
6. *Street sweepers before they begin their work*, 1868; NYHS.
7. *Newsboys waiting for papers*, 1867; LC.
8. *Newsboy on the street*, 1867; LC.
9. *Beggars*, 1877; NYHS.

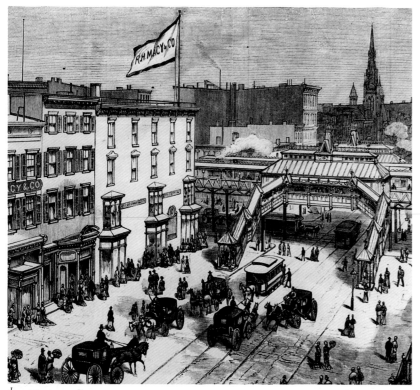

1.

3.

2.

4.

Developing a Transportation Network

New York's first transportation network was created by the Native Americans, who had a system of paths connecting their numerous settlements. Their paths ran from the Battery to the Bronx, covering the full length of Manhattan. There were extensive paths over all of Brooklyn, Queens, and Staten Island.

As the city grew from colony to city, new modes of regional public transportation appeared. By the mid-nineteenth century a loosely integrated transportation system evolved. There were horse-drawn stages, omnibuses, and streetcars that connected with the depots of ferries, ships, and railroads operating throughout the region.

Ferries operating on a regular schedule linked New York with Brooklyn, Hoboken, Jersey City, and Staten Island. Every five minutes from Grand Street and every ten minutes from Peck Slip, there were ferries to Williamsburg. In 1860 the East River ferries carried 32,845,950 passengers. During warm weather steamboats traveled between Manhattan and Glen Cove, New Rochelle, Croton-on-Hudson, and New Brunswick, New Jersey.

The principal mode of ground transportation was the horsecar, a streetcar pulled by a horse. The world's first such street railway was inaugurated in New York in 1832. Soon there were streetcar lines on major avenues. In 1858 the city's principal street railways carried 35 million passengers.

LONG ISLAND RAILROAD

SUNDAY MILK TRAIN

Will run as follows, until further notice.

	GOING EAST.		STATIONS.		GOING WEST.	
	A. M.	P. M.	Leave. Arr.		A. M.	P. M.
READ DOWN—Trains going East.	9 00	6 00	James Slip,	READ UP—Trains going West.	9 52	6 52
	9 30	6 30	Huntr's Point		9 10	6 10
	9 37	6 37	Woodside,		8 59	5 59
	9 42	6 42	Newtown,		8 55	5 55
	9 58	6 58	Jamaica,		8 45	5 45
	10 02	7 04	Willow Tree,		8 34	5 32
	10 07	7 12	Queens,		8 29	5 27
	10 16	7 22	Hyde Park,		8 19	5 17
	10 22	7 34	H. Branch,		8 12	5 09
	10 30	7 45	Westbury,		7 57	4 55
	10 41	7 55	Hicksville,		7 45	4 45
	10 56	8 10	Syosset,		7 30	4 30
			Arr. Leave.			

A. H. PALMER, Ass't Sup't.

Office L. I. R. R. Co., June 6th, 1861.

"Modern martyrdom may be succinctly defined as riding in a New York omnibus. The discomforts, inconveniences and annoyances of a trip in one of these vehicles are almost intolerable. From the beginning to the end of the journey a constant quarrel is progressing. The driver quarrels with the passengers and the passengers quarrel with the driver. There are quarrels about getting out and quarrels about getting in. There are quarrels about change and quarrels about ticket swindle. The driver swears at the passengers and the passengers harangue the driver through the strap hole—a position in which even Demosthenes could not be eloquent. . . . [T]he omnibus . . . a perfect Bedlam on wheels."
NEW YORK HERALD, OCTOBER 2, 1864

". . . it is utterly impossible to get down town in the morning, or up-town at night, with any comfort, either by railroad or by omnibus. All attempts to limit any of these vehicles to the number of passengers they will hold have been abandoned. Omnibuses already full are regularly stopped for fresh accessions, and those who have seats are compelled to give them up, or have stout men and women treading on their toes or tumbling into their laps during the whole journey. Any remonstrance on the part of passengers provokes insolence from the driver and sour looks from the new comers. . . . The fares are collected 'on entering,' . . . any dissatisfied person is at full liberty to leave at any moment, and give up his seat. . . ."
NEW YORK HERALD, JANUARY 6, 1860

1. *Gilbert Elevated Railway station, Sixth Avenue and Fourteenth Street, 1878; OYL.*
2. *On the horsecars, 9:00 A.M., 1870; OYL.*
3. *Grand Central Terminal, about 1870; NYHS. A transportation hub, where horsecars, omnibuses, and hansom cabs can be seen in the foreground.*
4. *On the horsecars, midnight, 1870; OYL.*
5. *Commuters and weekenders, rushing from a Long Island Railroad train to waiting cabs, 1873; QBPL.*
6. *Horsecar, 1867; OYL.*
7. *Long Island Railroad schedule, 1861; QBPL.*

1.

Firefighters in Action

The burning of a small log house at the foot of the Battery in 1658 demonstrated New Amsterdam's need for fire protection. When organized, this fire company consisted of 8 men, furnished with 250 buckets, hooks, and small ladders. Each member was expected to walk the street throughout the night, watching for fires. Under British rule inspection of flues and chimneys commenced, and every house was supplied with fire buckets. In 1731 two hand pumper fire engines were imported from London. In 1737 there was a volunteer force of 30. By 1770 there were eight engines and 170 men available. During the Revolutionary War two major fires occurred. On March 20, 1778, the Fire Department of the City of New York with a chief engineer and 6 subordinates was formed by an act of the state legislature. In 1785 Brooklyn's volunteer force had a captain and 5 men. In 1799 the Manhattan Company, the first of several private companies, provided a steady supply of water, supplementing rivers, springs, and wells. As the city continued to grow, there was an apparent need for expanded fire protection. Volunteer companies were formed, and by 1810 about 1,000 volunteers manned three hook and ladder companies and thirty-four engine companies. Originally men pulled their equipment; they were later replaced by horses. In 1842 the Croton Aqueduct increased water available to fight fires.

"Although the disreputable element in the Fire Department had been gradually growing less for some years, owing to the judicious and unrelenting weeding-out process in operation, still even at this date (the Fall of 1850), there were disagreeable and emphatic evidences of the existence of a rowdy crowd, upon whom a writ of ejectment should be served. At a fire in Gansevoort Street on the afternoon of August 7, Engine Company No. 34 detached the hose of Hose Company No. 35. At a fire in University Place on August 14, Engine Company No. 4 hindered Hose Company No. 35 from attaching to a hydrant. . . . Hose Company No. 16 assaulted Engine Company No. 19, and injured their apparatus whilst they were going to a fire on the morning of August 16. . . . Engine Company No. 19 was

proceeding up Third Avenue to an alarm of fire—doubtless raised for the express purpose—they were assailed by a large party of rowdies, several of their members seriously injured and driven from their engine, which was then wantonly upset and considerably damaged. Owing to threats made by persons connected with No. 16 there were good reasons for believing that the outrage had been perpetrated by them."

AUGUSTINE E. COSTELLO, *OUR FIREMEN*, 1887

1. "*Broadway, every day scene—the paid fire department—going to a fire,*" *undated; OYL.*
2. "*Fireman's Hall, Mercer Street,*" *1856; OYL.*
3. *Burning of the steeple of Old North Dutch Church, about 1868; OYL.*
4. *Tenement fire on Second Avenue, 1868; OYL. Seven families of about thirty people occupied this building. People on the upper floors were trapped by smoke in the hallway, Seven people died in the fire, and seven more succumbed later.*
5. *Demonstrating the "Little Giant," a chemical fire extinguisher, at the Brooklyn Navy Yard, 1874; OYL.*

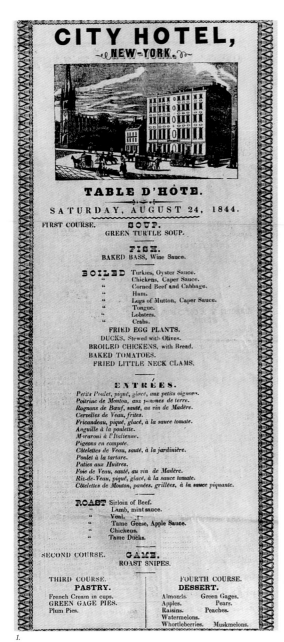

CITY HOTEL,
NEW-YORK.

TABLE D'HÔTE.

SATURDAY, AUGUST 24, 1844.

FIRST COURSE.   **SOUP.**
GREEN TURTLE SOUP.

FISH.
BAKED BASS, Wine Sauce.

BOILED   Turkies, Oyster Sauce.
"   Chickens, Caper Sauce.
"   Corned Beef and Cabbage.
"   Ham.
"   Legs of Mutton, Caper Sauce.
"   Tongue.
"   Lobsters.
"   Crabs.
FRIED EGG PLANTS.
DUCKS, Stewed with Olives.
BROILED CHICKENS, with Bread.
BAKED TOMATOES.
FRIED LITTLE NECK CLAMS.

ENTRÉES.

Petits Poulet, piqué, glacé, aux petits oignons.
Poitrine de Mouton, aux pommes de terre.
Rognons de Bœuf, sauté, au vin de Madère.
Cervelles de Veau, frites.
Fricandeau, piqué, glacé, à la sauce tomate.
Anguille à la poulette.
Macaroni à l'Italienne.
Pigeons en compote.
Côtelettes de Veau, sauté, à la jardinière.
Poulet à la tartare.
Pâtés aux Huîtres.
Foie de Veau, sauté, au vin de Madère.
Riz-de-Veau, piqué, glacé, à la sauce tomate.
Côtelettes de Mouton, panées, grillées, à la sauce piquante.

ROAST   Sirloin of Beef.
"   Lamb, mint sauce.
"   Veal.
"   Tame Geese, Apple Sauce.
"   Chickens.
"   Tame Ducks.

SECOND COURSE.   **GAME.**
ROAST SNIPES.

THIRD COURSE. **PASTRY.**	FOURTH COURSE. **DESSERT.**	
French Cream in cups.	Almonds.	Green Gages.
GREEN GAGE PIES.	Apples.	Pears.
Plum Pies.	Raisins.	Peaches.
	Watermelons.	
	Whortleberries.	Muskmelons.

1.

The New Yorkers' Birthright: Good Food and Fancy Shops

Good restaurants and fashionable stores have been ever-present in New York. Residents have never been their sole patrons but have always shared them with visitors, many of whom have stayed in hotels. Before there were hotels, taverns provided accommodations. The City Hotel, on lower Broadway, begun in 1794, was probably the first building erected in this country specifically for use as a hotel. By the mid-nineteenth century a group of luxury hotels was being built on Broadway. In addition to accommodating travelers, hotels offered sumptuous meals in their dining rooms and provided a setting for social events.

3.

4.

THE MARKETS
"Two thirds of the people of New York deal with 'corner groceries' and 'provision stores,' consequently there are very few markets in the city. The principal are the Fulton Market on East River, at the foot of Fulton Street . . . , the Jefferson, at the corner of Sixth and Greenwich Avenues; and the Tompkins Market, opposite the Cooper Institute. The Washington Market is more of a wholesale than a retail establishment, as is also the Fulton Market. The supplies of meat, fish, and vegetables brought to the city, are originally sent to the wholesale dealers at these markets, to be sold on commission."
EDWARD WINSLOW MARTIN, *THE SECRETS OF A GREAT CITY*, 1868

MARK LEVY & BROTHERS,
49 MAIDEN LANE,
New-York,

IMPORTERS OF French and English Stationery,

Fancy Goods, PLAYING AND VISITING CARDS,

HAIR, TOOTH AND NAIL BRUSHES, COMBS, MIRRORS,

WORK-BOXES, DESKS,

PORTE MONNAIES, PURSES, BRONZES, PAPIER MACHE ARTICLES,

CUTLERY, INKSTANDS,

English, French and American Writing Paper and Envelopes,

WATER COLORS, MATHEMATICAL INSTRUMENTS

AND A GENERAL ASSORTMENT OF FRENCH, ENGLISH AND GERMAN STATIONERY AND FANCY GOODS.

5.

SUTRO BROTHERS,

Manufacturers and Importers of

SOUTACHE, HERCULES, TUBULAR, SQUARE, AND

FANCY BRAIDS,

FOR TRIMMING AND ORNAMENTAL WORK.

Rick-Rack, Star-Braid,
Feather-Edge, Gold-Braid.

IMPORTERS OF FINE SILK HAT BANDS.

109, 111 & 113 GRAND ST., One Door West of Broadway, NEW YORK.

6.

7.

RESTAURANTS

"Thousands of persons, sometimes entire families, live in rooms, and either take their meals at restaurants or have them sent to them. This has become so common that it ceases to attract attention in the city, but strangers are struck with it and are quick to notice the bad effects of it.

"Living at restaurants begets irregularity in the meal hours and thus promotes bad health; and the absence of the restraints which the table of a family at home, or even the public board of a hotel, imposes, is the beginning of a looseness of manners, which is generally sure to be followed by a similar defect in morals."

EDWARD WINSLOW MARTIN, *THE SECRETS OF A GREAT CITY*, 1868

HOTEL DINING

"This [the Metropolitan] has been the most successful hotel in the city. and has a world-wide celebrity for good dinners; and, although the house is not as new or as elegant in its appointments, as some more recently constructed, the excellence of its cuisine, the neatness, order, and quiet which pervades every department, together with the promptness and attention of the proprietors and servants, renders it one of the most desirable houses in the city."

A SOUTH CAROLINIAN, *GLIMPSES OF NEW YORK CITY*, 1852

1. *City Hotel menu, 1844; NYHS.*
2. *Fifth Avenue Hotel, Fifth Avenue and Twenty-third Street, 1858; MCNY.*
3. *Oyster stands in Fulton Market, undated; OYL. New York City was surrounded by waters containing rich oyster beds; consequently, oysters were extremely popular.*
4. *Fresh watermelon for sale at the Fulton Market, undated; OYL.*
5. *Advertisement, 1860; SI.*
6. *Advertisement, about 1870; SI.*
7. *Shopping on Broadway, 1870; MCNY. Among the fashionable stores on Broadway around this time were: A. T. Stewart & Co. (Ninth and Tenth), Arnold Constable (Nineteenth), and Lord & Taylor (Twentieth).*

Poverty, Charity, and the Homeless

"To form an accurate idea, we must *see*, not read of . . . the famous 'Five Points.' . . .

"We shall not need our hack, as it is only a short distance from the City Hall. . . . Let us go up Broadway to Anthony street, thence east down Anthony to the Points, it being only three short blocks, passing Elm and Centre streets to the citadel of this notorious rendezvous of crime and poverty. . . .

". . . You begin to see the squalid, boisterous-looking, drunken females, sitting upon the door-steps, or standing round the counter of a drinking hole. . . .

"See the squalid females, sottish males and half-starved urchins, perching about the windows, stoops and cellar doors, like buzzards on dead trees, viewing the dead carcass beneath. The population of the Points is about equally divided between whites and blacks. The blacks however are, for the most part, the rulers; they own and keep a majority of the drinking and dance-houses.

"We now pass through this alley into the area and up a flight of stairs. There lies a drunken female, screaming and yelling—only fit of delirium tremens. What a picture of the frailty of our race! We pass on. The next flight brings us upon a drunken beast in the shape of a man, rolling and pitching about upon the floor like a catfish in mud. Near by you see a poor little boy *pulling* at a piece of meat, the only meal he has had probably for twenty-four hours. Another flight. We enter an eight-by-ten room; what a scene presents itself—five or six bloated and haggard-looking brutes in human-form are sitting or lying around the room talking, some upon one thing, some upon another—all curs-

3.

ing and swearing in the most blasphemous manner—a sort of medley which is indescribable. At the stove sits a female cooking a meal . . . consisting of greens and pork. . . . What destitution! Not two shillings worth of furniture in the room, including the clothes upon *the bodies* of the inmates. . . . These poor wretches pay a few shillings per week, and take the chances whether they get a meal or not; they get a place upon the floor when they sleep at all events.

"You never knew the meaning of poverty and destitution till you saw these people, did you? 'No, never, never.'

"There are scenes and acts to be witnessed here which would make the blood of any man not accustomed to such sights almost freeze. . . .

"For two or three hundred yards square

there is not a house or person worthy of respect; but all seem to partake of the polluting atmosphere which floats about, *freely.*

"However, you will observe that the missionaries and the mechanics have made a descent upon this outlandish and heathenish portion of the city, and have left their marks. You will notice several new buildings going up; and as the officer told us at the beginning of our walk, it was safe here now. This has been brought about by the missionary."

A SOUTH CAROLINIAN, *GLIMPSES OF NEW YORK CITY,* 1852
(Although there is no doubt that despicable conditions existed in the Five Points area, non-New York commentators such as this person and Charles Dickens tended to exaggerate actual circumstances.)

1. Squatters living near Central Park, 1869; OYL.
2. Five Points Mission Building, 1866; OYL. Believing that poverty was the result of individual moral failure, the Ladies Home Missionary Society of the Methodist Episcopal Church founded the Five Points Mission. They conducted missionary services, had day and Sunday schools, and operated a free library. Approximately seven hundred children were involved in their programs.
3. Shelter for the homeless in a police station, 1873; OYL.

City of Vice

Life in New York had evolved as two worlds with a wide chasm separating the lives of the upper class from the lower class. The police and newspapers had convinced New Yorkers that an organized culture of crime and violence was maintained by gangsters, pickpockets, prostitutes, thieves, and thugs who were recently arrived immigrants. Crime was evident. In 1859, 23 percent of those arrested were American born, 55 percent were born in Ireland, 10 percent in Germany, 7 percent in England and Scotland, and 5 percent in other countries. In 1851, 25 percent of the city's criminals were less than twenty-one years of age.

THE THIEVES' EXCHANGE
"There is, in the Eighth Ward of the City, an 'Exchange,' where the light-fingered gentry congregate and interchange confidential intelligence, news of their profession, and exchange the stolen goods temporarily in their possession. Attached to this is the wareroom of the proprietor, who is simply a receiver of stolen goods. There are many of these places in the city.

"The agent of the New York Prison Association, in one of his reports, says:

"'When a burglar has successfully entered a store, and carried off a large amount of property, in the form of fine goods, this property itself is of no more use to him than the dust of the street. He does not want to wear lace or jewelry. He does not need watches or pencil-cases. He cannot eat

3.

cameos or vases. He, therefore, at once takes his plunder to his 'fence,' and receives from him, in money, such a price as is usually agreed upon. It is very difficult to ascertain, with any degree of exactness, what proportion of the value of the plunder is realized on the average by the thief; but from the best information we could obtain, we feel confident it does not exceed one sixth.'"

EDWARD WINSLOW MARTIN, *THE SECRETS OF A GREAT CITY*, 1868

PICKPOCKETS

"Strangers coming to New York should always be on the watch for pickpockets, and even natives are not careful enough in this respect. Picking pockets has been reduced to a science here, and is followed by many persons as a profession. It requires long practice and great skill, but these, when once acquired, make their possessor a dangerous member of the community. Women, by their lightness of touch and great facility in manipulating their victims, make the most dangerous operators in the city. The ferry boats, cars, stages, crowded halls, and public places afford the best opportunities to pickpockets for the exercise of their skill."

EDWARD WINSLOW MARTIN, *THE SECRETS OF A GREAT CITY*, 1868

1. *"Our River Privateers—Hudson River Pirates Boarding the Schooner C. Clemens, near Corlear's Hook, for Plunder and Murder, at 2 a.m., December 20, 1870"; OYL.*
2. *"The Thieves' Exchange—A Drinking Saloon Where Pawnbrokers go to Buy Stolen Goods," undated; OYL. The pawnbroker is depicted as an ethnic Jewish stereotype.*
3. *"A Mother's Startling Discovery—Mrs. Coin of Lafayette, New Jersey, Recognizes her Missing Daughter Among the 'Living Statues' in a New York Variety Show," undated; CP.*

1.

2.

Two Hundred and Four Thousand Irish in New York

In 1860, of New York's 813,669 residents, approximately 204,000 were Irish-born. Since the colonial period there had always been a presence of both Catholic and Protestant Irish. The city's first St. Patrick's Day Parade took place in 1766; it was organized by Irish soldiers serving in the colonies. In 1806 the Irish population had reached about 10,000. By 1815 the first St. Patrick's Cathedral had been built at Mott and Prince streets. In 1834 the Irish Catholic population was estimated to be between 30,000 and 40,000.

The Great Famine between 1845 and 1850 brought a flood of Irish to New York. By 1845 the Irish had become the city's largest ethnic group with an estimated 70,000 foreign-born people. Irish immigration continued. In 1860 there were 203,740 Irish-born

in New York and another 56,710 in Brooklyn. In New York they were concentrated in lower Manhattan in areas below Houston Street and with less density in other parts of the city. In the Sixth Ward, known as Little Ireland, they accounted for 42 percent of its residents in 1855. Bounded by Broadway on the west, Chatham Street on the south, Canal Street on the north, and the Bowery on the east, the Sixth Ward included the notorious Five Points area within its precincts.

3.

1. *Drawing illustrating architect James Ren-wick's design for St. Patrick's Cathedral on Fifth Avenue between Fiftieth and Fifty-first streets, 1869; LC. Renwick also designed Grace Church.*

2. *Brooklyn-born John Cardinal McCloskey, the first American cardinal, was invested on April 27, 1875, MCNY. He was the first president of St. John's College (now Fordham University). He dedicated St. Patrick's Cathedral, completed at a cost of $1.9 million, on May 25, 1879.*

3. *St. Patrick's Day Parade, going south into Union Square, 1874; MCNY.*

GREAT HONOR TO GOTHAM SAINT
". . . the great city of New York, the jewel of commerce as Ireland is the jewel of history, did honor to the festival of Ireland's saint by a procession which had in its ranks 30,000 solid, sturdy and warm-hearted sons of the Gael. Through the pelting, pitiless rain storm they marched over a route nine miles in length to the music of fifty-eight bands and with a greater number of banners and standards than were set up at the Field of the Cloth of Gold in days of yore. . . .

"The heavy rain storm, which continued throughout the day and part of the night previous, rendered the streets on the route of the procession wretchedly unfit for walking or marching, and yet on the nine miles of the route every available awning, door-way, vestibule and every window or balcony that could serve as a coign of vantage or place of observation was crowded with men, women and children. The route of procession was altogether too long, particularly in such miserable weather; but the enthusiasm that was displayed by the processionists and their friends completely ignored all such considerations of comfort. The heavy clouds above, full of rain, did not prevent the metropolis from putting on a gala appear-ance, and the American and Irish flags were displayed from nearly all the public build-ings, hotels and hundreds of private resi-dences and places of business along the route."
NEW YORK HERALD, MARCH 18, 1874

1.

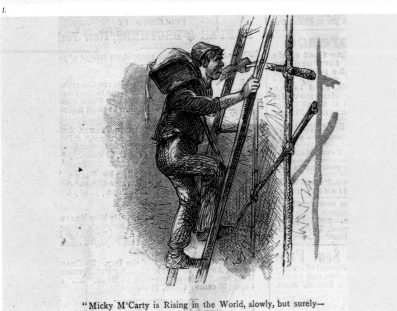

"Micky M'Carty is Rising in the World, slowly, but surely—

2.

3.

An Embattled Irish Image

Nativism, the fear of foreigners, is endemic in American society. Perhaps it was because they were the first large immigrant ethnic minority to appear on the New York horizon, no matter why, the Irish were victims of ethnic stereotyping. What happened to the Irish was repeated for the Jews, Italians, African-Americans, and every other ethnic group that chose to reside in New York. In cartoons, Irish men were depicted with human bodies and the physiognomy of baboons, as poverty-stricken, and as criminals. Like every other group, the Irish counted among themselves disreputable characters, criminals, and the poor.

"There is a disposition—unjust, but not unnatural under the circumstances—to confound and condemn in a body all people of Irish birth or parentage. This is wrong. We know of many instances in which Irishmen have been warm and efficient supporters of law. In the first Ward of this city the Irish porters and laborers have been formed into a guarding force, and have dispersed incipient riots, arrested a countryman of their own who was attempting to create a disturbance, and rescued one poor negro from the clutches of a mob. We are assured there are similar instances. It is highly important that the public should be enable to distinguish between these two classes—the riotous, and the orderly and industrious."
EVENING POST, JULY 17, 1863

4.

Irish Catholic-Protestant Conflict

By the 1870s Irish Catholics vastly outnumbered Irish Protestants. Called Orangemen and Ulstermen, the Protestants bore allegiance to William of Orange, the English Protestant king who assumed the throne in 1689. They did not want to be identified with Irish Catholics. Ulstermen celebrated Boyne Day, honoring William's victory over James II, on July 12, 1690. In 1824 they marched through an Irish Catholic neighborhood in Greenwich Village, resulting in a riot.

In 1871 Orangemen insisted on marching along Eighth Avenue on Boyne Day. They were pelted with rocks thrown by Catholics, and shots were fired by the police and militia. There were seventy-seven casualties with sixty-two, mostly Irish Catholics, dead.

1. "The Day We Celebrate," cartoon by Thomas Nast, 1867; NYHS. Depicting St. Patrick's Day, the cartoon sees the Irish as drunken, brawling baboons.
2. An Irish hod carrier, undated; CP.
3. The Irishman, shown as a baboon, was seen as a threat to American public schools, cartoon by Thomas Nast, 1872; NYHS.
4. The Orange riot of July 12, 1871; NYHS. Eighth Avenue at Twenty-fifth Street was the scene of militia firing on demonstrators. Paving stones and other missiles were thrown at the marching Protestant Orangemen and their police and militia protectors by Irish Catholics on the sidewalk and from surrounding buildings.

1.

2.

Two Hundred Thousand Germans in New York

In 1860 German-Americans accounted for 1 out of 4 of New York's 813,669 residents. Of the 200,000, 120,000 were German-born. Another 60,000 lived in the metropolitan area at that time. Prior to the Irish potato famines in the 1840s, the German community was growing more rapidly than the Irish.

There had been a German presence in New York since its founding as New Amsterdam in 1626 by Peter Minuit, a native of the German town of Wesel am Rhein. In 1702 there was a Lutheran church on Rector Street. In 1710 Palatine Germans settled in the city. Among them was John Peter Zenger, who became well known as a printer and publisher. The 1790 census reported about 2,500 Germans living in New York.

During the first half of the nineteenth century the Industrial Revolution began to transform the German states, causing social and economic disruption. Many Germans emigrated to the United States, seeking better economic opportunities. The 1848 Revolution brought liberals and intellectuals.

Those who settled in New York created a German-American community known as *Kleindeutschland* (Little Germany) on Manhattan's lower East Side. It was bounded by Division Street on the south, Mott Street and the Bowery on the west, Fourteenth Street to the north, and the river on the east.

At mid-century German population growth accelerated. *Kleindeutschland* contained four times as many German immigrants in 1855 as it had ten years earlier. The area was a mix of residential and commercial buildings, some wooden structures and others brick.

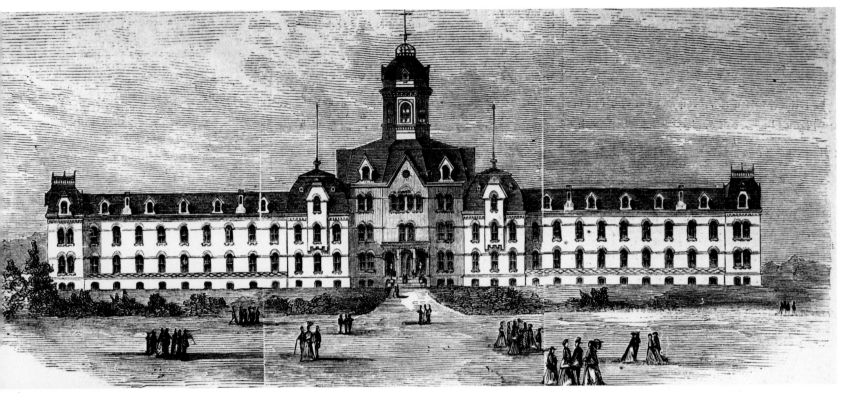

Some streets were covered with paving stones, and others were unpaved. The Thirteenth Ward, the area bounded by Norfolk Street on the west, Rivington Street on the north, Grand Street on the south, and the river on the east, housed some factories. Immigration intensified the demand for housing. Owners renovated existing buildings, renting basements, attics, lofts, and stables. Tenements accommodated most of the new arrivals. The Irish and the Germans shared neighborhoods and the miseries of tenement life. Many of these same buildings were occupied by Jewish and Italian immigrants when they settled in the city twenty, thirty, or forty years later.

Prior to the arrival of a considerable number of Germans in New York, there were no concentrations of immigrants who did not speak English. The Germans were the first of a long succession of groups of immigrants to establish ethnic enclaves in New York where foreign languages were spoken, different clothes were worn, and different kinds of foods were sold and served in restaurants. There were a number of German-language newspapers and magazines, among them *Puck*, which began as a German-language humor magazine.

1. *German-American parade moving through Union Square, 1868; OYL.*
2. *"Grand Picnic of the Sängerfest (festival of singing societies) at Jones' Wood," 1865; OYL.*
3. *The New German Hospital, 1867; OYL. As they prospered, Germans moved to new neighborhoods, such as Yorkville on Manhattan's Upper East Side. This building was constructed on Lexington Avenue between Seventy-sixth and Seventy-seventh streets. It was a predecessor of the present Lenox Hill Hospital.*
4. *Excursion of the New York Turners (gymnastic society), 1854; NYHS.*
5. *Turnhalle (home of gymnastic societies) in Williamsburg, about 1850; NYHS.*

85

New York's German-American community was composed of immigrants who came from different regions of Germany, who lived in different parts of the metropolitan area, who had a variety of occupations, and who had achieved different levels of economic success.

In 1870 the German immigrant population of New York represented these regions: Austria (4.1 percent), Prussia (43.8 percent), Hesse-Nassau (10.7 percent), Bavaria (17.4 percent), Wurttemberg (6.3 percent), Baden (9.1 percent), Hamburg (1.1 percent), Saxony (2.5 percent), and Hanover (5.0 percent). They were both Catholics and Protestants. Although Manhattan's *Kleindeutschland* was the center of New York's German-American life, Germans were spread across the metropolitan area. They had moved to Yorkville in

upper Manhattan, Williamsburg in Brooklyn, and sections of Queens. In 1875 out of a total population of 482,493, there were 53,359 German-born residents of Brooklyn.

By 1855 some occupations had become German preserves. There were seven thousand German tailors, thirty-seven hundred German shoemakers, and twenty-seven hundred German furniture makers. German bakers and tobacco workers were not far behind. Germans played a prominent role in the formation of the labor movement. The German unions reflected their occupations; there were German unions of furniture workers, piano makers, tailors, shoemakers, cigar makers, and bakers. They accounted for a large portion of the organized workers in the city and began to take leadership in the formation of a national labor organiza-

4.

tion. They published their own daily newspaper. Within their ranks, there were both socialists and Marxists.

Germans played a prominent role in the cultural life of the city. There were musicians and organized performing and singing societies. There were a German working class, middle class, and upper class. There were grocers and dry goods dealers. There were doctors, pharmacists, ministers, journalists, and teachers. And there was an elite of bankers, brewers, merchants, and industrialists

1. Eight Hour League demonstration in the Bowery, 1872; NYHS.
2. German beer hall, 1877; OYL.
3. German band, 1879; OYL.
4. Twenty-sixth annual fancy dress ball of the Liederkranz Society, 1879; NYHS. Organized in 1847 as an elite singing group, the Liederkranz Society had over a thousand members in 1869. It had its own building, Deutscher Liederkranz Halle, on East Fourth Street. This was replaced in 1881 with a new building on East Fifty-eighth Street.

EIGHT HOUR LEAGUE DEMON-STRATES

"The principal thoroughfares of the city rang with cheers yesterday. The workingmen's parade attracted crowds of spectators in the Bowery, in Broadway, in Fourteenth street and Twenty-third street, and all the other streets through which the procession passed. The houses in the Bowery near where the procession was formed displayed flags and the whole street was gay with the colors of the United States and Germany. As the majority of the workingmen in the parade are Germans, so the greater part of the spectators seemed to be of Teutonic origin. . . . Thousands who did not march in the procession stood on the sidewalks. . . ."
NEW YORK SUN, JUNE 11, 1872

1.

2.

From Orthodox to Reform Judaism

German Jews were a conspicuous part of *Kleindeutschland*, the Lower Manhattan German immigrant community. They arrived in increasing numbers, and their New York community grew. In 1846 there were seven thousand. By 1860 their number had increased to twenty thousand, and by 1875 it was estimated to be between thirty-five and forty-five thousand.

Congregation B'nai Jeshurun was formed in 1825 by German Jews who seceded from the Sephardic synagogue Shearith Israel. By 1845 two additional Orthodox German synagogues existed in *Kleindeutschland*, sharing the services of the same rabbi. Within the Jewish community there were those who practiced Orthodox rituals and others who were more secular.

However, the religious and secular elements cooperated in forming a number of mutual aid societies and fraternal orders. B'nai B'rith was founded on Essex Street in 1843 as a mutual aid society. Some German Jews participated in broader based non-Jewish German political and social organizations. Rabbi Isaac Mayer Wise, a proponent of the German reform movement, came to this country in 1846 and campaigned for religious reform, stressing the need to adapt Judaism to American conditions. Temple Emanu-el was New York's first Reform congregation. Its reforms consisted of conducting the service in English and inaugurating a choir. Since that time Orthodox and Reform congregations have continued to maintain their independence.

3.

4.

5.

6.

INSTALLATION AT EMANU-EL

"The Rev. Dr. James K. Gutheim was, on Saturday, with imposing ceremonies, installed as English minister [rabbi] of the magnificent new Jewish Temple Emanuel, corner of Fifth-ave. and Forty-third-st. The usual services having been conducted by the Rev. Dr. Rubin, the new minister was introduced by the Rev. Dr. Adler, the German minister. The latter then delivered the installation address, in which he referred to Dr. Gutheim's fifteen years' service in New Orleans, and expressed his confidence that his colleague would prove his title to the high reputation he had obtained in the South. After the singing of a hymn by the choir, the newly-installed minister delivered an impressive discourse."

NEW YORK DAILY TRIBUNE, NOVEMBER 16, 1868

1. Exterior of Temple Emanu-el, Fifth Avenue and Forty-third Street, 1868; LC.
2. Interior of Temple Emanu-el, 1868; LC. It had eighteen hundred seats on the main floor and eight hundred in the balcony.
3. Purim Ball at the Academy of Music, 1865; LC. Balls and dances were organized during this festival of redemption commemorating the events recounted in the Book of Esther.
4. Buffet at Hebrew Benevolent Association Charity Fair, 1870; OYL.
5. Rebecca at the Well at Hebrew Benevolent Association Charity Fair, 1870; OYL.
6. "Mrs. Rosenfeld's marriage ceremony according to the Orthodox ritual," 1870; OYL.

1.

2.

Four Hundred and Sixty-Five Protestant Churches in the Metropolitan Area

The Dutch Reformed Church was the accepted religion of the founders of New Amsterdam. Calvinists (Dutch Reformed, French Reformed, and English Puritan) were allowed to build churches and worship publicly. Other Protestants (such as German Lutherans) were tolerated, but could not worship in public. Jews were reluctantly accepted. Catholics were not welcomed; the few living in the colony were not allowed to worship in public.

When the British took control, they introduced the Church of England and permitted religious freedom for all groups except Catholics, who were unable to establish their own church until after the Revolution. In 1786 St. Peters on Barclay Street was formally dedicated. By 1774 New York had eighteen houses of worship: three Anglican,

three Presbyterian, two German Lutheran, one German Reformed, three Dutch Reformed, one Huguenot, one Methodist, one Baptist, one Moravian, one Quaker meeting house, and one Jewish synagogue. In 1786 representatives of Trinity Church met with delegates from parishes in Jamaica, Newtown, Flushing, Hempstead, and Rye to form the Episcopal Diocese of New York.

Like most other parts of the United States, New York remained mostly Protestant until Irish and German Catholics began to arrive in the 1840s and 1850s. By 1855 there were estimated to be 465 Protestant churches in the metropolitan area with: 11 African Methodist Episcopal, 46 Baptist, 22 Congregationalist, 1 Disciples of Christ, 88 Episcopal, 4 Evangelical, 9 Friends, 7 Lutheran, 93 Methodist, 3 Moravian, 69

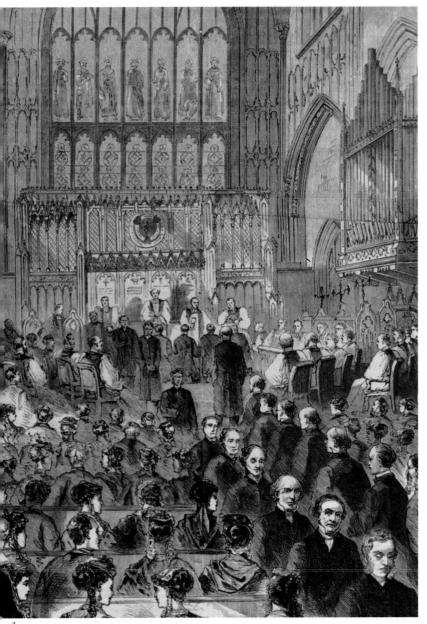

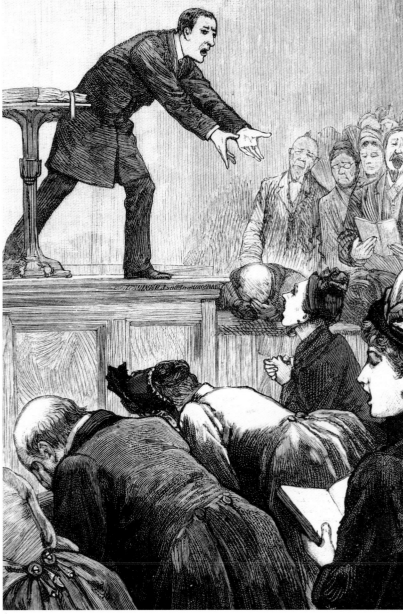

Presbyterian, 52 Reformed, 5 Unitarian, 5 Universalist, and 50 other denominations. At the same time, there were 53 Roman Catholic parishes and 11 Jewish synagogues.

1. St. George's Episcopal Church, Beekman Street, undated; OYL. Formed as a chapel of Trinity Church in 1752, St. George's became independent in 1811.

2. Baptism in Grace Church, Broadway and Tenth Street, 1869; NYHS. Designed by architect James Renwick (also the architect of St. Patrick's Cathedral), this Episcopal church was founded in 1808.

3. Triennial Convention of the Protestant Episcopal Church at Trinity Church, Broadway and Wall Street, 1868; NYHS. An Anglican church, Trinity was formed by royal charter from William III in 1697.

4. A religious revival meeting, 1868; NYHS. Methodist Episcopal "revivalist" meetings were extremely popular, drawing huge crowds.

Public Schools, Parochial Schools, Colleges, and Universities

In 1842 the work of the Public School Society led to the formation of the city's public school system. There was an elected board of education whose members held decidedly Protestant views. Faced with Protestant proselytizing in "godless" public schools, Catholics organized a separate parochial school system that combined secular subjects with Catholic teachings and allowed no individual interpretation of the Bible. Clergy conducted classes in church basements and other informal locations. About 1840 parochial schools provided education for four to five thousand of the nine to ten thousand Catholic children. Over the next fifteen years the number of students in parochial schools tripled.

In the eighteenth century, educational institutions were often affiliated with religious institutions. King's College was the city's first institution of higher learning; it began in Trinity Church on Wall Street in 1754. Closed during the Revolution, it reopened as Columbia College in 1784. The General Theological Seminary was formed in 1817, and the Union Theological Seminary in 1836. The University of the City of New York, later renamed New York University, was established in 1831. Rutgers Female Institute, the first college exclusively for women, opened in 1838. St. John's College, which later became Fordham University, was the first Catholic college in the metropolitan area. In 1847 the College of the City University of New York was formed by a citywide referendum.

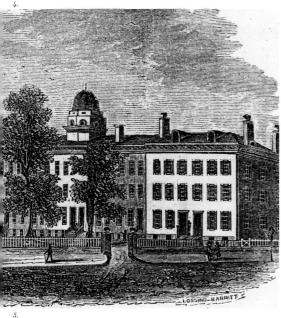

"In the regular orders of command, the teacher's voice should seldom, or never, be heard. Approbation, and displeasure too, may often be as well expressed by looks and gestures as by words; and sometimes better. Such is the language of nature, and the medium of the first moral lessons of infancy, —and therefore well understood. In giving orders, signs are always preferable to words. A gentle tap on the desk with the forefinger, a single and slight sound of the bell, or a slight clap of the hands, will sooner command and fix attention than noise or blustering. Gentle sounds act by sympathy on the nervous system, and enforce silence and order, when once the school is accustomed to such a mode of discipline. But noise is never effectually prevented by noise; or, if thus repressed, it is only for the moment; and it returns as a spring recoils on the removal of a weight. 'A silent teacher makes a silent school.'"

A MANUAL OF THE SYSTEM OF DISCIPLINE FOR THE SCHOOLS OF THE PUBLIC SCHOOL SOCIETY, 1850

1. *Grammar School 55, 140 West Twentieth Street, 1873–1876; MCNY.*
2. *Cooper Union for the Advancement of Science and Art, Astor Place, 1867; MCNY. From 1857 to 1859 inventor, manufacturer, and philanthropist Peter Cooper established this institution to provide free education for gifted students of the working class.*
3. *St. John's College (later Fordham University), Bronx. undated; MCNY.*
4. *University of the City of New York (later New York University), undated; OYL.*
5. *Columbia University, undated; OYL.*
6. *Christmas reception at Grammar School 51, on West Forty-fourth Street, undated; CP. The play* The Sick Man Cured *was performed.*

2.

1.

4.

3.

Around the Town
1850s–1870s

ON BROADWAY

"The more noise, the more confusion, the greater the crowd, the better the lookers on and crowders seem to like it, and the world from the match-boy to the gentlemen of leisure, resort there to see the confusion, the uproar, and the sights while all enjoy it alike. The din, this driving, this omnibus-thunder, this squeezing, this jamming, crowding, and at times smashing, is the exhilarating music which charms the multitude and draws its thousands within the whirl. This is Broadway—this *makes* Broadway. Take from it these elements, the charm is gone."

NEW YORK DAILY TRIBUNE, JULY 17, 1852

THE BOWERY

". . . Decent people forsook it, and the poorer and more disreputable classes took possession. Finally, it became notorious. It was known all over the country for its roughs or 'Bowery B'hoys,' as they were called, its rowdy firemen and its doubtful women. In short, it was the paradise of the worst element of New York. . . . And the Bowery girl—who shall describe her? She was a 'Bowery b'hoy' in petticoats; unlike him in this, however, that she loved the greatest combination of bright colors, while he clung religiously to red and black. . . .

"The Bowery is devoted mainly to the cheap trade. The children of Israel abound here. The display of the goods in the shops is flashy, and not often attractive. Few persons who have the means to buy elsewhere

care to purchase an article in the Bowery, as those familiar with it know there are few reliable dealers in the street. . . .

"Pawnbrokers' shops, 'Cheap Johns,' third-class hotels, dance houses, fifth-rate lodging houses, low class theatres, and concert saloons, abound in the lower part of the street. . . .

"As different as the scene, is the crowd thronging this street from that which is rushing along Broadway. Like that, it represents all nationalities, but it is a crowd peculiar to the Bowery. . . .

"Respectable people avoid the Bowery as far as possible at night. Every species of crime and vice is abroad at this time watching for its victims. "

JAMES D. MCCABE, JR., *LIGHTS AND SHADOWS OF NEW YORK LIFE,* 1872

THE FULTON MARKET
"We saw a display of fruits, vegetables, and flowers from all parts of the world. . . . Messina oranges, a heap of pineapples from the Bahamas, and bunches of ripe bananas from Cuba . . . Alpine strawberries in little Long Island baskets . . . a heap of Virginia water-melons. . . . There were Valpariso pumpkins, manna apples from Cuba, peaches from Delaware, lobsters from the coasts of Maine, milk from Goshen, chickens from Bucks County, Pennsylvania, hens from Cochin China, potatoes from Bermuda, peas, beans and squashes from Long Island, white-fish from Lake Michigan; there was beef that had been fattened on the banks of the Ohio; hams smoked in Westphalia; sausages stuffed in Bologna; . . . ."
EVENING MIRROR, 1850

1. *Street scene. about 1870; BURNS.*
2. *"Scene in front of a popular hotel at five o'clock," about 1870; CP.*
3. *Broadway facing south from the corner of Canal Street, 1866–1867; MCNY.*
4. *Street acrobat, 1871; OYL.* Harper's Weekly *provided this description: "They used to be called 'tumblers;" but now they are 'contortionists,' 'gymnasts,' and 'acrobats.' Just in proportion as they have lost power and skill, these street performers have assumed more grandly sounding titles."*
5. *West side of Hudson Street north of Chambers Street, about 1865; NYHS.*
6. *Exterior of Washington Market, about 1879; NYHS.*
7. *Interior of Washington Market, 1874; NYHS.*
8. *392 South Street, about 1876; MCNY.*

1.

2.

3.

Democrats and Republicans

In mid-century, political allegiance was determined by one's economic position—wealth or poverty—and by one's heritage—native-born American or immigrant. The Whigs, formed in 1834, remained a viable political entity for twenty years. During that time they elected five mayors. They represented the affluent native-born. Horace Greeley, founder of the *New York Tribune*, was one of their supporters.

The national Republican party, formed in 1854, soon replaced the Whigs in New York City. The Democratic party, formed in the early nineteenth century, several decades later built its constituency among the working class and immigrants. Tammany Hall, originally a fraternal group, became a political organization.

As Irish and German immigrants arrived,

the Democrats and Tammany politicians cultivated them. During the 1830s, Tammany effectively organized a system of citywide leadership in which neighborhood saloons became its cornerstone. By 1855, in eight wards east of Broadway, where most of the new German and Irish immigrants lived, naturalized voters outnumbered native-born voters by three to two. The Irish, more than the Germans, were attracted to politics and soon became Tammany functionaries. Irish Tammany politicians like Big Tim Sullivan in the Bowery and George Washington Plunkitt in Hell's Kitchen built constituencies by catering to voter needs. Sullivan bought food and clothing and paid rent for the poor. Plunkitt appeared at wakes and weddings for Irish, Germans, Italians, and Jews; he bought gifts for brides and flowers

4.

for funerals; he obtained licenses for push cart operators, provided shelter for fire victims and bail for prisoners.

William M. (Boss) Tweed was the most visible politician of the era. From alderman representing the Seventh Ward in 1851, he rose in eight years to become a member of the Tammany Hall general committee. He and his ward heelers built a large and powerful political base by courting the support of Catholics and by helping feed, clothe, and shelter immigrants and the poor. In 1863 Tweed was named chairman of the Democratic General Committee of New York County and was chosen to lead the general committee of Tammany Hall. From this position he managed patronage and collected kickbacks. In 1871 his career began to disintegrate. Two years later he went on

trial and was convicted on 204 of 220 counts of corruption. Although Tweed himself was not Irish, the vast majority of Tammany operatives were Irish. In 1872 "Honest" John Kelly became the first of ten successive Irish-American Tammany bosses. He built a disciplined political machine that dominated New York City politics for generations.

1. New Tammany Hall building on East Fourteenth Street, 1868; NYHS.
2. "Selling pools on the mayoralty election at Johnson's, corner of Broadway and Twenty-eighth street," 1872; NYHS.
3. "The night before the election at a 'Political Headquarters' in the Bradley and O'Brien district—distributing money to the workers," 1871; NYHS.
4. Liberal Republicans' outdoor meeting near Cooper Union to ratify their ticket of Greeley and Brown, 1872; NYHS. Horace Greeley, who had built a career at the New York Tribune, *ran unsuccessfully as the Liberal Republicans' presidential candidate.*

Making It and Losing It

This was the age of "rags to riches" and the self-made man. The paragons were John Jacob Astor, an immigrant from Germany who became the nation's richest man in the 1840s and Cornelius Vanderbilt, who amassed his fortune in transportation and railroads. The national economy was growing, and there was money to be made by speculation in real estate and investment in the stock market. In 1845 it was estimated that there were 10 millionaires in New York; fifteen years later the estimate reached 115. There were ups and there were downs, and there were the "panics." In 1837 a panic occurred when commerce contracted. In 1857 a panic began on August 24; the Ohio Life & Trust Company declared bankruptcy, triggering hundreds of other failures.

1. Therese Viele and her maid, 1862; BURNS.
2. Preparing for the summer exodus, a Fifth Avenue belle superintending the packing of her Saratoga trunk in her dressing room, 1879; MCNY.
3. State Street, facing Battery Park, 1864; NYHS.
4. "Ruined," 1869; NYHS.

5.

7.

9.

6.

8.

10.

Up in Central Park

Planned by Frederick Law Olmsted and Calvert Vaux, covering an area of 843 acres, Central Park opened to the public in the winter of 1859. The city had used the right of eminent domain to acquire the site, some of which was occupied. The homes of Irish squatters scattered throughout the area and Seneca Village, an African-American community between Eighty-third and Eighty-eighth streets and Seventh and Eighth avenues, were demolished to make way for the park. The park was available to the rich and the poor. In 1868 Edward Winslow Martin said, "The effect of this magnificent pleasure ground has been most salutary. The thousands of poor persons in the great city have the means of breathing the pure fresh air and enjoying the beauties of nature on all their holiday occasions."

5. *Picnic in the park, 1865; MCNY.*
6. *Looking at the swans, 1868–1870; MCNY.*
7. *Carriages and the Mall, 1868–1870; MCNY.*
8. *Baseball day in the park, 1868–1870; MCNY.*
9. *Music Day in the park, 1868–1870; MCNY.*
10. *Music Day in the park, 1868–1870; MCNY.*

1.

2.

The Pleasures of the Rich

The rich established for themselves a common life that embraced politics, education, religion, recreation, and culture. Often they sent their sons and daughters to the same private schools, they attended the same fashionable churches, they belonged to the same limited number of restricted clubs, and they attended the same musical and theatrical performances. There was the Academy of Music, the Philharmonic Society, Daly's Fifth Avenue Theater, and the Astor Place Opera House. The rich were members of a number of clubs, such as the Union Club, established in 1836, and the New York Yacht Club, founded in 1844. They looked to Europe as the center of culture and inspiration; they built institutions that emulated those found in Britain and on the Continent.

CLUB LIFE
"Clubs are essentially English. Though every continental city in Europe has imitated the institution, yet the English club still remains *sui generis*. . . . On the continent the *café* takes the place of the club. . . . The light in which a Parisian, Austrian, or Russian views his club is not that of a *home*. And here lies the great difference between club-life abroad and club-life in London and New York, where a man's club is his home. It is here that he sees his friends, writes his letters, dines, and spends the greater part of the day. Respectability, in its most severe moments, can wish for no more decorous haunt for her husbands and sons to enter and take up their abode."
FRANCIS GERRY FAIRFIELD, *THE CLUBS OF NEW YORK*, 1873

3.

4.

THE YACHT REVIEW

"Several hours were passed in the most agreeable manner by the yachtmen conveying their lady guests from yacht to yacht. Music, of course, was provided on many of the yachts. . . . Guns were fired in a highly boisterous manner on a great many occasions, and colors were dipped and changed. . . . Then there was a luxurious repast worthy of DELMONICO. The courtesies of the day lasted several hours, the affair concluding with some manoeuvering by the yachts. . . . The New York Yacht Club is the oldest and unquestionably the best on this side of the Atlantic, and comprises some yachts that would put to the blush the best of the famous squadrons of England."

HARPER'S WEEKLY, JULY 7, 1866

1. Second annual review of the New York Yacht Club, 1868; OYL.
2. Boat race on the Harlem River, 1875; OYL.
3. Daly's Fifth Avenue Theater, 1875; MCNY. The audience is seen witnessing a performance in Augustin Daly's theater, in which the parquet seated about six hundred, the balcony four hundred, and the family circle five hundred.
4. Broadway Theater, 1859; OYL.

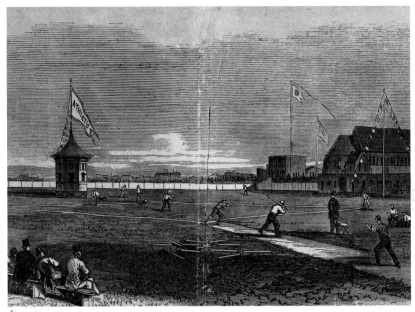

1.

2.

3.

Urban Recreation

Many immigrant groups brought athletic and sports traditions with them. In 1833 some Irish immigrants organized the East River Fishing Club. In 1840 a number of Scots organized the St. Andrews Curling Club. In 1844 English rowing enthusiasts formed a boat club. The Germans had turnvereins, gymnastic societies that were fixtures in *Kleindeutschland*. An Irish hurling and football club was organized. During the forties and fifties the English St. George's Cricket Club held matches with other New York amateur clubs and other clubs from as far away as Toronto. However, baseball seemed to capture everyone's imagination. When the Excelsior and Atlantic baseball clubs of Brooklyn played their championship match in 1860, there were twelve thousand spectators at the Brooklyn Excelsior Club.

A SPLENDID BATTING GAME
"Yesterday at 1 P.M. the reception committee of the Resolute Club, with two four-horse stages, duly drove up to the Lafarge House for the Philadelphians, and took the whole party over to the Union Ball Grounds, Brooklyn E.D., where at 3 P.M. both parties began playing in a match Athletic vs. Resolute. The most numerous concourse of spectators gathered at a match in Brooklyn this season were present on the occasion, a bevy of the fair ones of Williamsburgh gracing the scene with their presence. The banks surrounding the grounds were lined with hundreds of people, and what with the crowd, the field of players in uniform, and the number of banners on the several flagstaffs of the grounds, the scene presented was picturesque in the extreme.

4.

"Precisely at the hour appointed the game was commenced, and for the first three or four innings the contest was close, both parties playing finely, both as regards batting and fielding, the totals at the close of the fourth inning standing 9 to 8 in favor of the Athletics. From this point, however, the Philadelphians began to excel in batting, and on the sixth inning their display equaled that of the best ever seen on the grounds, and the locality is noted as being the scene of several brilliant encounters between the Atlantics, Eckfords and Mutuals. The advantage thus obtained was too great to be overcome, and soon afterward the contest closed in favor of the Athletics by a total score of 39 to 14, in a quickly played game of two and a half hours' duration."
NEW YORK TIMES, JUNE 10, 1865

THE VALUE OF SPORTS
"Right glad are we to find that manly sports and exercises are becoming so popular in America. This is as it should be; and it is good for the public health and morals. Once make Cricket and Base Ball and Quoits and Foot Ball and the rest of them national pastimes, and there will be little room left for big crimes to grow among us. It is bad diseased people who commit murders, and arson, and rapes and robberies—rarely or never, your robust fellow who has a sound stomach, and well-developed muscles."
NEW YORK ILLUSTRATED NEWS, AUGUST 4, 1860

1. *"Grand match between the Athletic Ball Club of Philadelphia, and the Resolute Club of Brooklyn," 1865; NYPL.*
2. *"The Foot-Race on 'Fashion Course,' Long Island," 1868; QBPL.*
3. *Archery practice on Staten Island, 1878; OYL.*
4. *View of Riverside Park, about 1875; OYL.*

1.

The Lure of the Beach

Those who worked and lived in New York needed to escape from the heat and congestion of the city in the summer. Two marvelous beaches, Coney Island and Rockaway Beach, were a relatively short distance by train or ferry from Manhattan; they were places to go to inhale the clear salt air and to relax.

As early as the 1820s Coney Island was being promoted as a resort with safe bathing, grand vistas, and gently rolling waves. The Gravesend and Coney Island Bridge and Road Company built the Coney Island House, a resort at the end of a toll road, a strategy designed to increase traffic on the road. The clientele of the Coney Island House were men of business and merchants who could afford both the time required to get there and the leisure time to relax. In 1844 Coney Island acquired its first entertainment enterprise, the Pavilion, a large tented structure with a dance floor. Steam-powered ferries delivered vacationers. Twenty years later the scene had changed. Parts of Coney Island were becoming an extension of New York's Bowery, providing honky-tonk amusements for a rough-and-ready crowd.

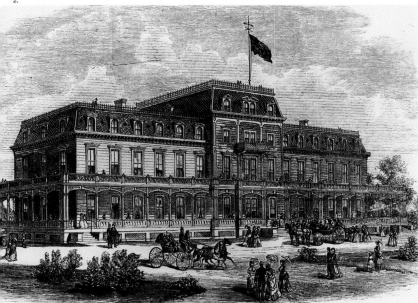

"We sailed down the bay in an antiquated steamer [in 1863], mid scenes of confusion and hilarity. At the landing there was a barn-like bar-room, more conspicuous than the dingy dining-room with two barrels at either end supporting boards used as a lunch or dining counter. Chops, chowder, steaks, etc., of a very inferior quality, were purveyed at the prices of fashionable restaurants in the metropolis.

"Three-card monte-men and swindlers occupied tables along the beach, which either for bathing purposes or promenade could not be surpassed. It is no exaggeration to say that respectable citizens, and especially ladies, could not visit this Island then without danger of robbbery. . . ."
CONEY ISLAND, AN ILLUSTRATED GUIDE TO THE SEA, 1883

THE SEASIDE HOME, NO NOBLER CHARITY EXISTS
"Since the Home opened, June 17, we have received each week a party of 160 children and mothers, making upwards of 800 who have enjoyed the benefits of the recreation. In many cases this would be better RE-creation, for the wonderful tonic of the sea air has restored to life children who had been given over by physicians.

"The experience of the summers of 1876 and 1877 demonstrates the value of sea air and bathing and good food in nearly all cases of Cholera Infantum, General Debility and Diseases of Children produced by the foul air of our crowded tenements."
CONEY ISLAND HERALD, AUGUST 31, 1878

1. *The beach at Coney Island, 1867; OYL.*
2. *The rescue of Jennie Fields from the surf at Far Rockaway Beach, 1870; QBPL.*
3. *The Woodsburgh House, Rockaway Beach, 1870; QBPL.*
4. *The working girl's excursion at Rockaway Beach, 1877; QBPL.*
5. *The working girl's excursion at Rockaway Beach, 1877; QBPL.*

By 1900 there was no longer an American frontier, there was an American empire. Not only had virtually all of the territory between the Atlantic and Pacific oceans become incorporated into the union, but also the United States had acquired Alaska, Guam, Hawaiian Islands, Midway Island, Philippine Islands, Wake Island, and Puerto Rico. In 1914 the Panama Canal was completed. European colonial empires had been built in the sixteenth century pursuing raw materials and markets for manufactured products. In the nineteenth century Europe's industrial revolution created excess production giving birth to the age of imperialism during which Britain, France, Germany, and Italy acquired colonies in Africa and Asia. Imperialism generated excess wealth, fueling the growth of London, Paris, and Berlin. It was during this period that these cities took on their particular splendor with monumental public buildings and broad avenues. If these cities were the capitals of European empires, then New York was the capital of the American empire.

Post–Civil War industrial and territorial expansion accelerated the growth of the American economy. By 1913, the United States had become the world's most productive industrial nation, exceeding the manufacturing output of Britain, France, and Germany combined. The great modern corporation had its origins at this time, and factories were being built throughout the country. The headquarters of many of these new industrial giants were located in New York. Vertical integration with owners and supervisors above and workers below was the guiding principle of management. Lower Manhattan became the location for the headquarters of many of these new corporations. Although the technological development of structural steel and the invention of elevators gave birth to the tall buildings that dominated the Lower Manhattan skyline, this new type of architectural structure reflected the organizational principles of these industrial and commercial enterprises based on centralized management.

In the late nineteenth century New York was the undisputed financial capital of the United States. In 1892 greater New York had 1,265 millionaires, 30 percent of the total for the entire country. Among them were an estimated sixty German Jews. Their fortunes were based in banking, brokerage, railroads, oil, mining, wholesaling, importing, shipping, food processing, publishing, manufacturing, and real estate.

Recognizing its national and international prominence, New Yorkers set out to build a city of appropriate scale and splendor. Brooklyn's Grand Army Plaza, completed in 1892, set the tone. In scale and setting it was reminiscent of the Arc de Triomphe in Paris. In keeping with an imperial vision, the Dewey Arch, erected on the southwest corner of Madison Square in 1899, was built to commemorate Commodore George Dewey's victory over the Spanish in Manila the previous year. The Dewey Arch did not survive. A full-scale plaster model used to solicit contributions, it was demolished the following year when Dewey's popularity was eclipsed by native New Yorker Theodore Roosevelt. As president, Roosevelt personified a new American spirit. He was the first president to play a role as a world statesman and the first chief executive to leave the country while in office.

Many of New York's public structures, such as Carnegie Hall, Columbia University, The Metropolitan Museum of Art, Plaza Hotel, Pennsylvania Station, and Grand Central Terminal, constructed during this era reflect America's and New York's new found sense of self-importance. There were events like Mrs. William K. Vanderbilt's ball, where her guests danced through the night in elaborate costumes; it was an extravaganza which some say has yet to be equaled.

Perhaps it was Manhattan's imperial spirit that lead to the consolidation of the five boroughs into Greater New York in 1898. Long discussed, much contemplated, and finally put to vote, it happened on January 1, 1898. New York became, after London, the world's second largest city. With a population of 3,360,000, Greater New York was now larger than Paris, Berlin, Tokyo and Vienna. Most of the world capitals were agglomerations of towns and villages consolidated into a larger entity. So, why not New York? And, there was Chicago growing fast on its heels.

When the five boroughs came together as Greater New York, a long-existing reality became a political fact. New York had been a metropolitan region since the Dutch established their colony on Manhattan Island. By the nineteenth century, a network of ferry boats linked separate communities and individual economies into one region. This ferry

Chapter Three
Imperial City: 1881–1914
The Eastern Europeans and
Italians Arrive

boat network embraced the five boroughs and parts of New Jersey not included in the Greater New York compact; however, they were at that time and continue to be integral parts of the New York metropolitan region.

Although bridges had already linked Manhattan with Brooklyn (Brooklyn Bridge—1883) and the Bronx (Washington—1888), three new East River bridges (Williamsburg—1903, Manhattan—1909, and Queensboro—1909) helped to integrate Brooklyn and Queens into the consolidated city. When the Interborough Rapid Transit Company began operating its subway system in 1904, the subways had not yet linked the boroughs; however, that was soon to come.

In Europe the industrial revolution and imperialism generated enormous wealth for one class and extreme poverty for another. For Jews living in Central and Eastern Europe, economic and social changes upset their occupational structure. Industrialization and modernization of agriculture began to displace them as petty merchants, peddlers, artisans, and teamsters. For Italian peasants, it became barely possible to extract enough from the land that they worked to avoid starvation. Prior to 1880, the majority of the immigrants entering the United States came from Northern and Western Europe. At this time, a radical shift began to take place. The percentages of Northern and Western Europeans dropped while the percentages of Eastern-Central and Southern Europeans (predominantly Jews and Italians) escalated. Between 1882

and 1914 about 2.0 million Jews entered the country.

For Jews, economic and social dislocations were not the sole reasons for their emigration. Coming from areas where virulent anti-Semitism was an issue, they left as pogroms in Russia intensified. Between 1881 and 1920, about 3.8 million Italians arrived. New York City was a preferred destination for many of these Jews and Italians.

Earlier waves of immigrants were processed at Castle Garden located at the tip of Manhattan. Ellis Island became their point of entry in 1892 after the federal government assumed responsibility for processing immigrants.

Although Jews and Italians were clearly in the majority, there were still a considerable number of immigrants arriving from Great Britain, Ireland, Germany, Scandinavia, Greece and from other parts of Europe and the Americas, including the West Indies.

In 1910, New York had a total population of 4,766,883 with 1,944,400 foreign-born residents. Of that number, there were about one million Jews and 340,000 Italians, with these two groups accounting for two-thirds of the city's immigrant population at that time.

Jews were evident, but mostly confined to their ghettos on Manhattan's Lower East Side and Brooklyn's Brownsville. Italians were concentrated in Manhattan's Little Italy. Having left difficult lives in their native lands, they found other harsh economic realities in New York. Both Jews and Italians worked in sweatshops on the Lower East Side and lived under miserable condi-

tions in tenements. Italians replaced the Irish and African-Americans as manual laborers. For Jews, the opportunity to practice their religion without restraint was a benefit. Those Jews with entrepreneurial skills could adapt them to their new situation by operating small businesses serving their neighborhoods. Some immigrant Jews became sweatshop operators exploiting both their relatives and countrymen. Hard lives on the Lower East Side and in Little Italy served to make them a breeding ground for crime.

When the Irish and Germans arrived earlier in the century, they established certain patterns and were involved in some experiences that Jews and Italians replicated at this time and that have since been shared with succeeding waves of immigrants. They came as workers to fill both skilled and unskilled niches in an expanding economy. They established their own ethnic enclaves with food stores, saloons, and restaurants. They created a variety of support mechanisms including immigrant aid organizations, churches and synagogues, town, country, and county associations, insurance brotherhoods, labor organizations, foreign language newspapers, and schools where the traditions of the homeland could be passed on to their children. For these first generation immigrants, becoming Americans was tempered by their desire to retain ethnic identity while becoming New Yorkers.

Below: The Brooklyn Bridge and the Manhattan Bridge, postcard, undated; QBPL. Preceding pages: Hester Street, photograph by Byron, 1898; MCNY.

BROOKLYN AND MANHATTAN BRIDGES, NEW YORK.

1.

Among Others, Eastern European Jews and Italians Arrive

When construction of the Erie Canal was completed in 1825, New York became the nation's principal port of entry for European immigrants. Some settled in New York, and others proceeded westward, first along the Hudson River and the Erie Canal to Buffalo, then on to various inland locations. When the railroads were built, they followed the same route and transported immigrants to the western regions of the country. Between 1820 and 1880 some 9,000,000 immigrants, from Western and Northern Europe, arrived in the United States. In a single decade, between 1880 and 1890, the number swelled to 4,735,484, half the number that had arrived in the previous sixty years.

Although immigrants from Northern and Western Europe continued to be part of the mix, the majority of new immigrants came from Southern and Eastern Europe. They were mostly Italians and Jews. Economic, political, and social conditions in Italy and Eastern Europe motivated their departures. For the Italians, most of whom came from the rural south and Sicily, it was dire poverty, a life without hope. As for Jews, they sought to escape religious persecution and the severe economic dislocations occasioned by the growth of urban economies.

A distinction was drawn between the "old immigrants" from Northern and Western Europe and the "new immigrants" from Southern and Eastern Europe. Clearly the old immigrants envisioned the new immigrants as a threat. Immigration Commissioner General Frank Pierce Sargent's comments in 1905 typified this attitude. He said, "Put me down in the beginning as being

2.

3.

fairly and unalterably opposed to what has been called the open door, for the time has come when every American citizen who is ambitious for the national future must regard with grave misgiving the mighty tide of immigration that, unless something is done, will soon poison or at least pollute the very fountainhead of American life and progress. Big as we are and blessed with an iron constitution, we cannot safely swallow such an endless-course dinner, so to say, without getting indigestion and perhaps national appendicitis."

Immigration Commissioner General Sargent continued: "Today there is an enormous alien population in our larger cities which is breeding crime and disease at a rate all the more dangerous because it is more or less hidden and insidious. . . . Under present conditions nearly one-half the immigrants who pass through this port never get beyond New York City and State, or the immediately contiguous territory. Unless something is done to discourage this gradual consolidation, it is my fear and belief that within five years the alien population of the country, or rather cities, will constitute a downright peril."

1. Immigrants on an Atlantic liner, about 1906; photograph by Edwin Levick, LC.
2. Statue of Liberty, 1894; photograph by J. S. Johnston, NYPL. Completed in 1886, the statue has become the symbol of America's welcome to newly arriving immigrants. Emma Lazarus's poem, to be found at the base of Miss Liberty, expresses this spirit. "Give me your tired, your poor, / Your huddled masses yearning to breathe free, / The wretched refuse of your teeming shore, / Send these, the homeless, tempest-tost to me: / I lift my lamp beside the golden door."
3. Italian immigrants aboard a ship on their way to America, 1906; LC.

1.

The Ellis Island Experience

With the tide of immigrants swelling, Castle Garden, the old immigration station, was no longer able to handle the deluge. On January 1, 1892, the federal government inaugurated Ellis Island as a new facility to process immigrants. The original buildings used to house the immigration center were destroyed by fire in 1897. A new fireproof structure (now the American Museum of Immigration) was opened on December 17, 1900. Planned to accommodate the various functions of the Immigration Service—medical examinations, interviews, and transportation arrangements—Ellis Island processed nearly sixteen million people before closing in 1924.

Most immigrants arrived from Europe by ship in steerage. They were transferred by barge to Ellis Island. Upon entering the main structure, they were given medical examinations, and a decision was made about their eligibility to enter this country. The Registry Room, a huge two-story amphitheater, was the processing center. Immigrants were placed row by row in alphabetical order and according to their nationalities. Approximately eight thousand people could be processed on an average day. In describing the shower facility, which could hold two hundred people, Assistant Immigration Commissioner McSweeney said in December 1900, "We expect to wash them once a day, and they will land on American soil clean, if nothing more."

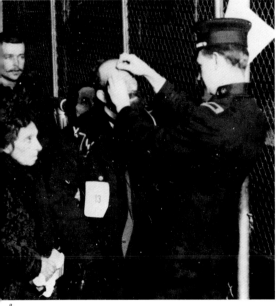

1. *Processing immigrants in the Registry Room at Ellis Island, about 1910; NYPL.*
2. *Ellis Island, about 1905; NYPL.*
3. *Examining eyes at Ellis Island, 1913; photograph by Underwood and Underwood, LC.*
4. *Italian immigrants on the deck of a ferry, looking at Manhattan from Ellis Island, 1905; photograph by Lewis Hine, NYPL.*

ON BEING AN IMMIGRANT

"The harsh manner of the immigration officers was a grievous surprise to me. As contrasted with the officials of my despotic country, those of a republic had been portrayed in my mind as paragons of refinement and cordiality. My anticipations were rudely belied. 'They are not a bit better than Cossacks,' I remarked to Gitelson. But they neither looked nor spoke like Cossacks; so their gruff voices were part of the uncanny scheme of things that surrounded me. These unfriendly voices flavored all America with a spirit of icy inhospitality that sent a chill through my very soul."

ABRAHAM CAHAN, *THE RISE OF DAVID LEVINSKY*

(Although depicting his arrival at Castle Garden, Abraham Cahan's description of the immigration bureaucracy could have been written a few years later to describe conditions at Ellis Island.)

1.

2.

Eastern European Jews

In 1880 only about one-sixth of the 250,000 Jews living in the United States were immigrants from Eastern Europe. In the succeeding decades the balance shifted dramatically. Eastern European Jews became a majority. Seeking to escape religious persecution and miserable economic conditions, millions of Jews fled Russia, Austria-Hungary, and other regions seeking havens in the United States.

The 1882 May laws enacted in Russia severely restricted Jewish residence and activities. In 1891, 20,000 Jews were banished from Moscow. The 1903 pogrom in Kishinev, in southern Russia, where 49 people were killed and more than 500 injured, was a fuse that ignited a tidal wave of immigrants. Between 1900 and 1914, 1,500,000 arrived. The peak year was 1906,

with a total of 152,000 Jews or 14 percent of all immigrants for that year. They were primarily families; 56.6 percent were males, and 43.4 percent females; one-fourth of the total was children under the age of fourteen. It was predominantly a young group. Between 1899 and 1909, 69.8 percent were in the age group from fourteen to forty-four.

Jewish immigration deviated from the norm in occupational distribution. Compared with 20 percent for immigrants as a whole, 64 percent of Jewish immigrants were skilled workers. Of the young people who left Russia, 60 percent were in the clothing trades. Others were small shopkeepers. Thus they were well equipped to fill niches in areas of America's expanding economy. For most of the Eastern European Jews, New York was the port of entry. Many stayed

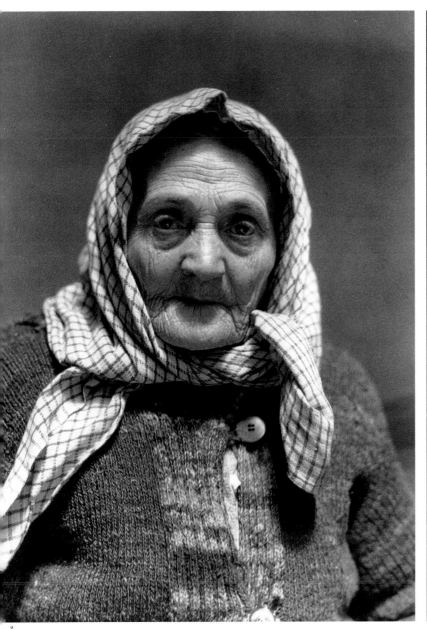

while others moved on to Jewish neighborhoods in Boston, Chicago, Cleveland, Detroit, and Philadelphia similar to Manhattan's Lower East Side and Brooklyn's Brownsville. Between 1880 and 1910 about 1,400,000 Eastern European Jews settled in New York, becoming one-fourth of the city's total population.

I DISCOVER AMERICA

"The immigrant's arrival in his new country is like a second birth to him. Imagine a new-born babe in possession of a fully developed intellect. Would it ever forget its entry into the world? Neither does the immigrant ever forget his entry into a country which is, to him, a new world in the profoundest sense of the term and in which he expects to pass the rest of this life. I conjure up the gorgeousness of the spectacle as it appeared to me on that clear June morning. . . . It was all so utterly unlike anything I had ever seen or dreamed of before. It unfolded itself like a divine revelation. I was in a trance or in something clearly resembling one.

"'This . . . is America!'"

ABRAHAM CAHAN, *THE RISE OF DAVID LEVIN-SKY*

1. *Armenian Jew, about 1914; photograph by Lewis Hine, NYPL.*
2. *Young Russian Jew, 1905; photograph by Lewis Hine, NYPL.*
3. *Grandmother, Ellis Island, about 1914; photograph by Lewis Hine, NYPL.*
4. *Man, about 1914; photograph by Lewis Hine, NYPL.*

1.

2.

Italians

Although few in number, Italians had made a considerable contribution to New York's cultural life. Lorenzo Da Ponte, Mozart's librettist for *The Marriage of Figaro, Don Giovanni*, and *Cosi Fan Tutte*, settled in New York and was responsible for bringing the first Italian opera companies to the city. He was appointed the first professor of Italian at Columbia College in 1830. In the wake of Da Ponte's efforts, numerous Italian dancers and opera singers performed on New York stages. In 1850 and 1851, Giuseppe Garibaldi, liberator of Italy, took temporary refuge in the Staten Island home of the disputed inventor of the telephone Antonio Meucci.

There was a dramatic rise in the city's Italian population around 1880. In 1865 there had been 955 native-born Italians

in New York. By 1880 the number had increased to 12,223, and by 1890 it had jumped to 39,951. Dire economic conditions in Italy provoked a wave of emigration that brought Italians to the United States, Brazil, Africa, and Australia. Particularly in the regions of Calabria and Sicily, peasants saw no futures for themselves or their families. It was customary for an Italian male to seek work in a foreign land, come back to his town or village, find a wife, and bring her and their children to their foreign home. Some were sojourners who always hoped to save enough to purchase a home in Italy. After years abroad some wanted to return to their villages to die. Many in this generation of Italian immigrants saw America only as a refuge, not a permanent home.

Between 1901 and 1910 Italian immigra-

tion reached 2,045,877, one of the largest numbers of immigrants from an individual country. Although all Italian immigrants did not settle in New York City, a high percentage did. Concentrated in Little Italy, an area roughly bounded by Broadway on the west, the Bowery on the east, Canal Street on the south, and Houston Street on the north, they formed residential clusters: Neapolitans and Calabrians on Mulberry Bend, Genovese on Baxter Street in the Five Points area, and Sicilians on Elizabeth Street.

LEAVING A SICILIAN VILLAGE
"When the train moved, there was a heart-breaking cry like the anguished roar that bursts from a crowd at the instant of a great calamity. All the people raised their arms and waved handkerchiefs. From the windows of the cars the leaning figures of the young men and women strained; they seemed suspended in air and kissed the hands of old people as the train departed.

"A woman left the crowd and ran screaming. . . . 'Say hello to him, remind him that I'm waiting; make him send me the money for the trip; tell him that I'm waiting; that if I don't leave, I'll die.'"

ANGELO MOSSO, *VITA MODERNA DEGLI ITALIANI*

1. Italian woman at Ellis Island, about 1910; photograph by Augustus Francis Sherman, NYPL.
2. In the luggage storage area of Ellis Island, 1905; photograph by Lewis Hine, NYPL.
3. Immigrants detained at Ellis Island taking time to be happy, 1905; photograph by Lewis Hine, NYPL.
4. Mother and child sitting outside the detention cell at Ellis Island, 1905; photograph by Lewis Hine, NYPL.

1.

2.

Gypsies, West Indians, Scots, and Dutch

According to the census of April 15, 1910, there were 1,944,357 foreign-born persons residing in New York City. Although a large percentage of the immigrants arriving in the United States during the first decades of this century were Eastern European Jews and Italians, there were a large number from other locations. Between 1901 and 1910, 120,469 came from Scotland, 48,262 from the Netherlands, and 107,548 from the West Indies, of which Jamaicans would have been a considerable number. It is likely that many of the Dutch and Scots moved to other locations. However, between 1900 and 1910 New York's population from Great Britain, of which the Scots would have been a part, increased by 13,000.

When the government of Serbia placed restrictions on nomadism, the first large group of Gypsies came to New York. Most of them settled on the Lower East Side in areas populated by other people from the Balkans. More Jamaicans arrived around 1900. Slavery under the British in the West Indies was less harsh than the plantation system in the South. Jamaicans saw themselves as separate culturally and socially from native-born African-Americans. Jamaicans who arrived at the beginning of this century settled in both Harlem and Brooklyn; they proceeded to establish their own organizations and identity.

3.

4.

1. *Gypsies at Ellis Island, about 1910; photograph by Augustus Francis Sherman, NYPL.*
2. *Women from Guadeloupe at Ellis Island, about 1910; photograph by Augustus Francis Sherman, NYPL.*
3. *Scottish children at Ellis Island, about 1910; photograph by Augustus Francis Sherman, NYPL.*
4. *Dutch children at Ellis Island, about 1910; photograph by Augustus Francis Sherman, NYPL.*

1.

Hardly a Friendly Welcome

1. *"They Would Close to the New-Comer the Bridge That Carried Them and Their Fathers Over,"* Puck, *January 11, 1893; SI. Puck, a humor magazine published in New York, was founded in 1876 as a German-language publication and in 1877 began an English-language edition. It attracted some of the best cartoonists of the day. In politics it was identified with the Democrats. By the 1880s, its circulation had reached ninety thousand*

2. *"New Trans-Atlantic Hebrew Line, for the Exclusive Use of 'The Persecuted,'"* Puck, *January 19, 1881; AJHS.*

3. *"An age of infernal machines, but this is the worst of them all,"* The Judge, *May 27, 1882; CSI. The caricature is of an Italian street musician. The Judge, a humor magazine published in New York, was founded in*

1881 *by several cartoonists from* Puck. *In politics it was identified with the Republicans. Its circulation reached eighty-five thousand before the turn of the century.*

4. *"Uncle Sam's Tenement House,"* The Judge, *April 1, 1882, AJHS.*

2.

3.

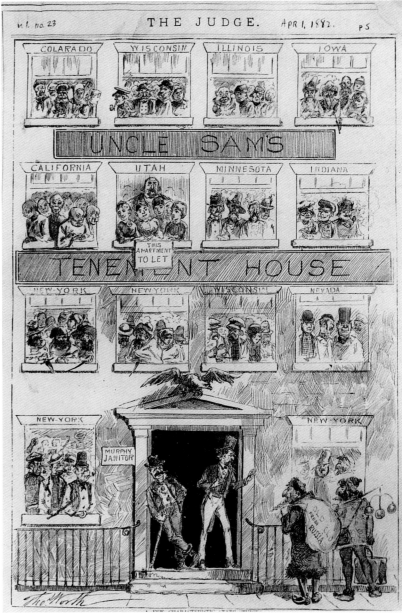

4.

1.

2.

Ethnic Stereotypes

At the turn of the century, ethnic stereotyping was a common practice in business, entertainment, and society. To produce and market products that utilized ethnic stereotypes was never questioned. To refer to another person as a member of a particular group in derogatory terms was a social convention. Race and ethnicity identified burlesque and vaudeville acts in which the performers themselves became the stereotypes of the groups they represented. Each spoke his or her own language and wore clothes characteristic of that ethnic group. Irish comics, in dialect, engaged in physical routines, German comics spoke in heavily accented English, Italians were always happy-go-lucky characters, and Jewish comics sang and told jokes in Yiddish. African-Americans were billed as "coons," and white performers played in "black face." To distinguish themselves from white performers in black face, African-Americans Bert Williams and George Walker called their act the Two Real Coons.

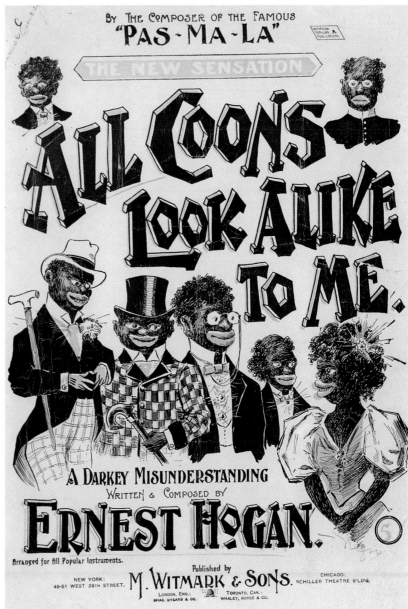

3.

4.

1. Advertisement, about 1900; SI.
2. "Muldoon's Jokes: A Select Collection of the Sayings and Doings of Clarence Muldoon," 1902; SI.
3. Sheet music, 1908; SI.
4. Sheet music, 1896; NYPL/SC. Lyricist and composer Ernest Hogan was an African-American.

1.

2.

3.

From the Battery to Little Italy and the Lower East Side

Although the processing of immigrants began to take place at Ellis Island after 1892 (the new permanent facility did not open until 1900), immigrants experienced their first physical contact with New York when they exited from the Barge Office, at the foot of Manhattan facing Battery Park. Here they would be greeted by friends, relatives, and representatives of immigrant aid societies or accosted by a relentless horde of hustlers, among them boardinghouse operators and *padrones* offering virtual bondage employment to Italians, all seeking to defraud the new arrivals. From the Battery, their next destination was, if Italian, Little Italy and, if Jewish, the Lower East Side.

1. *Immigrants arriving at the Barge Office, Battery Park, 1900; LC.*
2. *The Battery as seen from the water with Castle Garden in the foreground, 1883; NYHS.*
3. *Italian immigrants in Battery Park outside the Barge Office, 1896; photograph by Alice Austen, SIHS.*
4. *Mulberry Street, Little Italy, 1906; LC.*
5. *Hester Street, Lower East Side, undated; LC.*

4.

5.

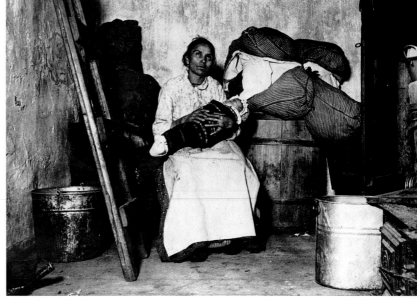

Tenements in Little Italy and on the Lower East Side

Tenements were the product of an expanding economy requiring living space for workers. The first tenements, built during the middle of the nineteenth century in lower Manhattan, were simple, functional four-story structures with four unventilated apartments per floor erected on lots twenty-five feet wide and one hundred feet deep. These buildings were occupied mostly by arriving Irish and German immigrants. Few had running water, and most had communal privies, either in the basement or backyard. In 1867 the state legislature enacted the Tenement House Law, which sought better living conditions. In 1879 *Plumber and Sanitary Engineer* organized a competition for the improved design of tenements. What is known as the dumbbell tenement, which provided for a ten-by-thirteen-foot airshaft

between buildings, won the prize. It was used as the pattern for future tenement buildings in other parts of the city. With the expansion of the public transportation network (principally elevated trains) tenements were built on its perimeter.

Although tenements were found in many neighborhoods, there was an extremely high concentration of them in Little Italy and on the Lower East Side. According to an 1893 Board of Health census, out of a total New York City population of 1,891,306, there were 1,332,773 people living in 39,138 tenements. In 1890 the Lower East Side's Eleventh Ward, bounded by the East River, Fourteenth Street on the north, Avenue B on the west, and Rivington Street on the south, at the time one of the most heavily populated areas in the world, had a density

of 800.47 persons per acre. (In 1881 a part of Bombay had 759.66 per acre.)

Citizen action seeking to improve the lot of tenement dwellers succeeded in passing the Tenement House Law of 1901. It required that buildings have side courts four feet wide and backyards eleven feet deep. It also mandated creation of a Tenement House Department, which administered improvements made to "old law" tenements and enforced standards for new tenements.

At the turn of the century Jews and Italians were the principal occupants of lower Manhattan's tenements. Statistics indicate that there was a lower death rate among Jewish tenement dwellers than Italians. The Health Department attributed this difference to Italians having difficulty adapting to a colder climate and to Jewish adherence to

religious traditions that embody sanitary laws. Statistics aside, these buildings were still unhealthy places to live.

Lillian Wald was instrumental in creating public health services ministering to the poor living in tenements and was involved in formation of the Henry Street Settlement. The Children's Aid Society played an active and continuous role in these neighborhoods.

1. Rear tenement, Roosevelt Street, 1890; photograph by Jacob Riis, MCNY.
2. Italian woman and child, Jersey Street, 1890; photograph by Jacob Riis, MCNY.
3. "Five cents a spot," about 1889; photograph by Jacob Riis, MCNY.
4. Ready for the Sabbath Eve in a coal cellar, Ludlow Street, about 1890; photograph by Jacob Riis, MCNY.
5. Combined bath and laundry in tenement sink, about 1910; photograph by Lewis Hine, NYPL.
6. Broom handle Christmas tree, about 1890; CAS.

1.

3.

2.

4.

Mulberry Street and Hester Street

Mulberry Street was Little Italy, and Hester Street was the Jewish Lower East Side. Each became the symbol of its ethnic group. Separated by only a few blocks, the people who lived in these adjacent neighborhoods had different and shared experiences. With extremely crowded living conditions in tenements, the street became a virtual living room where social exchange, commerce, and recreation took place. On a typical Friday morning Hester Street was a pre-Sabbath marketplace housing double rows of pushcarts tended by vendors selling fruits, vegetables, fish, fowl, and meat products that appealed to the Eastern European Jewish palate. Their cries, "*Gutes frucht! Gutes frucht! Metziehs! Drei pennies die whole lot!*" ("Good fruit! Good fruit! Bargains! Three

pennies for the whole lot!"), were the sound track for this spectacle. English was hardly spoken; one would hear Yiddish, German, Hungarian, Romanian, and Russian. On the periphery there were retail shops selling housewares and clothing.

No one ever paid the asking price. It was an accepted fact that the pushcart vendor or shopkeeper's first price marked the start of a negotiating session lasting fifteen minutes. If the shopkeeper asked eight dollars, the purchaser might offer four. Given time, they would settle for six. No one complained; the time invested in haggling was a form of recreation in an otherwise dreary life.

THE ITALIANS OF NEW YORK

"With all his conspicuous faults, the swarthy Italian immigrant has his redeeming traits. He is as honest as he is hot-headed. There are no burglars in the Rogues' Gallery; the ex-brigand toils peacefully with pickaxe and shovel on American ground. His boy occasionally shows, as a pick-pocket, the results of his training with the toughs of the Sixth Ward slums. . . . The women are faithful wives and devoted mothers. Their vivid and picturesque costumes lend a tinge of color to the otherwise dull monotony of the slums they inhabit. The Italian is gay, lighthearted and, if his fur is not stroked the wrong way, inoffensive as a child. Where his headquarters is, in the Mulberry Street Bend, these vile dens flourish and gather about them all the wrecks, the utterly wretched, the hopelessly lost, on the lowest slope of depraved humanity. And out of their misery, he makes a profit."

JACOB RIIS, *HOW THE OTHER HALF LIVES*

1. *"Stale" bread, about 1900; LC.*
2. *"Fresh air for the baby," 1910; photograph by Lewis Hine, NYPL.*
3. *Women buying eggs on Hester Street, 1895; photograph by Alice Austen, SIHS.*
4. *Pushcart peddler, about 1900; NYPL.*
5. *Hester Street, about 1900; MCNY.*
6. *Hester Street, 1898; photograph by Byron, MCNY. A similar scene might be found in the Brownsville section of Brooklyn. It was a largely Jewish slum with crowded tenements, sweatshops, and street peddlers.*
7. *Peddler selling clothes, about 1900; LC.*

1.

2.

3.

Street Kids

For better or for worse, the street was the home of the young boys who were both American residents and foreign immigrants. They worked and played on the streets. They were newsboys and shoeshine boys. They gambled at craps and cards. They were vagrants and they were toughs.

"The Street Arab is as much of an institution in New York as Newspaper Row, to which he gravitates naturally, following his Bohemian instinct. Crowded out of the tenements to shift for himself, and quite ready to do it, he meets there the host of adventurous runaways from every State in the Union and from across the sea, whom New York attracts with a queer fascination, as it attracts the older emmigrants from all parts of the world. . . .

"The Street Arab has all the faults and all the virtues of the lawless life he leads. Vagabond that he is, acknowledging no authority and owing no allegiance to anybody or anything, with his grimy fist raised against society whenever it tries to coerce him, he is as bright and sharp as the weasel, which, among all the predatory beasts, he

4.

5.

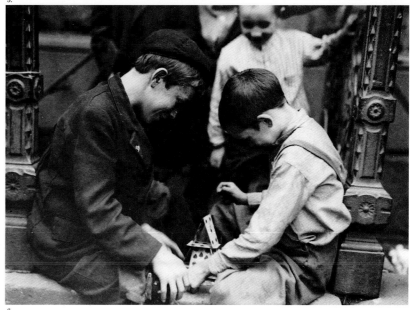
6.

most resembles. His sturdy independence, love of freedom and absolute self-reliance, together with his rude sense of justice that enables him to govern his little community, not always in accordance with municipal law or city ordinances, but often a good deal closer to the saving line of 'doing to others as one would be done by'—these are strong handles by which those who know how can catch the boy and make him useful . . . . There is scarcely a learned profession, or branch of honorable business, that has not in the last twenty years borrowed some of its brightest light from the poverty and gloom of New York's streets."

JACOB RIIS, *HOW THE OTHER HALF LIVES*

"'How about the gangs?' inquired the sociologist. 'Did you ever belong to one?'

"'Did I? Why, of course. But, then, there are at least three kinds of gangs. First, there's the really tough gang. The boys who belong to this kind of gang meet at corners to make trouble. They fight, and sometimes they hold up other boys and make them give up money. . . .

"'Then, there was another kind, and I think that most of the gangs they have now belong to this class. These boys hang around a corner and flirt with girls and amuse themselves. . . .

"'The third kind of gang . . . was just a social gang, formed chiefly for the purpose of playing games and especially baseball."

NEW YORK TRIBUNE, SEPTEMBER 2, 1900

1. *Bootblacks in City Hall Park, 1896; photograph by Alice Austen, SIHS.*
2. *Playing in a lumberyard, 1910; photograph by Lewis Hine, NYPL.*
3. *Street Arabs in Mulberry Street, about 1889; photograph by Jacob Riis, MCNY.*
4. *Mullen's Alley, about 1889; photograph by Jacob Riis, MCNY.*
5. *Group of newsboys, midnight on the Brooklyn Bridge, about 1910; photograph by Lewis Hine, NYPL.*
6. *Street kids playing cards, about 1910; photograph by Lewis Hine, NYPL.*

1.

2.

3.

East Side Love of Learning

Cultural adaptation and assimilation were abetted by two American institutions: the public schools and the public libraries. The public school system indoctrinated the children of immigrant parents with American values. They were taught to read, write, and speak English and to salute the flag. Public libraries offered unlimited opportunities for the intellectually curious. Coming from a variety of homelands and backgrounds, most immigrants had one thing in common: the desire that their children obtain a public school elementary and secondary education and be able to prosper more than their parents. For some, colleges and universities were possibilities. This was particularly prevalent among Eastern European Jews.

"'It is enough that I am a merchant,' said a long-gabardined peddler yesterday. 'What is such a life? What can I do for my people or myself? My boy shall be a lawyer, learned and respected of men. And it is for that I stand here, sometimes when my feet ache so that I would gladly go and rest. My boy shall have knowledge. He shall go to college.'

"College! That is the aim and ambition of hundreds of them. The father, bent beneath the load of coats he is carrying to the factory or trudging along with his pushcart, dreams of a better life than his own for the boy or girl who is so dear to his heart. When the evening comes and the day's work is over, he sits in the little tenement, at the

doorstop or on the sidewalk, and instills into his children's minds the necessity for knowledge. He points to his own life—how meager, sordid, and poor it is—and he tells them that to avoid it they must study hard and learn much."

NEW YORK TRIBUNE, SEPTEMBER 18, 1898

"Long lines of children reaching down two flights of stairs and into the street may not infrequently be seen at the Chatham Square branch of the New York Public Library when school closes at three o'clock in the afternoon. On the newsstands round about only Yiddish and Italian newspapers are sold. These are read by the grown-up people. Meanwhile, the children are drawing books in English at the rate of 1,000 a day. Little wonder the branch is waiting anxiously for the completion of its new quarters, the second Carnegie building at Nos. 31 and 33 East Broadway, which would have been ready now had it not been for the strike in the building trades."

NEW YORK EVENING POST, OCTOBER 3, 1901

1. *Boys' public school roof playground, about 1897; photograph by Jacob Riis, MCNY.*
2. *Taking the Pledge of Allegiance at the Mott Street Industrial School, 1892; photograph by Jacob Riis, LC.*
3. *"Pietro learning to write," Jersey Street, about 1890; photograph by Jacob Riis, LC.*
4. *Unidentified school group, about 1900; MCA.*
5. *Aguilar branch of the New York Public Library in the Educational Alliance, 127 East Broadway, about 1900; NYPL. In 1898, 194,492 books were borrowed from this library.*
6. *Girls with librarian, about 1912; photograph by Lewis Hine, NYPL.*

1.

2.

Schleppers

In *The Joys of Yiddish*, Leo Rosten says that *shlep* is derived from the German verb *schleppen*, meaning "to drag." With reference to the sweatshop era, the term can be applied to the people who carried heavy burdens and were the most visible symbol of the men's and women's clothing industry. A common sight on the streets of lower Manhattan, they functioned as the transport infrastructure that linked one tenement sweatshop with another.

Throughout the nineteenth century ready-made clothing was the product of piecework manufacturing. Patternmaking, cutting, and inspection were performed under one roof, but most of the sewing operations were done off premises. The mid-century invention of the sewing machine transformed clothing manufacturing. First there were hand- and foot-powered sewing machines, and later there were electric-powered machines. New immigrants provided a supply of cheap labor for the expanding ready-made clothing industry. Traditionally Jewish men had been tailors in Eastern Europe and Italian women were skilled seamstresses. Together they were the bulwark of the needle trades. The contracting system, which had been the structure of the ready-made clothing industry since its infancy, involved a central location where designing, cutting, and sample making took place.

3.

4.

Sewing, pressing, and finishing were done outside in sweatshops or at home. Shleppers—men, women, and children—carried garments from one location to another as the various processes were completed.

PIECEWORK SHIRT MANUFACTURING
"More modern methods have introduced intricacy, and perfect shapeliness and durability are now secured by the multiplication of parts. A first-class white shirt of the present day now contains not less than thirty-eight separate pieces and in the various processes of cutting, sewing, inspection, laundrying and packing, passes through twenty-five to thirty hands before completion. . . . The subdivision of labor is quite minute, and incredible facility combined with unerring accuracy is gained by the special training given by years of practice at one thing and one thing only."
THE HABERDASHER, 1887

1. Jewish man carrying unfinished garments from one sweatshop to another, about 1910; photograph by Lewis Hine, NCEY.
2. Italian woman carrying unfinished garments from one sweatshop to another, 1912; photograph by Lewis Hine, LC.
3. Italian woman carrying unfinished garments from one sweatshop to another, 1912; photograph by Lewis Hine, LC.
4. Italian woman carrying an enormous empty dry goods box for some distance along Bleecker Street, 1912; photograph by Lewis Hine, LC. She was carrying the box to her home, where it would be used for kindling.

135

1.

The Immigrant Worker's Life: Sweatshops, Manual Labor, Homework, Tragedies, and Strikes

In addition to housing sweatshops, tenement apartments were the site of tasks associated with clothing manufacturing performed by women, children, and entire families. Although sweatshops continued to be at the core of the clothing industry, their position was gradually eroded by the introduction of the factory system, in which all the workers were concentrated in one place. As described in the *Outlook* of November 21, 1903, "Down either side of the long factory table forty operators bend over machines, and each one sews the twentieth part of a coat. One man makes hundreds of pockets." Since it was virtually impossible to organize sweatshop workers, the growth of the factory system led to the rise of the needle trades unions, the International Ladies' Garment Workers' Union and the Amalga-

mated Clothing Workers of America, which fought for improved working conditions.

While Italian women worked in the needle trades, Italian men replaced the Irish as the principal group of manual laborers. They worked on construction of streets, subways, and residential and office buildings. While German and Eastern European Jews ran sweatshops that exploited Jewish workers, Italian immigrants were victimized by the padrone system, in which Italian labor contractors exploited Italian workers.

2.

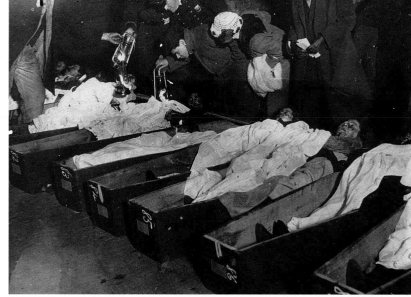

4.

3.

5.

THE PADRONE (LABOR CONTRACTOR)

"I once witnessed the departure of a party of laborers and I shall never forget the sight. . . . [O]ur conversation was interrupted by the appearance of the contractor; the groups dissolved, the men took leave of their wives and friends, kissed once more their children, and made a rush for the carts. Then the train started for the railroad station, where the laborers were to be taken to their unknown destination. Of course, this destination and the wages and the nature of work have been agreed upon in some informal way. But the contract is a sham. I do not believe there is a single instance in which a contract was honestly fulfilled by the contractor."

FORUM, APRIL 1893

THE TRIANGLE FIRE

"The fire began in the eighth story. The flames licked and shot their way up the other two stories. All three floors were occupied by the Triangle Waist Company. . . . The first signs that persons on the street knew that these three top stories had turned into red furnaces in which human creatures were being caught and incinerated was when screaming men and women and boys and girls crowded out on the many window ledges and threw themselves into the streets far below. They jumped with their clothing ablaze. The hair of some of the girls streamed up aflame as they leaped. Thud after thud sounded on the pavement."

NEW YORK WORLD, MARCH 26, 1911

1. *Sweatshop of Mr. Goldstein, 1910; photograph by Lewis Hine, NYPL.*
2. *Family making garters, about 1910; photograph by Lewis Hine, LC.*
3. *Italian street laborers working under the Sixth Avenue elevated, 1910; photograph by Lewis Hine, NYPL.*
4. *Triangle fire victims, Washington Place and Greene Street, 1911; BB. One hundred and forty-six workers, mostly Jewish women, died. This tragedy led to strong legislation dealing with working conditions in the garment industry.*
5. *Italian and Jewish garment workers demonstrating to demand union representation, Union Square, 1913; LC.*

1.

2.

On Becoming "American Jews"

NEW NAMES FOR EAST SIDERS

"The directory makers are experiencing less difficulty every year with the names of the Russian and Polish Jews on the East Side of New York. The names with which they are burdened when they come to this country are made pronounceable by the children or the teachers when the second generation goes to school . . . are written differently, and in most cases, bear no resemblance to the roots from which they were taken. . . .

"A long-bearded pushcart man was asked in court recently, 'What is your name?'

"'Yaikef Rabinowski,' he answered.

"The magistrate evidently thought that was the man's family name and asked, 'What's your Christian name?'"

NEW YORK TRIBUNE, JULY 3, 1898

PETITIONS FOR NAME CHANGES

"Petition (17 Aug. 1885) of Jacob Hirschfeld, age 29, residing at 1912 Second Avenue . . . has been employed at diverse stock brokers offices on Wall and New Streets, using the name of Jacob Field. He is now in the stock brokerage business at 7 New St. and wishes to change his name to Jacob Field."

"Petition (11 July 1892) of William Abraham, aged over 21, residing at 323 E. 3rd St., unmarried. His father, Morris Rogozinski, came to the U.S. in 1866 and assumed the name Abraham. . . . He states that as the name Rogozinski and Abraham are of Semitic origin, it will be to his material and pecuniary advantage to bear a name that will not be so distinctive . . . William Abraham Rodgers."

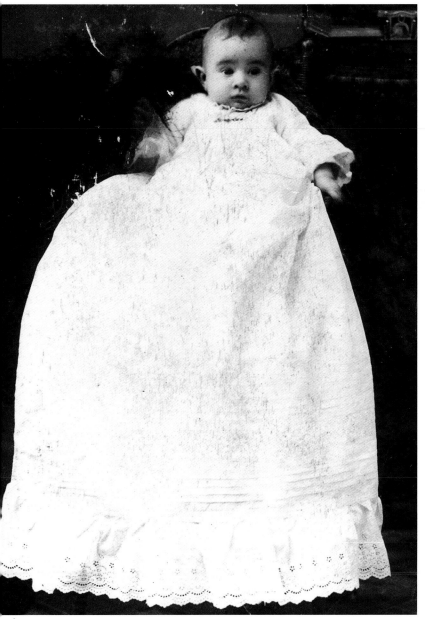

3.

4.

RUSH TO BE NATURALIZED

"This is what is known as the 'busy season' in naturalization work at the United States District Court. . . .

"Both lines were made up, for the most part, of Russian Jews and Italians, though an occasional Irishman and German insisted on his right to have an earlier hearing than an ordinary *dago*. At rare intervals still, an Englishman appeard to acknowledge his willingness to forswear his allegiance to the Queen. . . .

"At any time in the course of recent weeks, visitors to the Italian and Jewish quarter would have found male members of a family who were of voting age poring over slips of paper prepared and distributed by the local leaders. Nearly all the candidates had these same slips with them, upon which

their eyes were riveted up to the moment that the Commissioner took them in charge. A translation of these modest treatises upon the American Constitution . . . were all printed in the languages with which the candidate is most familiar. . . ."

NEW YORK EVENING POST, AUGUST 7, 1900

1. Jack and Regina Spillinger, about 1900; photograph by Joseph Fischl Studio, 1442 Third Avenue, Manhattan, YIVO.

2. Unidentified woman, about 1900; photograph by H. Caplan Studio, 27 Manhattan Avenue, Brooklyn, YIVO.

3. Unidentified child, about 1900; photograph by Feinberg Studio, 226 Bowery, Manhattan, YIVO.

4. Unidentified child, about 1900; photograph by Paley Studio, 41 Division Street, Manhattan, YIVO.

1.

The Black Bourgeoisie

Three well-defined social classes existed among African-Americans in northern cities: upper, middle, and lower. The term "black bourgeoisie" has been associated with the upper class. Although skin color was paramount in determining social status in the South, it was not the only factor in the North, where occupation, education, income, and standard of living were given weight. At the turn of the century the upper class consisted of doctors, dentists, lawyers, ministers, businessmen, and schoolteachers. A notch below were entertainers, who were often financially successful. Those in the middle were clerical workers and domestics, and those at the bottom were manual laborers. According to the 1890 census, only 30 percent of New York's black male population was employed outside domestic and personal service occupations. More black women than white women were domestics. Male and female black domestics were employed as servants, waiters, laundresses, and janitors. Most black men were unskilled workers; they were draymen, hackmen, teamsters, porters, packers, and messengers. Although black participation increased in industrial jobs between 1900 and 1910, they found themselves in competition with European immigrants. The black monopoly over the position of servants in first-class hotels, good restaurants, and private clubs was waning. Italians and Greeks began to replace them.

2.

3.

1. *Dr. W. E. B. Du Bois, his wife, Nina Gomer Du Bois and daughter, Yolande, about 1905; NYPL/SC. In 1910 the black liberals who had formed the Niagara Movement joined forces with white liberals to create the National Association for the Advancement of Colored People with offices in New York. Dr. Du Bois became the NAACP's director of publicity and research and editor of its magazine, Crisis.*
2. *Women from the Virgin Islands, about 1900; NYPL/SC.*
3. *Young and Young, a husband and wife dance team, about 1900; NYPL/SC.*

HIS GRANDFATHER'S HUGUENOT HERITAGE

"Louis XIV drove two Huguenots, Jacques and Louis Du Bois, into wild Ulster County, New York. One of them in the third or fourth generation had a descendant, Dr. James Du Bois, a gay, rich bachelor, who made his money in the Bahamas, where he and the Gilberts had plantations. There he took a beautiful little mulatto slave as his mistress, and two sons were born: Alexander in 1803 and John, later. They were fine, straight, clear-eyed boys, white enough to 'pass.' He brought them to America and put Alexander in the celebrated Cheshire School, in Connecticut. Here he often visited him, but one last time, fell dead. He left no

will, and his relations made short shrift of these sons. They gathered in the property, apprenticed grandfather as a shoemaker; then droped him."

W. E. B. DU BOIS, *DARKWATER*

1.

2.

3.

Sixty Thousand African-Americans in Manhattan and the Other Boroughs in 1900

With a total population of 3,437,202 in 1900, there were 60,666 African-Americans (less than 2 percent) in all boroughs and 36,246 in Manhattan. They were segregated in several neighborhoods with concentrations around Pennsylvania Station (Seventh Avenue and 33d Street) and San Juan Hill (Amsterdam Avenue between 60th and 64th streets). There were nearly half as many— 18,367—living in Brooklyn with the Bedford area as a center of activity; they had literary societies and a number of churches, and they built the Brooklyn Home for Colored Aged. In the Bronx they were on Brook and Morris avenues near 161st Street. Although fewer in number, they were also present in Queens and Staten Island.

RACE RIOT

"For four hours last night Eighth Avenue, from Thirtieth to Forty-second Street, was a scene of the wildest disorder that this city has witnessed in years. The hard feeling between the white people and the Negroes in that district, which has been smoldering for many years and which received fresh fuel by the death of Policeman Thorpe, who was stabbed last Sunday by a Negro, burst forth last night into a race riot which was not subdued until the reserve force of four police precincts numbering in all over 100 men, headed by Chief Devery himself, were called to the scene and succeeded in clearing the streets by a liberal use of their night sticks.

4.

"As a result of the riot a considerable number of wounded Negroes were attended to by surgeons at the Roosevelt Hospital. The greater number of those who were injured, however, preferred to remain in their houses, being afraid to trust themselves to the mercy of the crowds on the streets while on the way to a police station or hospital.

"Every car [streetcar] passing up or down Eighth Avenue between the hours of 8 and 11 was stopped by the crowd, and every Negro on board was dragged out, hustled about and beaten until he was able to break away from his assailants and escape into a house or down a side street. The police contented themselves with trying to protect the Negroes, and it was remarked by many witnesses that they made little or no attempt to arrest any of their assailants. The police of the West Thirty-seventh Street station first tried to stop the disturbance by urging the crowd to move on, but were finally forced to charge upon the crowd with drawn clubs."

NEW YORK TIMES, AUGUST 16, 1900

1. African-Americans at Seventh Avenue and West Thirtieth Street, Manhattan, 1904; photograph by Byron, MCNY.
2. African-Americans at Seventh Avenue and West Thirtieth Street, Manhattan, 1904; photograph by Byron, MCNY.
3. Unidentified minister, Manhattan, about 1890; photograph by Tonnelle Company, NYPL/SC.
4. Unidentified man with oxcart, Staten Island, about 1890; SIHS. Most African-Americans in New York were either laborers or domestic servants. An African-American involved in agriculture was an anomaly; however, Staten Island still had a considerable amount of farmland at this time.

1.

2.

3.

Seven Hundred and Fifty Thousand Germans in *Kleindeutschland* and Beyond

Between 1880 and 1889, 1,445,181 Germans emigrated to the United States. In 1900 there were 750,000 Germans living in New York City, of whom 210,723 were German-born. The total population of New York City (following consolidation in 1898, including Brooklyn) was 3,360,000. Therefore, nearly 1 out of every 5 persons was German-American.

During the 1840s and 1850s Germans established *Kleindeutschland*, the area on the Lower East Side between the Bowery and Mott Street on the west, the river on the east, Division Street on the south, and Fourteenth Street on the north.

Kleindeutschland was one of the city's first ethnic neighborhoods. Within its precincts were to be found people speaking a different language, worshiping in different churches, and eating different foods. They established immigrant aid organizations, turnvereins, groups promoting health and physical exercise for young men; and dozens of daily and weekly German-language newspapers and magazines. The *New York Staats-Zeitung und Herold*, a consolidation of several newspapers, was published until 1974. *Puck*, the satirical magazine, first published in a German edition in 1876 and in an English edition the next year, occupied buildings on the southeast corner of Houston and Lafayette streets that were constructed between 1886 and 1889. *Kleindeutschland* gave birth to a unique New York institution, the delicatessen, which was later modified by Eastern European Jews.

As one of New York's first ethnic neigh-

144

borhoods *Kleindeutschland* established a number of patterns that have been repeated by every ethnic group to arrive in New York. First the new immigrants settled in a specific area of the city. The next generation, rising socially and economically, moved to new neighborhoods, in this case Yorkville, Har lem, the Bronx, Brooklyn, and Queens. The parents remained in *Kleindeutschland*, as did the churches, stores, and social organizations. Children and grandchildren visited *Kleindeutschland* but did not live there.

1. *Koch family reunion at Joseph Witzel's College Point View Hotel, Queens, about 1900; QBPL. Among those identified in the photograph are Adolph Koch, a butcher who supplied meat to the Witzels, as had his father, Ferdinand, before, and William Bayerele, a "big" butter-and-egg man.*
2. *German Savings Bank at Fourth Avenue (now Park Avenue South) and Fourteenth Street, 1907; photograph by Byron, MCNY.*
3. *Fleischmann's Vienna Model Bakery at the northeast corner of Broadway and Tenth Street, 1898; photograph by Byron, MCNY.*
4. *Golden wedding of the Guttenberg family at 110 West 110th Street, 1902; photograph by Byron, MCNY.*
5. *The Hoffman House Bar, on Fifth Avenue facing Madison Square, 1898; MCNY.*
6. *A "beer baron's mansion," the home of*

brewer August Horrmann, Grymes Hill, Staten Island, about 1900; SIHS. Horrmann was a partner in the Rubsam and Horrmann Brewery on Staten Island.

Germans in the Other Boroughs

German-American communities were not homogeneous. They reflected the regional differences and diversity of their homeland. Austrians were generally included among the Germans. Since the area that had become Germany was predominantly Catholic in the south and Protestant in the north, German immigrants followed this division. However, another division arose within the German immigrant community. There were some who were church-oriented, both Catholics and Lutherans, and some who were club-oriented. Their organizations were modeled on the rich variety of activities that had grown up among the middle and working classes in German cities by the mid-nineteenth century. Informal neighborhood gatherings gave way to organized *kaf-feeklatsches*, singing societies, and debating societies.

In 1890 *Kleindeutschland* contained 23 percent of New York's German population; Williamsburg and Bushwick in Brooklyn combined had 35 percent. In the Bronx the Germans settled in Morrisania and Melrose. Cortlandt Avenue, was called Dutch Broadway because of its concentration of German shops, beer halls, turnvereins, and singing societies. In Queens Germans were in Astoria. Conrad Poppenhusen established the India Rubber Comb Company in what is now College Point, Queens, with adjacent housing for workers, many of whom were German. There were German bakers and brewers on Staten Island.

3.

4.

5.

6.

1. St. John's Lutheran Church, College Point, Queens, 1907; photograph by Jacob Weiners, Jr., PI.
2. Poster announcing Masquerade Ball, College Point, Queens, 1908; QBPL.
3. August and Wilhelmina Geipel, Astoria, Queens, about 1900; LGWA.
4. The Geipel family in front of their home, Astoria, Queens, about 1900; LGWA.
5. The Schlubachs, Staten Island, 1907; photograph by Alice Austen, SIHS.
6. Cider Vinegar Shop (Apfel-Wein Stube) on ground floor and Steinmetz Real Estate and Insurance office on second floor, Bronx, about 1900; BCHS.

1.

Pinochle, Picnics, and Disaster

College Point, Queens, sits at the junction of Flushing Bay and the East River. In the late nineteenth and early twentieth centuries its Irish and German hotels with huge adjacent private parks hosted outings, picnics, and family reunions for large contingents of immigrants. They boasted easy access from Manhattan, Brooklyn, and locations on Long Island via the Long Island Railroad, ferries, and trolleys. They offered meals at all hours and bountiful supplies of beer on tap. They were bucolic refuges for families in the midst of a teeming city. A network of such sites existed along the water in Brooklyn, the Bronx, Queens, and Nassau County. Excursion boats and ferries brought thousands of people to these places for summer outings.

At nine on the morning of June 15, 1904, the excursion boat *General Slocum* departed from the East Third Street pier with an estimated 1,300 to 1,400 women and children aboard. St. Mark's German Lutheran Church of 323 East Sixth Street had chartered the boat, destined for an outing at Locust Point on the north shore of Long Island. The ship caught fire in the rough waters of Hell Gate. It was a horrible scene, The life preservers were useless, and 1,021 women and children died. *Kleindeutschland* was decimated by the disaster. To obliterate their loss, many Germans abandoned their Lower Manhattan neighborhood. When Germans moved out, Jews and Italians moved in.

2.

STORIES THE SURVIVORS TELL

"Herman Lembeck, 14 years old, of 14 East Ninth street, was picked up by the launch Kills and brought to Riker's Island.

"'I was with my mother, two brothers and two sisters on the hurricane deck,' the boy said. 'We saw a lot of smoke and flames coming from below and mother got scared. Just then Dr. Haas, the minister, came running up to us. He said that it was nothing but some coffee burning and begged us to be calm.

"'He then went off looking for his own family. We stood holding on to mother and then the deck broke underneath us. I lost hold of mother and fell into the water. When I came up I saw my sister Dora hanging on to the paddle wheel. I looked for her after I was picked up but she was gone.'

"Freda Gardiner, of 420 Willis avenue, was one of a number of children rescued by a rowboat off East 138th street. She had been with her aunt on the main deck.

"'We were all laughing,' said the child, 'because my aunt had said she was afraid on such a big boat. When the first cry of fire came, Aunt Louise told me to hold on to her hand, but the crowd came rushing at us and swept her away from me. A big man picked me up in his arms and held me in front of him, but he couldn't keep his feet.

"'I fell over the rail, and when I came up I grabbed a big piece of timber. A man in the water tried to grab hold of me and when he missed me I saw him go down. The rowboat came up just as I was about to let go the log. I was so weak.'"

NEW YORK SUN, JUNE 16, 1904

1. Pinochle game on the lawn at Witzel's Point View Hotel, College Point, Queens, about 1900; PI.
2. St. Vincent's Home, Brooklyn, picnic at Witzel's Point View Hotel, College Point, Queens, about 1900; PI. Although Witzel's catered to a German clientele, ethnic groups of every origin picnicked there.

1.

Breweries and Beer Gardens

What is considered American beer has German lager beer at its root. Immigrant Germans brought their beer-making skills with them and immediately established breweries whose products, long a staple of German society, were consumed not only by Germans but by other New Yorkers. There were breweries in every part of the city. In 1879 Manhattan had seventy-eight, and Brooklyn forty-three. German Jews were among brewery owners. The beer garden, a German convention, was introduced to this country and became a fixture in every German neighborhood. Saloons had their adjacent gardens, often supporting a grape arbor providing shade on hot summer days.

1. Workers at the Rubsam & Horrmann Brewery, Staten Island, about 1890; SIHS.
2. Calendar of S. Liebmann's Sons Brewing Co., Brooklyn, celebrating its fiftieth anniversary, 1905; BPL.
3. Angenbroich's Riverside House with its summer garden, College Point, Queens, about 1900; QBPL.
4. In the garden at Joseph Witzel's Point View Hotel, College Point, Queens, about 1900; QBPL.

3.

2.

4.

1.

Developing Irish Pride

In 1890 the combined populations of Manhattan, the Bronx, and Brooklyn totaled 2,321,644. Of that total, 595,720 were of Irish stock. When the Irish first arrived in great numbers in the mid-nineteenth century, they established an ethnic enclave on the Lower East Side. In 1890 they were widely settled through Manhattan, the Bronx, and Brooklyn, with the greatest density in Manhattan above Fifty-ninth Street on both the east and west sides. In 1875 there were 84,011 in Queens and 35,196 on Staten Island.

By 1900 the majority of Irish-Americans had not emerged from the working class, but significant numbers had moved up in the ranks of business and the professions. Irishmen were strongly represented in the

building trades and white-collar professional work. Irishwomen had jobs in teaching, nursing, and clerical work. With this went the sense of pride and accomplishment involved in mainstream participation. Irish-American voters supported the Democratic party, and Tammany Hall was their instrument of political power. However, William R. Grace, a successful businessman who was a proponent of Tammany Hall reform, was New York's first Irish-born Roman Catholic mayor and served two terms. Princeton-educated George B. McClellan was persuaded by Tammany boss Charles F. Murphy to run for mayor. Elected in 1903, he served two terms.

2.

"To call the members of the Hibernian race foreigners would be an anomaly, as they are an integral part of Americanism. The Irish have become an integral part of us, and even those of us who may be descended from passengers on the Mayflower can hardly look upon them as foreigners. Once here, the Irish have bound us so closely to that little isle whence they came that we can no longer look upon Ireland as a foreign country. . . . Everyone in the United States knows that the 'Old Country' can refer only to the Emerald Isle. . . . We feel that, after the United States, Ireland is the country in which we take the most interest. This very remarkable psychological state is due entirely to the Irishman's wonderfully passionate patriotism. . . . But the Irishman's love for his new home has never made him relegate America to a second place."

EDITORIAL, *BROOKLYN DAILY EAGLE*, 1916. (Although this chapter spans the period from 1881 to 1915, the spirit of this editorial, written in 1916, is associated with events occurring within that time.)

1. Mayor George B. McClellan at the opening of the first section of the subway, City Hall, 1904; photograph by Edwin Levick, MCNY.
2. St. Patrick's Day parade, Fifth Avenue and Fifty-ninth Street, 1904; MCNY.

1.

2.

A Distinctive Class Structure

At the turn of the century there were rich Irish and poor Irish. There were Irish living in mansions on Fifth Avenue, and there were Irish living in poverty throughout the city. Despite the success of some, the majority of the Irish remained in the working class well into the twentieth century. There was a continuous influx of new immigrants. Of the 595,720 residents of Irish stock in 1890, 275,156 were Irish-born. The new arrivals came from rural areas and filled niches in the unskilled-labor market. Second-generation Irish became part of the skilled work force in woodworking, metalworking, construction, and clothing industries, where they played an important role in the growth of the trade union movement.

1. John D. Crimmins, about 1890; MCNY. He lived in a mansion at 40 East Sixty-eighth Street and was a partner in the family construction business, at the time one of the city's largest employers. The firm built major municipal and state public works projects, including the Croton Aqueduct.
2. John E. McDonald, about 1900; MCNY.
3. The Short Tail Gang (Corlears Hook) under the pier at the foot of Jackson Street, about 1890; photograph by Jacob Riis, MCNY. The Short Tail Gang was one of a number of Irish gangs—thieves and muggers—who had been operating in the Fourth Ward for a long time.
4. Chuck Conners, about 1899; photograph by Byron, MCNY. A legendary Bowery charac-

3.

5.

ter, *Conners is seen holding forth in Barney Flynn's Old Tree House at the corner of the Bowery and Pell Street. One of his principal occupations was taking parties of the well-to-do slumming around the Bowery and Chinatown, where he offered a fake opium den as the pièce de résistance. In 1904 he published a book,* Bowery Life, *written in the slang of the day.*

5. Steve Brodie's bar, about 1890; MCNY. A native of the Five Points area, Brodie was most famous for his 1886 undocumented leap from the Brooklyn Bridge. In 1890 he opened a bar at 114 Bowery that became the haunt of sports celebrities.

LETTER TO HIS MOTHER

"Now that I am here a while, I like it better than ever. New York is a grand handsome city. But you would hardly know you had left Ireland, there are so many Irish people here. Some of them are become rich. Some of them are big men in government. For most of us it is hard work, but there is plenty of it and the pay is all right. They are always building things here. Tom worked on the great bridge they made over the river to Brooklyn a year or two ago. Now he has got me a job working with him on the new streets they are making in this city. There is always something going on if a man wants work. Soon I will be sending you some

money I have saved. I know that will help you and you will not feel so bad about how I had to leave you."

PATRICK MURPHY, SEPTEMBER 15, 1885

1.

2.

Irish Immigration
Continues

Irish immigration continued unabated.
Between 1881 and 1890, 655,482 Irish emigrated to the United States. Between 1891
and 1900 the figure was 388,416, and
between 1901 and 1910 it was 339,065. As
always, a large percentage of the new Irish
immigrants preferred to settle in New York.
In 1890 the number of native-born Irish
residing in New York and Brooklyn totaled
249,466, and in 1900, for the consolidated
city, it was 275,156.

If Irish immigrant men were restricted in
their employment opportunities, the situation for women was worse. They could work
in factories and restaurants or become
maids. Upper-class New Yorkers considered
housecleaning degrading. Parents of non-
Irish immigrants did not encourage their
daughters to become domestics; they were

concerned about their living in strangers'
homes. However, this was not an issue for
young Irishwomen. For them, domestic service meant comfortable living conditions,
decent food, clean clothing, and a taste of
higher-income living. With free room and
board, they did better economically than if
they had worked in restaurants or factories.
They saved their money, sent millions home
to relatives, and contributed to the Catholic
Church. Ethnic groups developed some form
of association that brought immigrants
together to share in a sense of community
they could not otherwise achieve in a foreign country. For the Irish it was the county
organizations representing people emigrat-
ing from specific counties in Ireland. There
were both men's and women's county organizations. In 1910 there were twenty-six

3.

ladies' county organizations. Thursday was "maids night out." For this reason most of the women's organizations met on that night. For Irishwomen in domestic service there was little opportunity for social interaction with the opposite sex. Therefore, ladies' county societies organized dances and socials in halls around the city, giving the women an opportunity to meet men of the same ethnic background. The men's county societies organized socials and dances with similar purposes.

A LADIES' SOCIETY BALL NOTICE
"The inducement we offer to the fellows who come to patronize our ball are [sic] probably the greatest on earth, namely the Kings Co. beauties. You may ask are they more beautiful than any other county girls. Well, they certainly must be, for it was only last year they could muster up single ones enough to form a young ladies association. They are grabbed up the minute they land, so that it was only allowing those who were just after being married to join the association that they ever managed to form it. With such an attraction I'm sure we will be able to find standing room for men."
IRISH-AMERICAN, NOVEMBER 26, 1910

1. Emigrant Industrial Savings Bank, about 1890; EB. Founded in 1850 as an adjunct of the Irish Emigrant Society, this began as a bank for the city's Irish population, providing savings accounts, small loans, and transfers of funds to relatives in Ireland.
No longer just for the Irish, today it is called the Emigrant Savings Bank.
2. The Austen family's three servants, Kate, Hannah, and Mary, 1890; photograph by Alice Austen, SIHS.
3. Irish immigrants arriving, about 1905.

Establishing a Chinese Community

In 1870 there were 120 Chinese living in lower Manhattan. They were mostly sailors who had married American women and decided to stay here. In 1880 there were 105,465 Chinese in the United States, mostly males, with 853 in New York City. In 1882 the Chinese Exclusion Act terminated open immigration; underground immigration followed. Anti-Chinese sentiment in the West, where Chinese laborers had built the railroads, brought some to New York. By 1900 New York City had 6,521 Chinese inhabitants. It was both a reclusive and independent community. There was a struggle between maintaining traditional values and accepting American ones. Of all New York's ethnic communities, it is the one that

remained most isolated from the process of acculturation. Chinese language, food, dress, and community organizations persisted. There were family organizations made up of people having a common family name. The Chinese Consolidated Benevolent Association, an umbrella organization, served as a tribunal. Everyone paid a two-dollar membership. There was one strictly American organization, a Boy Scout troop. One of the evils of China, the opium den, was imported to New York. Most outsiders knew only two types of Chinese business activity: restaurants and laundries. A business directory of the period lists bakers, carpenters, cigar makers, court interpreters, doctors, drugstores, editors, electricians, fruit stands, gro-

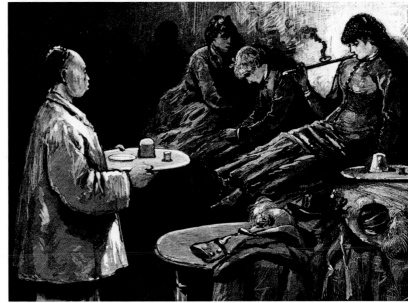

cery stores, jewelry stores, laundry supplies, machine shops, meat stores, noodle makers, novelty stores, poultry stores, restaurants, restaurant supplies, tailors, typesetters, and wagon peddlers.

AN OPIUM DEN

"There is but one pipe, one lamp, and one cook to each smoking layout.... Opium could not be smoked like tobacco. A pill is good for one long draw. After that the cook moulds another. A smoker would just as soon choose a gallows as an armchair for smoking purposes. He likes to curl down on a mattress placed on the floor in the quietest corner of a Tenderloin flat, and smoke there with no light but the tiny yellow spear from the layout lamp....

"The influence of dope is evidently a fine langour, a complete mental rest. The problems of life no longer appear. Existence is peace."

STEPHEN CRANE, *NEW YORK SUN*, MAY 27, 1896

1. *Unidentified businessman, about 1900; MCA. This man had adopted Western clothing.*
2. *Unidentified young woman in communion dress, about 1900; MCA. The Catholic Church played a major role in transforming Chinese into Americans.*
3. *Restaurant at 24 Pell Street, 1905; photograph by Byron, MCNY.*
4. *Chinatown street scene, about 1905; LC.*
5. *Preparing to receive friends on Chinese New Year's, 1908; LC.*
6. *A Pell Street opium den frequented by working women, 1883; NYHS.*

1.

Old Immigrants versus New Immigrants

Toleration of differences has become a precept of New York life. However, distinction between groups has been equally strong. This contradiction has often been evident. Fear of newly arrived groups has been a repeated pattern in the city's history. After each new group joins the mainstream, it finds the newest arrivals a threat. As group relations evolved, prejudice and xenophobia were handmaidens. At the end of the nineteenth century the public expression of such attitudes was never questioned.

1. "Extremes Meet—Crowded by Choice—Packed by Necessity," Puck, August 10, 1881; PC. With the sign THE 'MILLIGAN' APARTMENT HOUSE, ROOMS TO LET, on the side of the building, the Irish are clearly seen as a threat and as undesirable.
2. "The Dream of the Jews Realized," The Judge, 1882; AJHS. The John Smith & Co. sign is being replaced by a Moses Eichstein & Co. sign. This cartoon refers to Jews buying stores that were formerly owned and operated by Gentiles.

1.

2.

3.

The New York and Brooklyn Bridge

New York (Manhattan) and Brooklyn were two separate municipalities. It had become clear to politicians, government officials, and business people that the destinies of the two cities were linked. In April 1867 the state legislature authorized a private company to build an East River bridge. In the same year John Roebling submitted his report *To the President and Directors of the New York Bridge Company on the Proposed East River Bridge.* Born in Germany in 1806, Roebling settled in western Pennsylvania. He first applied his engineering talents to the development of aqueducts to carry canalboats over the Delaware River. When completed in 1855, his design for a bridge over the river at Niagara Falls incorporated the use of four wire cables 10 inches in diameter. Utilizing the same cable suspension system,

he was commissioned to design bridges in Pittsburgh (completed in 1860) and in Cincinnati (completed in 1867). His twenty-one-year-old son, Washington, supervised construction of the Pittsburgh bridge. In 1869 John Roebling died as the result of an accident that occurred while he was making observations to determine the location of the Brooklyn masonry tower. Washington Roebling was appointed to succeed his father as chief engineer. Construction began in January 1870. In December of that year Washington Roebling was stricken with caisson disease, also called bends; it is caused by working below water level, as was necessary to excavate the bases of the stone towers. Again in 1872, he was the victim of this disease. Becoming a virtual invalid, he directed the completion of the

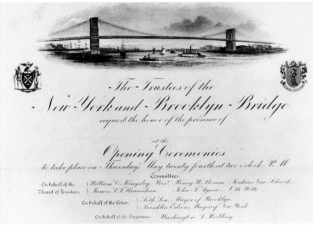

bridge from the sickbed of his Brooklyn Heights home; Emily, his wife, transmitted his orders to the engineers.

The Irish, with the highest percentage of unskilled workers in the city, were dominant among the construction crews. After thirteen years of hazardous work in which twenty-seven men lost their lives, the "Eighth Wonder of the World," the then world's longest suspension bridge was dedicated on May 24, 1883. The towers of this monument to engineering genius dominated the Brooklyn and Manhattan skylines.

1. Bridge under construction, 1877; NYHS. The view is toward Manhattan; the temporary footbridge can be seen in the foreground.
2. Visitors on the footbridge, undated; MCNY. The sign says, "Safe for Only 25 Men at One Time. Do Not Walk Close Together. Nor Run. Jump. or Trot. Break Step! W. A. Roebling. Eng'r in Chg."
3. Workers assembled as the thirty-ninth course of masonry on the New York tower was completed, 1872; NYHS.
4. The completed bridge, undated; MCNY.
5. Invitation to the opening ceremonies on May 24, 1883; NYHS.
6. Commemoraritve postcard, 1883; NYHS.

THE NEW ROAD TO BROOKLYN
"Anybody with a cent and a little patience was welcome yesterday to try the new road between Brooklyn and New York, or to regard the bridge as a summer resort and pass the day on it. A great number of people must have missed their sleep on Thursday night to enjoy the novelty as soon as possible. From the time the Brooklyn gates were opened at 11:20 that night and the New York gates at 11:50 a steady stream of people poured in at each end. They loitered over the planking and enjoyed the moonlight effects on city and river. . . .

"Soon after 5 o'clock a rush set in from Brooklyn. Men and women . . . at the rate of one hundred a minute."
NEW YORK SUN, MAY 26, 1883

163

The Greater New York.

Liberal AND Independent.

Progressive AND Patriotic.

Vote for Consolidation of the Cities of Brooklyn and New York.
Consolidation Means Employment to Thousands of Workingmen

VOL. I. NO. 4.   BROOKLYN, SATURDAY, NOVEMBER 3, 1894.   PRICE 3 CEN

1.

2.

1898: Consolidation and Creating Greater New York

3.

From the time of the first European settlement, New York encompassed more than Manhattan Island. Brooklyn grew as an independent city, and surrounding areas functioned as part of a metropolitan region. In 1833, 1850, 1851, and 1856, consolidation of Manhattan and Brooklyn was proposed. It was not taken seriously until 1868, when Andrew Green, who had been instrumental in the creation of Central Park, became its advocate. In 1890 the state legislature created a commission "to inquire into the expediency of consolidating the various municipalities in the State of New York occupying the several islands in the harbor of New York."

Many Brooklyn residents were skeptical of the advantages of consolidation, believing

4.

that it would deprive them of local control over taxes, expenditures, and development policies. In 1894 the affected communities approved a nonbinding referendum by a vote of 176,170 in favor and 131,706 opposed. In 1896 Governor Levi Morton appointed a charter commission. On May 4, 1897, the commission's charter, to be implemented on January 1, 1898, was approved by the legislature. The new municipality, Greater New York, consisting of Manhattan, Brooklyn, Queens, the Bronx, and Staten Island, had a total population of 3,360,000 covering an area of approximately 359 square miles. Democrat Robert Van Wyck was elected mayor of the consolidated city on November 2, 1897.

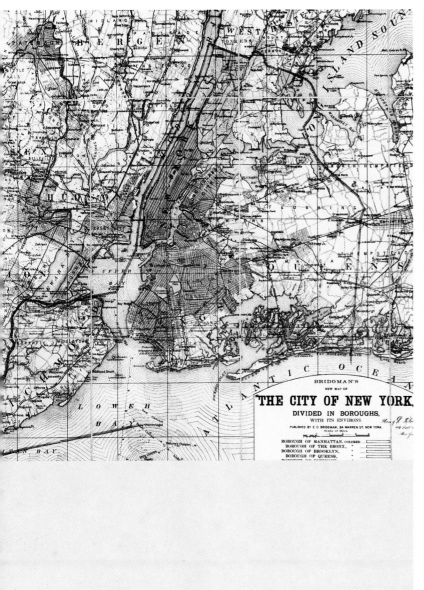

5.

6.

BENEFIT TO NEW YORK

"That New York will be greatly benefited from annexation of Brooklyn, by reason of New York's aggrandizement being placed in one instant in the proud position of second city in size in the world, is conceded. The consolidated city will at once have a population 500,000 greater than Paris, and be three-quarters as large as London; for we will have, by the act of consolidation, a population exceeding 3,000,000 and that, too, without the annexation of far distant suburbs, a process that we ridicule in western cities, but by the simple process of welding New York, Kings County and Long Island City into one city, even if no other territory should be included. And, furthermore, create a city so large that no Ring or Hall can pos-

sibly control it. Therefore, the natural tendencies of the consolidated city will be towards good government.

"Now comes a new feature in the consolidation movement . . . the wonderfully rapid growth of Chicago, the danger of its shortly passing New York and becoming the first city in the land, compelling New York to play second to Chicago forever after in everything, no matter what—business, music, society, politics, the drama, everything. Much against the New Yorker's will, he is obliged to admit that Chicago is growing very much faster than New York, and in fact it is destined to overtake New York in from three to five years."

THE GREATER NEW YORK. REASONS WHY

1. The Greater New York, a Brooklyn publication dedicated to supporting the consolidation movement, 1894; QBPL.
2. Detail of newspaper masthead, 1888; QBPL.
3. Staten Island elevated railway, about 1890; RMP.
4. Detail of newspaper advertisement, about 1890; QBPL.
5. Map of Greater New York, 1898; NYPL.
6. Fifth Avenue on Easter Sunday, about 1898; OYL.

1.

Symbols of Metropolitan Growth: Tall Buildings and the Elevated System

By the end of the nineteenth century New York was a teeming metropolis with an active port, an expanding industrial base, a booming commercial sector, and growing population. In the twenty-five years between 1865 and 1890 the city's population had doubled from 726,386 to 1,515,301. In 1865, there were 412,909 native-born residents and 313,477 foreign-born. In 1890 there were 875,358 native-born and 639,943 foreign-born. Of the foreign-born, 210,723 were German and 190,418 were Irish.

This growth was visible in two phenomena: the increased physical density and height of office and commercial buildings and the geographical spread of residences and businesses to undeveloped areas in the Bronx, Manhattan, and Brooklyn contiguous to elevated railway routes. By the 1880s Brooklyn

had its own downtown business and commercial district centered at Fulton and Joralemon streets. By the 1890s Manhattan's commercial and residential areas had been developed as far north as 125th Street on the East Side and central Harlem on the West Side.

Lower Manhattan evolved as the region's commercial center. Growing businesses required more space for their clerical and administrative personnel. Tall buildings were the logical homes for new enterprises. The Otis Brothers' development of passenger and freight elevators made it possible to erect multistory buildings.

An oft-repeated pattern was initiated. To increase the density of land use, an older building with few floors was replaced by a new taller one. There was fierce competition

2.

to erect the tallest building. When the twenty-six-story Pulitzer Building was completed in 1890, it was the world's tallest. By 1899 it had lost its title to the neighboring St. Paul Building, which later in the year was replaced by the thirty-two-story Park Row Building. These buildings became corporate or personal symbols; they were designed to draw attention to themselves and to project the image of the firm or individual that they represented rather than provide owners with maximum financial return.

The elevated railway with three hundred locomotives and one thousand cars carried 215,000,000 passengers annually over a system that ran from the Battery to Harlem in Manhattan and to 171st Street and Third Avenue in the Bronx. On the East Side

there were lines on Second Avenue and Third Avenue. On the West Side there were lines on Sixth and Ninth avenues. In Brooklyn there were elevated lines on Myrtle Avenue, Adams, Fulton, and York Streets, Broadway, and Fifth Avenue. Commercial centers, such as Greeley Square at Sixth Avenue and Thirty-fourth Street, developed around elevated terminals. The city continued to grow with new clusters of commercial buildings around transportation hubs and residential areas stretching in between.

1. City Hall Park, about 1905; QBPL. To the east of City Hall are the Pulitzer Building (with dome) and the Tribune Building.
2. Sixth Avenue elevated's Greeley Square Station, 1898; photograph by Byron, MCNY.

1.

The Building Boom

From the last decade of the nineteenth century to the first years of World War I, New York experienced an incredible physical transformation. Fueled by both commercial and industrial growth, New York for the first time considered itself equivalent to London and Paris in population size, economic importance, and cultural activities. Architects, planners, and business and civic leaders, aware of this new sense of scale, gave expression to it by building office towers, department stores, apartment buildings, concert halls, museums, schools, colleges, libraries, parks, roads, bridges, public monuments, and a transportation infrastructure linking all of them together.

A CATALOG OF CONSTRUCTION
1890—Madison Square Garden
1891—Carnegie Hall; Century Association; New York Botanical Garden
1892—Art Students League; Columbus Circle; Washington Memorial Arch
1894—Grand Army Plaza; Harvard Club; Metropolitan Club; Protestant Welfare Agencies Building
1896—Siegel-Cooper department store
1897—Grant's Tomb; Congregation Shearith Israel Synagogue
1898—Low Memorial Library, Columbia University
1899—Bronx Zoo; New York Yacht Club
1900—University Club
1901—Macy's Herald Square department store; New York Chamber of Commerce

1902—Carnegie mansion; Metropolitan
Museum of Art (Fifth Avenue facade)
1903—Flatiron Building; Lyceum Theater;
Luna Park, Coney Island; New Amsterdam
Theater; New York Stock Exchange;
General Sherman statue, Williamsburg
Bridge
1904—Ansonia Hotel; opening of IRT sub-
way; St. Regis Hotel
1905—College of the City of New York;
Sixty-ninth Regiment Armory
1906—B. Altman and Company
1907—Pierpont Morgan Library; Plaza Hotel;
U.S. Customs House
1908—Alwyn Court; Apthorp; Brooklyn
Academy of Music; New-York Historical
Society; Singer Tower
1909—Grand Concourse; Manhattan Bridge;

Metropolitan Life Insurance Company;
Police Department Central Headquarters;
Queensboro Bridge
1910—Pennsylvania Station
1911—Cathedral of St. John the Divine; New
York Public Library
1912—Forest Hills Gardens
1913—Grand Central Terminal; New York
Times Building; Woolworth Building
1914—Frick mansion; Municipal Building;
Knickerbocker Club; St. Thomas Church
1915—Brooklyn Museum; Yale Club

*1. Driving the last rivet, Metropolitan Life
Tower, 1908; CP. It became a tradition for
business executives to drive the last rivet
when a major building was completed.*
*2. Flatiron (Fuller) Building, about 1903;
OYL. At Fifth Avenue and Twenty-third
Street, it was the first tall building north of
City Hall.*
*3. Woolworth Building under construction,
about 1912; CP. The owners acknowledged
that this building was planned more as an
advertisement for Woolworth stores than as a
real estate investment.*

1.

Building the Subway

New York's growth has been conditioned by its geography. With Manhattan, a narrow island having water on all sides, being the driving force of the city's development, density and congestion have been endemic to New York life. The 1811 Manhattan gridiron street plan guaranteed that traffic congestion would never abate. At the end of the nineteenth century New York was becoming a different place: bigger, more densely populated, and more congested. Lower Manhattan was the center of commercial activity, and the Lower East Side was bulging with tenements. In 1865 surface transportation carried 79,618,818 passengers annually. In 1872 with elevated railways in operation, the number grew to 138,889,349. By 1886 surface lines and elevated railways carried 321,911,727 passengers annually. The grow-

ing middle class wanted to live away from congestion in new neighborhoods in Manhattan and the boroughs. Available modes of transportation, horse-drawn streetcars and elevated trains traveling at ten miles an hour, made commuting to distant locations onerous.

Technical developments, like the recent availability of electrical power, offered an alternative: subway trains traveling at forty to fifty miles an hour. In the wake of governmental and political problems, New York's commercial elite created a solution. On March 24, 1900, Mayor Robert Van Wyck turned the first spadeful of earth for the thirty-five-million-dollar subway system. On October 27, 1904, the Interborough Rapid Transit Company began operation of its 20.8-mile system, with 15 miles under-

ground and 5.8 miles of viaduct construction. The first line ran from City Hall to Grand Central, across Forty-second Street, and north on Broadway.

Although the subway was immediately acknowledged as a glorious solution, unanticipated problems arose. It was crowded and hot. Designed to accommodate 350,000 per day, it attracted 425,000 daily riders. The electrical systems generated heat, and the waterproofing barrier at the stations trapped the heat. During its first summer of operation it was 5.6 percent hotter underground than aboveground.

1. Tunnel construction, 1903; TM. Of the 20.8-mile system, 4.54 miles were tunnels.
2. Cut-and-cover construction, 1903; OYL. Of the 20.8-mile system, 10.46 miles were cut and covered. As an economy measure, it was decided to build as much as possible of the subway system directly beneath the surface of city streets because the city owned the property.
3. Opening ceremonies, October 27, 1904; MCNY. Although the subway was a civic project with broad community support, four people contributed to the final character of the system: financier August Belmont, Jr., contractor John B. McDonald, engineer William Barclay Parsons, and architect C. Grant La Farge.
4. Subway entrance and exit kiosks, 1904; LC.

BIRTH OF SUBWAY CRUSH
"Indescribable scenes of crowding and confusion, never before paralleled in this city, marked the throwing open of the subway to the general public last night. . . .

"Men fought, kicked and pummelled one another in their mad desire to reach the subway ticket offices or to ride on the trains. Women were dragged out, either screaming in hysterics or in a swooning condition; gray haired men pleaded for mercy; boys were knocked down, and only escaped by a miracle being trampled under foot. The presence of the police averted what would undoubtedly have been panic, after panic, with wholesale loss of life."
NEW YORK TRIBUNE, OCTOBER 28, 1904

1.

2.

3.

The Streets of New York, 1890–1905

"In New York all roads lead not to Rome, but to the Battery. There the city had its beginnings; and to-day, after three centuries of municipal existence and of steady expansion northward, the stupendous commercial and financial interests of the metropolis are still in that vicinity. The trains of the elevated railroads all run to the Battery, and all the principal street-car lines tend in that direction. . . .

"Broadway, which starts from Bowling Green, is one of the longest and grandest business thoroughfares in the world. It is not always imposing, but it is always interesting; and in general appearance, variety of scenes and impressive air of business and social activities, it has, all in all, no rival on either continent. . . .

"Here is the retail shopping district, from 10th Street to above 23rd Street. . . . [The] prominent retail establishments are the wonder and the admiration of all who see them, and in extent and in variety of goods they are not surpassed elsewhere in the world. . . .

"Fifth Avenue is celebrated the world over as the grand residence street of the aristocratic and wealthy families of the metropolis. In recent years business has encroached upon its boundaries, but despite all it still retains its prestige and its brilliant character. . . .

"Madison Avenue, which, only a block away, runs parallel with Fifth Avenue, contains the Villard Florentine palace, part of which is now the home of Whitelaw Reid, the editor of the *Tribune* and ex-United-States Minister to France. . . .

"Sixth Avenue rivals Broadway, 14th Street and 23rd Street in its retail stores. Several of the large dry-goods establishments are there, and hundreds of smaller shops. . . .

"Seventh Avenue, extending from Greenwich Avenue to Central Park, is a residence-street for people of moderate means, and has many retail stores. . . .

"Eighth Avenue is the West-Side cheap thoroughfare. The upper part of the avenue toward 59th Street is respectable, and contains several notable public buildings.

"Central Park West is that part of Eighth Avenue that faces Central Park from 59th Street to 110th Street. It is a beautiful street, and is being built up with artistic and expensive private houses and handsome apartment-hotels. The Dakota, the San Remo, the San Carlo, and the La Grange, are among the finest houses of their kind in the city. . . .

"The Bowery is historic ground. In the good old pre-colonial days it was a pleasant country lane running between the 'Boweries' or farms of the worthy Dutch burghers. Its rural character departed years and years ago, and for a long time its name was synonymous with all the worst phases of vice in the slums of the great city."

KING'S HANDBOOK OF NEW YORK CITY

1. *Broadway and 23d Street, about 1889; OYL.*
2. *East 125th Street and Third Avenue, about 1895; MCNY.*
3. *"In the City Where Nobody Cares," sheet music, 1908; MCNY.*
4. *Newsboys, South Ferry, Battery Park, 1895; photograph by Alice Austen, SIHS.*
5. *Messenger boy, Broadway and 30th Street, 1896; photograph by Alice Austen, SIHS.*
6. *Newsgirl, 23d Street station, Sixth Avenue elevated, 1895; photograph by Alice Austen, SIHS.*
7. *Street sweeper, 1895; photograph by Alice Austen, SIHS.*

Within the image:

MONTAUK THEATRE

PIANOS

M.V. CARBERRY, PHOTOGRAPHER

"HOMES FURNISHED 1⁰⁰ PER WEEK"

MULLINS & SONS

78-84 MYRTLE AVE.

1.

In Brooklyn

When the Brooklyn Bridge was completed in 1883, the first physical link between Brooklyn and Manhattan was established. The upper levels were dedicated to cable cars, and the lower levels carried horse-drawn carriages and wagons. Both Manhattan and Brooklyn had their own networks of streetcars and elevated railways; the Brooklyn Bridge provided a connection that required transferring from one conveyance to another to complete a journey.

In 1890 Brooklyn's population numbered 806,343. Approximately 466,800 were native born, and the remainder foreign-born immigrants, with 94,798 from Germany, 84,738 from Ireland, and 34,512 from Great Britain. Prior to consolidation, Brooklyn had been the nation's fourth-largest city, with New York, Philadelphia, and Chicago ahead. Sugar refining was its largest industry, producing more than half of all the sugar consumed in the United States. There were slaughterhouses, oil refineries, foundries, and printing plants. In downtown Brooklyn there were commercial, industrial, and residential areas, with the Navy Yard and waterfront on the periphery. Williamsburg was commercial, industrial, and residential. Brooklyn Heights and Park Slope were primarily residential. Flatbush was being transformed from village to urban center. With the expansion of public transportation, other areas contiguous to the elevated and streetcars were experiencing similar changes.

With consolidation in 1898, Brooklyn might have lost its political independence.

2.

However, this did not stunt its growth. By 1900 its population had reached 1,000,000 and in 1905 there were more than 100,000 factory workers.

1. *Fulton Street at De Kalb Avenue, about 1905; BHS. Downtown Brooklyn was a dense area of office buildings and commercial structures with residential Brooklyn Heights only a few blocks away. The Fulton Street elevated tracks are seen stretching through the heart of the downtown shopping and theater district to Grand Army Plaza.*
2. *Gordon L. Ford family in their library at 97 Clark Street, Brooklyn Heights, 1889; NYHS. Emily Ellsworth is seated in the lower left.*

1.

In the Bronx and Queens

Consolidation in 1898 amalgamated Manhattan with the four other boroughs. However, sections of the Bronx had already been incorporated into New York City. The towns of Kingsbridge, Morrisania, and West Farms were annexed in 1874. In the 1890s there was strong support in parts of Eastchester, Pelham, and Wakefield for consolidation. In 1895 areas West of the Bronx River became part of New York City.

In the 1890s and 1900s the Bronx was transformed from a group of villages into an urbanized continuation of Manhattan. First the railroads and then the subway provided a transportation link. The Bronx became a second settlement destination for many immigrants who first established themselves in Manhattan's ethnic neighborhoods. The Germans settled in Morrisania, where they

built breweries and beer gardens. Italians moved to Belmont and Melrose. The Irish were in Fordham, Highbridge, Kingsbridge, Melrose, Morrisania, and Mott Haven. The Jews were in Fordham, along the Grand Concourse, in Morrisania, and in Tremont.

In 1890 the area that became the borough of Queens had a population of 87,050; by the turn of the century it was 152,999, and by 1910 it had increased to 284,041. What had been a series of villages and towns lying in the midst of farmland became urbanized. The Long Island Railroad brought Queens within commuting distance of Manhattan. When the Queensboro Bridge was opened to traffic in 1909, it provided automobile and trolley access to Manhattan. Established communities like Long Island City, Jamaica, Flushing, and Newtown expanded. During

2.

3.

4.

the last decade of the nineteenth century and the beginning of the twentieth century, real estate developers created new communities: St. Albans in 1892, Bellerose in 1897, Auburndale in 1901, Forest Hills in 1906, Laurelton in 1906, South Ozone Park in 1907, Beechhurst in 1907, Malba in 1908, Howard Beach in 1911, Forest Hills Gardens in 1912, and Kew Gardens in 1912. Where there had been open fields, there were now paved streets, sidewalks, streetcar tracks, shops, stores, and acres of detached houses.

1. Intersection of Jamaica Avenue (Fulton Street) and 160th Street (Washington Street), Jamaica, Queens, 1915; photograph by Frederick J. Weber, QBPL.
2. Cimini & Co. ice wagon, Bronx, undated; BCHS.
3. William Morlang in front of his furniture and bedding store at 1054 Washington Avenue (near 166th Street), Bronx, about 1890; BCHS.
4. Hepburn's National Pharmacy, College Point, Queens, 1902; PI.

1.

The Public School System

A public school system was established in Manhattan in 1842. However, there were independent schools, some of which had religious orientations. In the minds of many German and Irish Roman Catholic immigrants the public schools were perceived as Protestant. The elementary school curriculum stressed basic instruction in language, arithmetic, singing, drawing, and calisthenics with science, history, and civics taught in the higher grades. In Manhattan and Brooklyn there were separate "colored" schools for blacks until the 1880s. Continuing the separation of church and state, the 1894 state constitutional convention enacted a ban on state aid to religious schools. In April 1896 Governor Levi Morton signed a law centralizing the New York City public school system, ending all neighborhood participation in school management and creating a single Board of Education. When the consolidation of Greater New York was implemented in 1898, the centralized school system was prepared to incorporate the separate schools of the boroughs into one unified system. Governor Morton's action was hailed as one of the most important decisions to be made affecting public education. It served as a model for cities throughout the country. At the time of consolidation the school population was swelling with the children of new immigrants. In 1898 there were approximately one half million students in the Greater New York public school system.

1. Morris High School class at the New York Botanical Garden, about 1900; BCHS. Founded in 1897, Morris High School in the Bronx was one of the first public high schools in the city.

2. Getting working papers, Brooklyn (Boys) Continuing Education School, about 1900; QBPL.

3. Class of Miss Agnes A. Lawlor, teacher of English and music, P.S. 27, Queens, about 1900; PI.

4. P.S. 7, Astoria, Queens, about 1900; QBPL.

CITIZENS IN THE MAKING

"The training of future citizens is the first duty of the public schools. . . .

"The principal and teachers, supported at present by the Health Officer, must deal with the question of cleanliness, not as a mere matter of appearance but rather as an absolute necessity. . . . Only by insisting—doubly insisting—on clean hands and faces can the teacher lay the foundation for habits of cleanliness. The next step is to insist on combed hair, then on cleaned shoes or boots, and it is not a rare sight to see a monitor or teacher placed at the entrance of an assembly room as Inspector-General of faces, hair, and shoes."

NEW YORK EVENING POST, JANUARY 10, 1903

1.

Calisthenics in the Public Schools

Personal health and public health were two linked issues. As New York became more congested and industrial and as immigrants continued to arrive, there was increasing concern about public health. The air was polluted by Brooklyn oil refineries and foundries; the streets were laden with horse manure and garbage; the disposal of sewage was a problem. With the memory of cholera epidemics in 1832 and 1849, there was fear that such outbreaks might occur again. The Metropolitan Board of Health was established in 1866 to prevent and cure diseases, to inspect houses, and to enforce health laws and the sanitary code. In 1901 twelve thousand cases of tuberculosis were reported; the disease was responsible for one out of four deaths of those between fifteen and sixty-five.

Calisthenics (systematic exercises performed in a group without apparatus) were considered a desirable health practice for schoolchildren and of value in the prevention of disease.

2.

1 and 2. Calisthenics classes in New York City public schools, about 1900; NYPL. It was customary for schoolchildren to have calisthenics on a regular basis.

LET WOMEN STICK TO LIGHTER AND GRACEFUL FORMS OF EXERCISE, SAYS HARVARD'S PHYSICAL DIRECTOR

"According to opinions expressed by authorities who addressed the Public School Physical Training Society at a mass meeting held last evening at the hall of the Board of Education in Fifty-ninth Street, woman for her own good should not strive to emulate man in the more strenuous forms of athletics, particularly competitive games, and should pursue physical training merely for recreation and pleasure. . . .

"The forms of gymnastics to which woman should confine herself Dr. Sargent classified thus: All forms of dancing, calisthenics, and light gymnastics, archery, lawn tennis, swimming, field hockey, lacrosse, sprint running, bicycling, rowing, canoeing, golf, skating, fencing and all gymnastic plays and games."
NEW YORK TIMES, MARCH 31, 1906

1.

Barnard, Blaikie, Brearley, and Browning

Private school education has been a factor in New York life since the Dutch Reformed Church established the Collegiate School for boys in 1628. The Trinity School opened its doors in 1709, and the Columbia Grammar and Preparatory School was created in 1764. In 1784 the Regents of the University of the State of New York were created to oversee academies providing secondary education and Columbia College. The Regents assigned one of their first charters in 1787 to Erasmus Hall Academy in Flatbush (Brooklyn), which was then operating both a day school and a boarding school.

Throughout the nineteenth century private and public schools coexisted. The public school system served the needs of the growing middle class and new immigrants. Private schools were for the children of the established rich families, many of whom received their schooling from tutors. New York's turn-of-the-century economic boom generated a new commercial and industrial elite that preferred to send their children to private schools. Together the old rich families and the new rich families provided support for a number of new private schools. Some were exclusively for boys or for girls, and others were coed. Most were nonsectarian; however, some were Catholic or Protestant. Among these new private schools were: Allen-Stevenson, boys (1883), Brearley, girls (1884), Brooklyn Friends, coed (1867), Browning, boys (1888), Buckley, boys

(1913), Chapin, girls (1901), Convent of the Sacred Heart, girls (1881), Dwight, coed (1880), Ethical Culture, coed (1878), Horace Mann, coed (1887), Nightingale-Bamford, girls (1903), Riverdale Country School, coed (1907), St. Bernard's, boys (1904), and Spence, girls (1892).

1. *Brearley School class of 1911; BRS. A girls' school which has always prided itself on educational innovation and liberal social and political attitudes, it was the first of the private schools to admit German Jewish students.*

2. *The Fifth Avenue School, 20 West Fifty-ninth Street, about 1900; MCNY. A private school that taught William Blaikie's method of gymnastics.*

3. *Browning School, 1895; MCNY. Founded in 1888, the school was at 27 West Fifty-fifth Street. One of its first students was John D. Rockefeller, Jr., who attended from 1889 to 1893.*

4. *Barnard College students, about 1900; photograph by Byron, MCNY. Because Columbia*

did not admit female students, Barnard was founded in 1889 as the undergraduate college for women within Columbia University.

1.

The Police, Gangs, Criminals, and "Peck's Bad Boy"

No one questioned that New York's social structure was clearly divided between the rich and the poor. Criminals were visible among the city's population. The role of the police was, and continues to be, protecting the good citizens from the bad ones. Corruption within the police force was a recurring problem that tarnished its image. A close affiliation between police and politicians engendered this situation because the Irish were well represented in both the police force and in Tammany Hall. The machine dispensed jobs on the police force at the neighborhood and ward levels. According to the 1860 census, there were 309 Irish-born police officers and 84 from Germany. In 1869 there were 32 Irish police captains and none who had been born in Germany. Irish policemen represented an elite within their ethnic community. Despite the fact that the majority of the people whom an Irish police officer might arrest would be Irish, (the Irish having developed a reputation for brawling, rioting, and membership in organized gangs), they were never accused of treating their Irish brethren more favorably than any other group.

There were numerous unaffiliated criminals and an extensive network of organized gangs. For a while Manhattan below Forty-second Street was divided into a series of rival gang territories with clearly defined boundaries that were guarded by members. There were the Eastmans, Five Pointers, Gas Housers, Gophers, and Hudson Dusters. The Five Pointers, with fifteen hundred members, operated in the area between Broadway and the Bowery and Fourteenth

Street and City Hall. When the Eastmans and Five Pointers fought over territorial rights in a number of pitched battles, an estimated thirty gang members were killed. In addition to the large gangs, there were smaller ones with fewer members operating in more restricted turf.

1. *A policeman on school duty, Seventh Avenue and 116th Street, 1899; photograph by Byron, MCNY.*
2. *"Bandit's Roost," Mulberry Street, about 1890; photograph by Jacob Riis, MCNY.*
3. *"William Peck, alias Peck's Bad Boy, alias Parks. Pickpocket. Description: Twenty-six years old in 1886. Born in New York. . . . Billy Peck is one of a new gang of pickpockets which are continually springing up in New York City."*
4. *"Mary Busby, alias Johnson, alias Mitchell. Pickpocket and shoplifter. Forty-eight years old in 1886. Born in England. . . . Harry Busby, alias Broken-nose Busby, her husband, is an old New York pickpocket and 'stall.'"*
5. *"Augustus Gregory, alias Geo. Schwenecke. Hotel thief. Description: Twenty years old in*

1886. *Born in United States of German parents . . . in prison in Colorado, and after he was liberated he worked all the hotels in the principal cities from there to New York."*
6. *"Tillie Pheiffer, alias Martin, alias Kate Collins. Hotel and house sneak. Thirty-six years old in 1886. Born in France. . . . She sometimes hires out as a servant and robs her employers; but her specialty is to enter a hotel or flat . . . secures whatever is handy and decamps."*
Photos 3, 4, 5, and 6, all dated 1886; from BURNS.

185

1.

"Our Firemen"

In 1865 the state legislature created the Metropolitan Fire Department, a paid force of seven hundred in Manhattan and Brooklyn. Prior to that, volunteer fire companies responded to alarms. These fire companies, like the police department, were closely associated with Tammany Hall. William M. (Boss Tweed) Tweed formed Americus Engine Company No. 6 in 1848, using it as a base from which to expand his political power. Seven mayors after 1835 had been members of volunteer fire companies. Rivalries between the volunteer companies was intense. Racing to be the first to arrive, they often brawled at the scene of the fire. The Irish were more prominent than Germans in these fire companies.

In 1866 the Metropolitan Fire Depart-

ment was reorganized following a military model in which specialization, discipline, and merit were encouraged. New techniques and fire-fighting equipment, such as taller ladders, steam engines with greater pumping pressure, and a fireboat, were introduced. In 1878 there were 972 fire alarm boxes; 654 were attached to poles, 25 were within city institutions, 131 in public school buildings, and 161 connected to theaters, hotels, factories, and other private buildings in Manhattan. The introduction of the civil service in 1884 encouraged professionalism and discouraged political interference.

FIRE ALARMS

"In early days before the introduction of the telegraphic system, notice was given of a fire by the ringing of bells. In 1835 it was ordered that a watchman be stationed constantly in the cupola of City Hall to give the alarm. The bell was rung during the continuance of the fire, the locality of the blaze being indicated by ringing the bell in a prescribed manner, and by hanging out at night a light in the direction of the fire, and by day a flag. The watchhouses and markets had bells which were utilized for the same purpose, and the churches also rang their bells. . . . In 1842 the city was divided into districts, and each district into sections, and a certain number of strokes for each section indicated the location of the fire. Each bell had its peculiar tone which a fireman soon learned, and could tell at once where the conflagration was."

AUGUSTINE E. COSTELLO, *OUR FIREMEN*

1. Eagle Hook and Ladder Company Number 1, College Point, Queens, about 1905; photo by Jacob Wieners, Jr., PI. Within fire-fighting companies, there were four distinct divisions: engine companies, hose companies, hook and ladder companies, and hydrant companies.
2. Fire Captain Philip Steiger, about 1915; QBPL.
3. Fire alarm signals, town of Newtown, Queens, 1882; QBPL.

187

1.

The Office Work Revolution

Between 1893 and 1897 the clerical staff of the Metropolitan Life Insurance Company doubled in size from 530 to 1,080 persons, a barometer of a major revolution affecting the office workplace. Throughout the nineteenth century manual labor was being transformed by industrial processes that increased an individual factory worker's productivity. The invention of the telegraph, the telephone, the typewriter, and electrical transmission transformed clerical office work. The invention of the elevator made it possible to construct tall buildings where concentrations of clerical and administrative personnel could be accommodated. Processing of data was mechanized and accelerated. As the factory worker's productivity had multiplied, so had the office worker's. New industries involving commercial transactions

were born, and old ones were revitalized. The Metropolitan Life Insurance Company needed a larger work force because its business continued to expand. In 1910 it had $2,216,000 of insurance in force, nearly ten times the amount held by any one life insurance company in 1870. In 1901 the annual turnover of shares on the New York Stock Exchange reached an all-time high of 319 percent. As the nation's largest commercial center New York watched its office work force expand dramatically to service the growing volume of transactions taking place. According to the 1910 census, approximately 37 percent of all New York City males could be classified as having an occupation pursuing professional, managerial, and entrepreneurial skills. Between 1890 and 1910 the number of white-collar work-

2.

3.

ers in Manhattan nearly doubled from 153,000 to 292,000. As the proportion of men in nonmanual jobs rose, the proportion in manual jobs fell. In 1900 white Anglo-Saxon Protestants were at the top of the occupational ladder; they were dominant in commerce and the professions; they were attorneys, bankers, doctors, stockbrokers, and wholesalers.

1. George Borgfeldt Co., 1910; photograph by Byron, MCNY.
2. Telephone exchange, 1896; photograph by Byron, MCNY.
3. Trading floor of the New York Stock Exchange, 1900; NYSE. The ticker tape communicated changing stock prices to distant customers by the Western Union Company.

THE BUILDINGS OCCUPIED BY THE

GREENHUT-SIEGEL COOPER CO., NEW YORK CITY

The World's Largest Store that has grown great because of the remarkable low prices on high class thoroughly dependable merchandise of a superior style–elegance. Every creation being an exclusive, authorative New York style, bearing the imprint of a Master's hand, planned especially to appeal to Women who admire smart apparel.

GREENHUT-SIEGEL COOPER CO.

1.

3.

Our splendid store renders shopping a pleasure. Our low prices for elegant goods are the magnets that attract crowds from all parts.

Our Genuine Alaska Seal Sacques from $85 00
Plush Sacques................. .... 11 95
Beautiful Manchester Plush Sacques..................... .... 18 95

and numerous other styles at equally startling prices.

BLOOMINGDALE BROS.

3d Ave., 59th & 60th Sts.,
NEW YORK.

4.

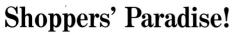

Shoppers' Paradise!

The evolution of shopping from the dry goods emporium to the department store illustrates the growth of mass consumption of mass-produced clothing and household products. This trajectory can be followed in the various stores owned and operated by A. T. Stewart. A native of Lisburn, Antrim, Ireland, he arrived in New York in 1823. In the same year he established a dry goods store at 283 Broadway. In 1846 he opened his "marble palace" at 280 Broadway. Offering a policy of one retail price for all customers, low markups, and unrestricted browsing through a large selection of merchandise, he became one of New York's leading merchants. In 1862 he built his "iron palace" (believed to be one of the first buildings in the city with a cast-iron facade) on Broadway between Ninth and Tenth streets.

Department stores like A. T. Stewart's afforded the opportunity to shop for a variety of merchandise in one multifloor establishment instead of having to go to a series of specialty shops. There was democratization of consumption. People were welcomed and encouraged to make purchases. Apparel for the entire family could be found under one roof. Furniture was displayed in an elaborate series of apartmentlike rooms. Department stores often described service as the secret of their success. They attempted to make spending money a comfortable, convenient, and ego-gratifying experience.

5.

1. *Greenhut-Siegel-Cooper department store, Sixth Avenue between Eighteenth and Nineteenth streets, undated; OYL. When it opened in 1896 as Siegel-Cooper, it occupied eighteen acres of floor space and offered an art gallery, a dental clinic, a nursery, a post office, and a theater. In 1911 Greenhut & Company which was directly across the street on Sixth Avenue in the building formerly occupied by B. Altman & Company, merged with Siegel-Cooper.*
2. *Cardboard fan advertising R. H. Macy & Company, 1902; SI. Founded in 1858, the store was purchased in 1888 by German Jews, Isidor and Nathan Straus, who erected the "world's largest department store" at Thirty-fourth and Sixth Avenue in 1902.*
3. *Vogel Brothers, 605–609 Broadway, 1880; NYHS. A traditional dry goods emporium,*

which sold a limited line of goods: men's, boys', and children's clothing.
4. *Advertisement for Bloomingdale's, 1885; LC. Located along the Third Avenue elevated railway, it attracted customers from all parts of the city.*
5. *The Siegel-Cooper bargain counter, about 1897; photograph by Byron, MCNY.*

CASHING IN CHRISTMAS GIFTS
"One of the busiest seasons in the department stores is immediately following the holidays, when people are taking back Christmas gifts. . . .

"The old time shopper wandered from counter to counter looking about, unable to decide between the many articles displayed. Now a woman has her list made up and does not buy on impulse to repent at leisure.

"The fact that the public recognizes this exchange habit as part of the routine is shown in the fact that whereas formerly people were always tearing the tags off the goods sent out as gifts now presents are sent with every help to make an exchange easy."
NEW YORK SUN, JANUARY 13, 1907

1.

Manifestations of Wealth

According to an 1892 survey conducted by the *New York Tribune*, greater New York had 1,265 millionaires, 30 percent of the total for the entire country. Another 12 percent lived in the New York State portion of the metropolitan region, and still more lived in southern Connecticut and northern New Jersey. The 1892 *Tribune* survey further indicated that of New York's million-dollar fortunes, 13.7 percent were involved in banking and brokerage, 3.4 percent in railroads, 1.7 percent in oil or mining, 26.5 percent in wholesaling and importing, 6.8 percent in shipping, 7.7 percent in processing (sugar refining, brewing, tanning, and metal refining), 13.7 percent in manufacturing, 5.9 percent in publishing, and 12.0 percent in real estate.

In 1895 there were 298 mercantile and manufacturing firms worth more than a million dollars in the New York region. Corporate leaders found that New York offered them the best combination of commercial information, marketing facilities, and professional and technical services of any city in the country. There were architects, bankers, brokers, designers, engineers, and lawyers in abundance.

Men who had made their fortunes in other parts of the country were attracted to New York for both its business opportunities and its social life. Andrew Carnegie and Henry Clay Frick came from Pittsburgh, and John D. Rockefeller from Cleveland.

As new fortunes were accumulated, many of these new millionaires and their wives wanted to join the social circles of the established elite. There was a clear tension

between old money and new money. Mrs. William (Caroline Schermerhorn) Astor's annual balls on the third Monday in January were the social event to which all of such ambitions aspired to attend. However, her weekly dinner parties were restricted to the highest ranks of the city's elite. Lawyer Ward McAllister, Mrs. Astor's adviser, conceived of the "four hundred" (those invited to Mrs. Astor's balls because her ballroom could accommodate only that number) as defining "society."

1. The Astor residence (Caroline Astor and her son John Jacob Astor IV), Fifth Avenue and Sixty-fifth Street, 1900; photograph by Byron, MCNY. There was a row of millionaires' mansions along Fifth Avenue from Murray Hill to Ninetieth Street.
2. General Ward's carriage at the front door of his mansion on Grymes Hill, Staten Island, 1890; photograph by Alice Austen, SIHS.
3. Children learning to waltz at the Staten Island Women's Club, about 1900; photograph by Alice Austen, SIHS.
4. A. T. Stewart mansion, on the northwest corner of Fifth Avenue and Thirty-fourth Street, about 1883; NYHS.
5. Madison Avenue at Thirty-sixth Street, about 1888; OYL.

"I must here explain, that behind what I call the 'smart set' in society, there always stood the old, solid, substantial, and respected people. Families who held great social power as far back as the birth of this country, who were looked up to by society, and who always could, when they so wished, come forward and exercise their power, which, for one reason or another, they would take no active part, joining in it quietly, but not conspicuously. Ordinarily, they preferred, like the gods, to sit upon Olympus. . . . [The] heads of these families, feeling secure in their position, knowing that they had great power when they chose to exercise it, took no leading part in society's daily routine."
WARD MCALLISTER, *SOCIETY AS I HAVE FOUND IT*

1.

Where the Rich Lived

The rich lived mostly in grand houses along Fifth Avenue from Thirty-fourth to Nine-tieth streets and on the side streets contiguous to Fifth Avenue in this area. Although sizable brownstones were being built on the Upper West Side, they did not compare in size and elegance with their Upper East Side competitors. Riverside Drive was the exception; some large houses were built there.

With the development of the elevator and the availability of electricity, it became possible to build multistory apartment buildings as well as office towers. They were appearing in midtown, and on the Upper East Side and the Upper West Side. The Dakota at Central Park West and Seventy-second Street was the most significant example of this trend.

MRS. CARNEGIE'S HOUSE
"There are eighty rooms in the Carnegie house, and of these easily half are in the quarters below ground, that is, in the basement, cellar and sub-cellar. Here the plumbers have held possession for months, laying the foundation of personal comfort as it will be later enjoyed by the residents above the stairs. With $110,000 worth of heating apparatus and $55,000 worth of plumbing in its relation to water and the sewage system, there is reason to credit the statement that the Carnegie mansion will have the most perfect system of plumbing in the world. . . .

"One flight up from the basement brings one on a level with the carriage drive. In this hall are to be wonders unimagined and unwritten. Mr. Carnegie has given orders

2.

that the wood carving shall be the most ornate that is procurable. At the right of the front door is the room where the people who call on official business are to be received. At the left is the place where the organ will stand. It is said in regard to this organ that the manufacturers have proved themselves so grasping as to space that the architects recommend that in the future when a house is to be supplied with a church organ, the organ be built first and the house built around it. The organ is to cost $16,000. . . .

"From the arrangement of the rooms on the second floor it is evident that the house has been designed to meet the requirements of the family of the owner, for the entire second floor is devoted to the use of three persons. The windows of Mr. and Mrs. Car-

negie's private apartment overlook Central Park, the drive and the reservoir lake. This is like a view into a private park."
NEW YORK TRIBUNE, MAY 31, 1901

1. The drawing room of the Carnegie mansion at Fifth Avenue and Ninety-first Street, 1902; MCNY.
2. Dakota Apartments, Central Park West and Seventy-second Street, about 1890; MCNY. Completed in 1884 when there were few other buildings of its size on the Upper West Side, this new luxurious apartment house was named the Dakota because it was in what might be called the "western wilderness." The original tenants, who had to be able to afford sizable rents, were different from the people who inhabited the Upper East Side. Among the Dakota's early residents were John Browning, the founder of the Browning School, Gustav Schirmer, the music publisher, and Theodor Steinway, the piano manufacturer.

Mrs. Vanderbilt's Ball

All these photographs were taken in a photographer's studio prior to the ball and demonstrate costumes worn at the ball. They date from 1883; NYHS.
1. Mrs. William Haliburton Bridgham.
2. Roland Redmond.
3. Mrs. William K. Vanderbilt.
4. Francis R. Appleton.
5. Mrs. Cornelius Vanderbilt.

MARVELS OF FANCY DRESS
"Mrs. William K. Vanderbilt's fancy ball, which has created such a stir and din of preparation in fashionable circles for a month and more, was gorgeously accomplished last night. . . . In lavishness of expenditure and brilliancy of dress it far outdid any ball ever before given in this city. Twelve hundred invitations had been issued, and up to midnight perhaps 700 guests had arrived, and were in the full swing of the ball. It was a scene from fairy land. Mother Goose, the picture galleries, the courts and camps of Europe, Asia and opera bouffe, Audubon's 'Birds of America,' heathen myths and Christian legends and even from Mr. Diedrich Knickerbocker's invaluable notes on the fashions in New York a long time ago. All the revel of color in such a

3.

4.

5.

catalogue moved, gleaming with newness, in a garden of flowers under bright lights to soft music from hidden instruments. It is only at a fancy dress ball that men can make themselves really picturesque; and qualified voters, grave and gay, vied in the artistic quality, and in the cost as well, of their costumes, with the lovely women who adorned the evening.

"The work of decorating and preparing Mrs. Vanderbilt's magnificent new house for the ball went on all day. Wagon load after wagon load of palms and plants, drawn from conservatories all over the city, was delivered at the Fifty-second street entrance. Inside the house Mr. Klunder and several assistants were busy arranging the decorations. The final preparations of the guests threw Fifth and Madison avenues and the adjoining fashionable streets into a whirl in the evening. A stranger to the city would have noticed that something extraordinary was on foot. Carriages were flying about with unusual go, and there was much slamming of front doors as hair-dressers, milliners, costumers, and other tradespeople were admitted or let out. Toward 10 o'clock muffled forms slid down front stoops and jumped into waiting carriages. The curious bystanders caught a glimpse of bright color, or the flash of diamonds, or heard the clank of a sword striking the stone steps. . . .

"Winding through the crowd of princes, monks, cavaliers, Highlanders, queens, kings, dairy maids, bull fighters, knights, brigands, and nobles, the procession passed down the grand stairway and through the hall into a front room in the style of Francis I., twenty-five feet in width by forty in length, wainscotted richly and heavily in carved French walnut, and hung in dark red plush. Vast carved cabinets and an immense deep fireplace gave an air of antique grandeur to this room, from which the procession passed into a salon in the style of Louis XV, thirty feet in width by thirty-five in length, wainscotted in oak and enriched with carved work and gilding. The whole wainscoting of this apartment was brought from a chateau in France."

NEW YORK SUN, MARCH 27, 1883

"Our Crowd"

The first Jews arrived in New York in 1654, when twenty-three Sephardic Jews sought refuge in the Dutch colony. During the succeeding two centuries they were few in number, never being more than several thousand. When the tide of German immigration reached its peak in the mid-nineteenth century, a considerable number of Jews were part of it. Some settled in New York; others went to towns and rural areas throughout the developing country. They created networks of peddlers, wholesale dry goods merchants, lawyers, and bankers. Although not a part of the rapidly expanding corporate industrial economy in post–Civil War America, they created special niches for themselves in merchant banking and in

department stores. Firms like Kuhn, Loeb & Company had its roots in Cincinnati. The Lehmans were southern cotton brokers, and Nathan and Isidor Straus, whose family began as peddlers in rural Georgia, bought Macy's. They amassed fortunes equal to or perhaps greater than many Gentile businessmen. Their firms were Abraham & Straus, J. S. Bache & Company, August Belmont & Company, Goldman, Sachs & Company, M. Guggenheim's Sons, Kuhn, Loeb & Company, Lehman Brothers, Lewisohn Brothers, R. H. Macy & Company, J. & W. Seligman & Company, and Wertheim. They built mansions on upper Fifth Avenue (Otto Kahn at Ninety-first Street opposite Andrew Carnegie's, and the Warburgs' on the

corner of Ninety-second), but they were never invited to Mrs. Astor's balls. They formed their own social circle, "our crowd," which included the elite German Jews and their predecessors, the Sephardic Jews.

"Our crowd" saw themselves as distinct from the Eastern European Jews who were so evident. In the tradition of Jewish charity, they supported organizations like the Educational Alliance on the Lower East Side and the YMHAs (Young Men's Hebrew Association), which facilitated transformation of ghetto Jews into Americans. However, Jacob Schiff, one of the principals of Kuhn, Loeb & Company and a pillar of the German Jewish community, conceived of the Galveston Plan. Rather than be deposit-

ed in New York City, ghetto Jews would land in Galveston, Texas, and be sent to other parts of the country. It was not a very successful idea. Some Jews entered through Galveston, but most preferred New York.

1. Bridesmaids at a Warburg family wedding, about 1915; LC.
2. Arthur Loew family with its carriage in Central Park, about 1900; LC.
3. Julian Nathan, a descendant of a Sephardic Jewish family, with cart and groom in Central Park, about 1900; MCNY.
4. Simon Guggenheim, about 1908; LC. A member of the Guggenheim mining and banking family, he was founder of the John Simon Guggenheim Foundation, which makes annual prestigious grants in the arts, sciences, and education.
5. Mrs. Simon Guggenheim, around 1908; LC. She was a patron of the arts and an early member of the board of the Museum of Modern Art.

1.

Metropolitan Culture

As New York's importance continued to expand in commerce and industry, its civic leaders recognized that creating a group of major cultural institutions was a natural corollary. Constantly comparing New York with London and Paris, they wanted New York to belong to the constellation of great cities. To accomplish this, they set out to build opera houses, concert halls, libraries, museums, and great universities that would rival similar institutions that they had seen in Europe. The Metropolitan Museum of Art was established in 1870; by 1902 its buildings facing Fifth Avenue were completed. The American Museum of Natural History broke ground for its Central Park West complex in 1874. The Metropolitan Opera was formed in 1883, with its first home at Broadway and Thirty-ninth Street. In 1892

both Carnegie Hall and the Arts Students League opened their doors on West Fifty-seventh Street. Columbia University's Morningside Heights campus was being built in the 1890s and first decade of the next century. In 1908 the first building in the Audubon Terrace complex was completed. In the Broadway theater district the New Amsterdam and the Lyceum opened in 1903. In 1911 the New York Public Library opened its building at Fifth Avenue and Forty-second Street.

Having a resident community of actors, architects, artists, intellectuals, musicians, and writers was a logical outgrowth of such civic enthusiasm. They gave expression to the aspirations of civic leaders in the form of grand buildings, impressive public monuments, and musical and theatrical perfor-

mances. New York certainly was not London or Paris, but with civic patronage, the cultural community created many works of enduring value.

1. Century Association, 1889 illustration of building completed in 1891; LC. Century is one of the oldest and most prestigious social clubs in the city; its membership has been heavily weighted with artists, writers, and intellectuals.

2. William Merritt Chase in his studio in the Tenth Street Studios, about 1895; MCNY. Considered the dean of late-nineteenth-century American painters, Chase gave classes at the Art Students League that were extremely popular.

3. Augustus Saint Gaudens in his studio with his statue of General William Tecumseh Sherman, 1900; MCNY. Completed in 1903, this statue, which stands at Fifth Avenue and Fifty-ninth Street, is one of New York's most notable public monuments. It was given to the city by the generation that fought in the

Civil War. Saint Gaudens said that he wanted "to help commemorate them in a noble and dignified fashion worthy of their service."

1.

Traditionalists, Suffragists, and Strikers

Victorian mores confined women to roles of inferiority and servility to males. At the turn of the century the position of women in New York was determined both by class and by choice. If they were wealthy or middle class, they could choose to fulfill traditional roles as wives, mothers, and participants in polite social organizations, or they could choose to become activists in women's suffrage and labor issues. If working class, they had some of the same choices. Upper-class educated women served as the nucleus of the women's suffrage movement with support from a broad spectrum of the women's community. Lillian Wald was the first modern public health nurse and was instrumental in founding the Henry Street Settlement. Working-class women joined their male counterparts in the struggle

against exploitation and the demand for decent working conditions. One of their actions, the shirtwaist makers' strike of 1909, was a major event in labor history and contributed to improved working conditions. Cutting across class lines, a group of strikers was invited to tea at the Colony Club, the city's most exclusive women's club, to present their case to a sympathetic audience of four hundred women.

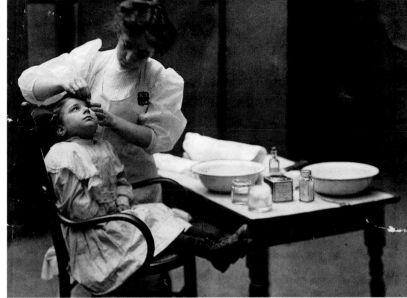

1. *Daughters of the American Revolution, 1898; photograph by Byron, MCNY.*
2. *Mrs. Borman Wells speaking at a women's suffrage meeting, 1907; photograph by George Grantham Bain, MCNY.*
3. *Demonstration of Jewish women workers, 1909; LC.*
4. *School nurse, about 1910; NYPL.*
5. *Women's suffrage parade on Fifth Avenue, 1913; NYHS. Fifth Avenue was the scene of the largest suffrage parades in the country. Under pressure from suffragists in 1913 the New York legislature agreed to a 1915 referendum on women's right to vote. It was defeated by eighty thousand votes in New York City and two hundred thousand statewide.*

WOMEN SHIRTWAIST MAKERS'
STRIKERS MEET IN CLINTON HALL

". . . the Women's Trade Union League was conducting an information bureau. This organization is under the leadership of certain social workers and 'organizers,' and is a sort of foster-mother to women's unions. . . .

"The girls in this room were in truth 'confused, frightened, excited.' Yiddish words, Yiddish gestures, here and there Italian chatter made a pandemonium.

"Vindictiveness, determination, anxiety leaked through the talk even where it was an unknown tongue. . . . And yet few of these girls were over twenty, many as young as twelve."

SARAH COMSTOCK IN *COLLIER'S* MAGAZINE,
DECEMBER 29, 1909

1.

2.

3.

4.

5.

Food: Ethnic and Elegant

Eating out has always been a New York passion, and there have always been places to get a meal. First there were taverns that provided food, drink, and lodging. By the mid-nineteenth century hotels had become more evident. They served elaborate four-course meals offering a choice of soups, fresh clams, boiled chicken, fish and meats, roasts, entrées with French names, pastries, and fruit.

The first American restaurant as we know it, originated by the Swiss brothers Giovanni and Pietro Delmonico on William Street, began serving food in 1827. Based on the Parisian model and managed by relatives and succeeding owners, Delmonico's estab-lished a model that was replicated through-out New York and the rest of the country.

Its name became synonymous with the ele-gant presentation of food. It catered to the rich and successful and had a farm in Brooklyn that supplied fresh fruits and veg-etables.

When the tide of immigrants from East-ern and Southern Europe swept New York, these foreigners brought with them a taste for their native foods and the ability to pre-pare them. A new type of restaurant and scores of stores supplying exclusively ethnic foods began to appear in immigrant neigh-borhoods throughout the city. The stores were small and specialized, reflecting pat-terns in their countries of origin. There were bakeries producing endless varieties of breads and pastries. There were butcher shops, fish stores, stores selling dairy prod-

6.

8.

9.

7.

10.

ucts, and others selling fruits and vegetables. The restaurants were modest because they catered to a hardworking, impoverished clientele and were seldom visited by other New Yorkers.

1. A thirteen-year-old Italian boy tending store, 1913; photograph by Lewis Hine, NYPL.
2. Greek restaurant, 1904; photograph by Byron, NYPL.
3. Pasta label, about 1900; SI.
4. Frankfurter vendor, about 1900; NYPL.
5. Baking bread in a brick oven, about 1915; photograph by Lewis Hine, NYPL
6. Mark Twain celebrating his seventieth birthday at Delmonico's, December 5, 1905; photograph by Byron, MCNY.
7. The kitchen at Delmonico's, 1902; photograph by Byron, MCNY.
8. Exterior of Delmonico's at southwest corner of Fifth Avenue and Twenty-sixth Street, 1910; OYL.
9. Pursell Mfg. Co., caterer's delivery wagon

on Park Avenue at Sixty-second Street, 1911; MCNY.
10. Bakers posing with Gustav Mayer's Vienna crackers, about 1890; SIHS.

1.

Central Park

"Central Park is one of the most beautiful and famous urban parks in the world. It covers the territory between Fifth and Eighth Avenues and 59th and 110th Streets, a tract over 2½ miles long by half a mile wide, including an area of 840 acres. There are about 400 acres of wooded ground, part of which is still in the natural state, while the rest has been improved by the planting of trees, shrubs and vines. There are nine miles of carriage-ways, six miles of bridle-paths, and thirty miles of foot-paths. The Park has been beautified with handsome architecture, landscape gardening, statues and other works of sculpture. There are nineteen entrances, over which it has been proposed to erect imposing arches, a plan that may yet be carried out. Transverse roads from east to west in open cuts below the level of

the Park, accommodate business traffic, which is not allowed within the park limits. Park-carriages are run for the convenience of visitors. . . .

"Starting from 59th Street, one comes first upon the Ball Ground, a ten-acre plot in the south-west corner, where the boys are privileged to play base-ball and cricket. Near this is the Dairy; and just to the north-east is the Carrousel, with swings for children. Adjoining is the Common, or Green, of sixteen acres where the sheep are pastured. On the east side, at Fifth Avenue and 64th Street, is the Menagerie, partly housed in the Arsenal, and partly in pens and wooden houses. There is a large and varied collection of wild animals, elephants, lions, hippopotami, tigers, bears, camels, seals, monkeys and birds. Just to the east of the Green

is the Mall, a grand promenade 200 feet wide and a third of a mile long, overshadowed by rows of noble elms. . . . To the north the Mall terminates in the Terrace, the chief architectural feature of the Park. There is an Esplanade on the shore of the lake, and the Bethesda Fountain stands there. A central stairway leads down to the Esplanade under the road, beneath which is a tiled hall with arched roof. . . .

"The Lake covers twenty acres, and is given over to pleasure-boats in the summer and skating in the winter. Beyond the lake is the Ramble, a spot beautiful with sylvan paths, waterfalls, natural groves, thickets of underbrush and exquisite bits of scenery. Next is the Receiving Reservoir for the city water, and on its margin rises the lofty terrace of the Belvedere, with a picturesque

tower fifty feet high, affording a magnificent view of Manhattan Island and all the surrounding country. To the east of the Reservoir are the Obelisk and the Metropolitan Museum of Art; and to the north again, the new Croton Reservoir, which fills nearly the entire width of the Park. . . .

"The place is much frequented in all seasons of the year. It is not unusual for 150,000 people to visit it on a single pleasant day in summer; and 15,000,000 visit it every year."

MOSES KING, *HANDBOOK OF NEW YORK CITY*

1. The annual May Day festival in Central Park, 1916; CB. As many as twenty thousand children congregated for these fetes. They participated in games and a ceremony honoring the elected king and queen. Similar events were held in Brooklyn's Prospect Park.
2. Orchestra concert, 1910; PARKS.
3. On the lake in the winter, about 1898; photograph by Byron, MCNY.
4. Grandpa and Mr. Dolnier in the Swan Boat, 1891; photograph by Alice Austen, SIHS.

207

1.

Going to the Beach

Although New York could boast of having two of the world's great urban parks, Central Park in Manhattan and Prospect Park in Brooklyn, summers in the city, with more people and more congestion, were getting more uncomfortable for both rich and poor. If you lived in a tenement, you might be able to sleep on the roof on a hot summer's night. If you lived in a mansion, it was still hot. With the refreshingly cool waters of the Atlantic only an hour away by ferry or longer by street railway, tens of thousands made frequent excursions to the beaches. There were two. The oldest, Coney Island, including Manhattan Beach, Brighton Beach, and West Brighton, was developed in the 1870s. Rockaway Beach was developed in succeeding decades, and its amusement park opened in 1901.

Both ferryboat and street railway operators were anxious to link their conveyances to the beaches. Busy five days a week transporting crowds back and forth to work, they could be busy seven days a week in the summer, transporting pleasure seekers to the beaches on weekends. William Engeman developed Brighton Beach with hotels, a fairgrounds, and a bathing pavilion for a broad cross section of social groups. Austin Corbin, a wealthy New York banker, developed Manhattan Beach as a high-class resort with the hope of creating a rival to Newport, Rhode Island. He also developed beachfront residential property in Rockaway. Nearby were three horse-racing tracks: Brighton Beach, Gravesend, and Sheepshead Bay. By 1900 Brooklyn was the horse racing capital of America.

2.

3.

West Brighton was developed more for the working class; it eventually became Coney Island, the amusement park. On arriving via the Prospect Park and Coney Island Railway, one would be confronted immediately with the three-hundred-foot Iron Tower that had been salvaged from the 1876 Philadelphia Centennial Exposition by Andrew Culver, builder of the railway. He wanted attractions at its terminus. There were others: saloons, restaurants, bathhouses, variety shows, games, and food vendors.

On Surf Avenue there was Lucy the Elephant, a seven-story wood and tin-skinned building weighing a hundred thousand tons, which had been constructed in the shape of an elephant. Containing thirty-four rooms, the structure reached a height of 150 feet at the top of the crescent resting on its

flagpole. It was essentially an indoor bazaar, and visitors entered through a door in the foot of the right hind leg. The July 11, 1885, edition of the *Scientific American* described its purpose as "to abstract the unwary dime from the inquisitive sightseer."

1. The Old Dominion Line's ferry docking at Rockaway Beach, about 1905; QBPL.
2. Going to the Brighton Beach racetrack on the Coney Island and Brooklyn Railroad, about 1897; photograph by Byron, MCNY.
3. The Beach at Coney Island, 1896; photograph by Byron, MCNY.

The Resorts

1. Luna Park, postcard, 1910; OYL. In 1893 and 1895 fires destroyed much of the entertainment district of West Brighton. In 1903, six years after George C. Tilyou opened Steeplechase Park, Fred Thompson and Elmer ("Skip") Dundy opened Luna Park, planned to appeal to a better clientele than Steeplechase. Luna Park was promoted as being entertaining and instructional. There were simulations of exotic places that most people had heard or read about but never visited. Middle Eastern architecture was its trade mark; there were historical re-creations of Eskimo settlements and Irish villages. In 1904 Dreamland, another entertainment park seeking to attract middle-class audiences, opened. Dreamland promoted genteel experiences devoid of pushing and shoving.

2. Steeplechase Park, postcard, about 1900; OYL. George C. Tilyou, whose family had been established in Coney Island, opened Steeplechase Park in 1897. His market was a working-class audience. He advertised "10 hours of fun for 10 cents." Steeplechase was big, brassy, and brazen. In 1901 Munsey's Magazine described Steeplechase as the essential Coney Island experience: "That, above all, is Coney Island's specialty; to toss, tumble, flop, jerk, jounce, jolt, and jostle you by means of mechanical contrivances, until your digestion is where your reason ought to be, and your reason has gone none knows whither."

3. Feltman's, postcard, about 1895; OYL. A combination restaurant and theme park, Feltman's offered shore dinners, a roller coaster, and other attractions with German

themes. *Charles Feltman, its German immigrant owner, claimed to have served two hundred thousand meals during an 1880s season. Various ethnic societies, lodges, and clubs held grand dinners there.*

4. Kite flying at Manhattan Beach, postcard. 1881; QBPL.

5. Entrance to Ocean Parkway, Rockaway Beach, postcard, about 1905; OYL. Coney Island had larger amusement parks.

6. William Auer's Steeplechase Camp, Ward Avenue, Rockaway Beach, postcard, about 1905; OYL. For those who could not afford hotels, there were tents.

"Manhattan Beach is now the recognized 'quiet day' sojourn on Coney Island, a corner where *pater familias* can bring his wife and daughters without fear of being jostled into bad temper and perhaps explosive language; where the *cuisine* is unexceptionable, and where trains are in such constant readiness as almost to amount to the high privilege of 'personal specials.' Here he knows that he can find a cool spot wherein to peruse his newspaper to the dulcet, yet drowsy, song of the would-be breakers, and without fear of the squeakings of the ever-facetious Mr. Punch, or the jarring din of the organ attached to the merry-go-round. If he is inclined to bathe, he can do so in a leisurely and becoming manner. . . ."

FRANK LESLIE'S ILLUSTRATED NEWSPAPER, AUGUST 6, 1881

LUNA PARK OPENS TO 200,000
"The biggest of the new shows at the park is the Great Train Robbery. It occupies several acres of ground. . . .

"A huge setting of mountains, cliffs, of railroad track, and a river, serve [*sic*] as a background for a real engine and two real cars, sets of train robbers, passengers, and a Sheriff's posse enacting a train hold-up in full detail.

"The train is seen winding down the mountain. A gang of mounted desperadoes watches it. . . . On one of the Pullmans is the magic name Rockefeller. This excites the robbers. They rush to the engine and drag out the engineer and fireman. Pistols are fired. Passengers shriek. . . . All are bustled out with 'Hands up!'"

NEW YORK TIMES, MAY 13, 1906

1.

The Automobile and Suburban Development

The street railways, the elevated railways, the building of the East River bridges, consolidation in 1898, and construction of the subway system all contributed to the physical growth of the city. Today much of the physical city that still stands was built before the arrival of automobiles. However, it was the automobile that accelerated growth in the boroughs, particularly in Queens and Staten Island, neither of which had extensive public transportation systems.

In 1858, forty years before gasoline-, steam-, or electric-powered vehicles were being seen on the streets of New York, Richard Dudgeon built a steam car that resembled a small traction engine with a bench seat on each side of the boiler. The wheels were solid wood shod with iron tires; it seated eight. He exhibited it in the Crys-

tal Palace; it was destroyed in the October 1858 fire that demolished the building.

During the decade from 1890 to 1900 the building of automobiles became an obsession for mechanics and small bicycle and carriage manufacturers. By 1900 there were six firms with nearly five hundred employees building automobiles in the New York area. Internal-combustion, steam, and electric vehicles were seen on the streets in increasing numbers. Although a practical form of transportation, the automobile captured the imagination of racing enthusiasts. There were Vanderbilt Cup races on Long Island, races at Brighton Beach, races in Morris Park, and Astor Cup races at the Sheepshead Bay Speedway. There were intercity races like the New York to Boston Endurance Run. In 1907 the three leaders were

QUARTER ACRE FOR A QUARTER A DAY
LITTLE FARMS. PRICE $500 AND UNDER; $10 DOWN $6 A MONTH
BOATING AND FISHING ALMOST AT YOUR DOOR
50 MINUTES FROM BROADWAY—ELEVEN CENT COMMUTATION FARE

BUNGALOWS BUILT

ON YOUR LITTLE FARM

TERMS:
Bungalow, $100 Down, $7 per Month
Bungalow, $150 Down, $10 per Month
Bungalow, $200 Down, $14 per Month

LITTLE FARMS
STATEN ISLAND
NEW YORK CITY

HOW WE PLANT THE LITTLE FARMS
FREE OF COST TO CUSTOMERS

ET FREE EXCURSION TICKETS

2.

KEY MAP

TO NORTH BEACH and 92d ST. FERRY

N.Y. & Q. CO. RY.
KINGSLAND AVE.

TO LONG ISLAND CITY and 34 ST. N.Y. via N.Y. & Q. Co. Ry.

CORONA STATION

LONG ISLAND RAILROAD

TO PENNSYLVANIA TERMINAL
33rd ST. and 7th AVENUE
when Terminal is finished
from the 34 St. Ferry to N.Y.

B.R.T. Co.

CORONA AVE.

TO FLUS

TO BROOKLYN via
Brooklyn Rapid T. Co.

GERRY AVE.

AVENUE

5th

SOUTH Q.B.

AVE.

ELMHURST-SOUTH
QUEENS BOROUGH
NEW YORK CITY

3.

BRYAN L. KENNELLY, - - AUCTIONEER
OFFICES, 156 BROADWAY. NEW YORK CITY

ABSOLUTE AUCTION SALE
By Order of the Executrix and Trustee of the
MARY A. GRISWOLD ESTATE
58 BEAUTIFULLY LOCATED LOTS
AND TWO DWELLINGS
Situated on Fieldston Road, West 252d St., Waldo Ave. and Riverdale Lane (253d St.), New York City.
10 MINUTES WALK FROM SUBWAY STATION AT 242d ST. & B'WAY
—AT—
RIVERDALE, N. Y. CITY

DWELLING HOUSE ON PROPERTY

ON THE GROUNDS
SATURDAY, MAY 7, 1910 AT 1 P.M.

70 Per Cent. May Remain on Mortgage for 3 Years at 5 Per Cent. Interest
Titles Insured and Policies of the Lawyers Title Insurance & Trust Co. Issued Free of Cost to Purchasers
Copies of this Book-Map and Further Particulars at AUCTIONEER'S OFFICE, 156 BROADWAY, NEW YORK CITY
Telephone 1547 Cortlandt

4.

the Aerocar, Packard, and Model K Ford. In October 1908 Henry Ford introduced the mass-produced Model T. It was a medium-size internal-combustion five-passenger touring car. By 1914 three hundred thousand were built annually. Other manufacturers emulated Ford's mass-production methods; horse-drawn vehicles dwindled slowly, and the streets of New York were permanently transformed by increasing numbers of internal-combustion cars, trucks, and buses. For most people living in Manhattan, owning a car was hardly a necessity, but for people living in the other boroughs, automobiles became increasingly more important.

Although automobiles were few in number at this time, in the boroughs other than Manhattan, developers continued to build new housing in areas adjacent to or accessi-

ble to public transportation. They also proceeded to convert open space, not contingent to public transportation, into housing, particularly individual dwellings.

1. Automobile at Union Turnpike and Utopia Parkway, Queens, about 1910; QBPL. Although called turnpikes and parkways, these roads were not yet paved, nor were most roads in outlying areas.
2. Staten Island real estate advertisement, about 1910; SIHS.
3. Elmhurst, Queens, real estate advertisement, about 1910; QBPL.
4. Riverdale, Bronx, real estate advertisement, 1910; OYL.

As the twentieth century unfolded, Europe was clearly at center stage. Its economy was buoyant; its culture and science were innovative; but it was wrapped in centuries-old competition and animosity. Wars had been fought, territories had been exchanged, and alliances had shifted. Another explosion was imminent. When the major European powers went to war, they were no longer seeking territorial gains. The Great War, as they called it, was a gigantic contest to determine their power in Europe and throughout the world. It was a bitter, ugly war fought in trenches and mud with barbed wire, artillery, machine guns, and poison gas, resulting in horrendous casualties: dead, wounded, and maimed.

Although neutral, the United States associated itself with the governments of the Allies (Britain, France, Russia, and Italy) against the Germans and Austro-Hungarians. Supplying the Allies with armaments was a boon to American industry. The loss of American ships and lives to German submarines became a deciding factor. On April 6, 1917, the United States Congress declared war. At this point it was no longer the Great War, it became the World War.

Conscription was authorized and mobilization was immediate. The first American troops landed in France on June 26, 1917. By the end of the following year, 2,084,000 American soldiers were in Europe. American participation assured an Allied victory. American losses were 112,432 dead and 203,044 wounded. New Yorkers went to war. On returning, some marched up Fifth Avenue, others hobbled on crutches.

Following the wartime surge, there was a short recession. Business boomed again in 1923. With increased industrial capacity and growing demand for consumer products like automobiles, refrigerators, washing machines, and vacuum cleaners, a robust economy with concomitant overconfidence gave birth to the "Roaring Twenties." The rest of the country participated, but much of the style, hoopla, and extravagance of this decade was generated in New York. In 1920, American women were finally granted their long-delayed right to vote with the ratification of the 19th Amendment. Florenz Ziegfeld's *Follies* created new icons of American female beauty. Over President Wilson's veto, Prohibition went into effect on January 16, 1920, but its enforcement was feeble. Speakeasies were omnipresent and booze flowed. To the rest of the country, New York symbolized glamour, sin, and sophistication. F. Scott Fitzgerald and his wife, Zelda, living high in New York, personified the flamboyant lifestyle of the twenties. With a grain of truth and a douse of distortion, the movies presented a New York that both did and did not exist. The motion picture industry abandoned New York for Hollywood in the previous decade, but transplanted New Yorkers who ran the industry converted Broadway productions into films and flaunted their nostalgia by manufacturing products depicting a fictional city. There were movies about high life, low life, and ethnic life: *Dead End, 42nd Street, Gold Diggers of 1933, Little Miss Broadway, King Kong, Manhattan Melodrama,* and *Street Scene.* Another image of the city was

projected in magazines like the *New Yorker* and *Vanity Fair*, which provided a coterie of authors and cartoonists with the opportunity to memorialize the era.

With the outbreak of war in Europe in 1914, the era of mass Eastern and Southern European emigration to the United States ended. The supply of cheap immigrant labor was cut off and a new source had to be developed. Millions of rural blacks living in Southern states were candidates for recruitment. It was reported that between April and October 1917, over one hundred thousand blacks had gone North with a considerable number settling in Harlem. The first blacks had moved to this largely white middle class and working class neighborhood, in 1905. Harlem soon became a place where African-Americans were the majority and where their presence gave the neighborhood a new and totally different personality.

By their numbers, native New York blacks and Southern blacks contributed to the transformed character of Harlem; however, they were not the only ones moving in. There were immigrants from the Caribbean and there were educated African-Americans from across the country whom Dr. W. E. B. DuBois called the "talented tenth." They created an American urban black culture and participated in the *Harlem Renaissance*, making Harlem the cultural capital of black America. There were writers like Langston Hughes, Claude McKay, Countee Cullen, and Zora Neale Hurston. There was jazz by Duke Ellington, Fletcher Henderson, and legions of musicians; there were dancers and singers performing at the Cotton Club and

Chapter Four
Sophisticated City: 1915–1945
The African-American
Presence Resonates

Connie's Inn. Harlem was hot and its afterglow radiated downtown. New York's business and social elites were regulars at Harlem clubs where blacks performed, but could not be patrons.

The first waves of Italian and Jewish immigrants settled in Manhattan's Little Italy and on the Lower East Side. As they prospered, some becoming middle class and others remaining working class, they moved to Brooklyn, the Bronx, Queens and Staten Island, creating replicas of their first settlement neighborhoods, although under much improved conditions in apartments and detached single houses. Similarly, the Irish and the Germans had been moving out of Manhattan, creating their own new ethnic enclaves. Movement to the outer boroughs was facilitated by expansion of the subway, which spanned the city's extremities.

The pervading sociological theory of the day described America as the great melting pot, where all of the peoples of the world who settled here would eventually merge into one generic identity. However, New York was a pot that never melted. Ethnic identity flourished. As Konrad Bercovici wrote in 1924, "A map of Europe superimposed upon the map of New York could prove that the different foreign sections of the city live in the same proximity to one another as in Europe: the Germans near the Austrians, the Russians and the Rumanians near the Hungarians, and the Greeks behind the Italians.... A reformation of the same grouping takes place every time the city expands. If the Italians move further up Harlem, the Greeks follow them, the Spanish join them, with the French always lagging behind and the Germans expanding eastward."

This cauldron of humanity gave birth to New York's unique amalgam of ethnicity and sophistication. Here's the chemistry. Colonial, commercial, and corporate elites borrowed heavily from European aristocracy and the *haute bourgeoisie*. The Irish, Germans, Italians, and Jews along with immigrants from dozens of other countries contributed their urban and rural identities. Rural and urban African-Americans added their vigor. When fused, a "New York style" emerged. It can be seen on the streets, in offices, in restaurants, wherever New Yorkers congregate. It can be described as the way they talk, the way they move, the way they do business, the way they shop, the way they ride the subway, the way they drive their cars, the way they eat, the way they dance, and most of all it can be described as the way they see themselves apart from all other human beings.

Between 1921 and 1929, the total output of the American economy increased by more than fifty percent. However, this came to an abrupt conclusion on Black Tuesday, October 29, 1929, when the stock market crashed. In a matter of weeks, stocks lost more than forty percent of their value. The ramifications of the crash were felt worldwide with European economies experiencing a similar decline. Unemployment sky-rocketed. Nationally, it reached 8,700,000 in 1930 and grew to 24,900,000 in 1933. There were Hoovervilles, encampments of unemployed, in Central Park. There were destitute people of all nationalities in bread lines or selling apples on the street. Out of desperation, some people resorted to suicide.

While the 1939 World's Fair shed a note of optimism, war clouds were again gathering in Europe and Asia. Hitler came to power in Germany in 1933 with the avowed intention of conquering Europe and annihilating European Jewry. He formed alliances with expansionist fascist Italy and Japan. Seeking refuge, a substantial number of European artists and intellectuals came to New York, altering the city's cultural life. In September 1939, Hitler unleashed his blitzkreig, ultimately controlling most of the European land mass. England was bombed and Russia invaded. In February 1939, the pro-Hitler German-American Bund had a rally at Madison Square Garden while Jews demonstrated outside. Again, America stood aside, finally entering the war after the Japanese bombed Pearl Harbor in 1941. Americans were back on the Continent fighting against the Germans and at the same time engaged in combat with Japan in the Pacific. New York served as a staging area for the military. It was also a favorite location for soldiers and sailors on leave. Victory came in Europe when the Allied and Soviet armies forced the Germans to surrender. Shortly after President Truman authorized dropping atomic bombs on Hiroshima and Nagasaki, the Japanese capitulated.

p. 216: Electric streetcar, undated; RMP. Below: Airplane, La Guardia Airport, 1940; MCNY.

Preceding pages: Empire State Building under construction, photograph by Lewis Hine, 1930; MCNY.

1.

Moving into Harlem

At the northern end of Manhattan, Harlem was originally settled by Dutch farmers and remained an urban outpost until the 1880s when the expanding elevated railway system linked it to the rest of the city. Brownstones, apartment buildings, and tenements were built to accommodate middle-class and working-class whites. In 1900 the African-American population of Manhattan numbered 36,246; it was segregated in several neighborhoods, with concentrations around Pennsylvania Station (Seventh Avenue and 33d Street) and San Juan Hill (Amsterdam Avenue between 60th and 64th streets).

As the value of Harlem real estate began to drop for purely market reasons—landlords built too many apartments, and the el didn't serve the whole neighborhood—blacks began to move in. In 1905 they were established on 133d and 134th streets between Lenox and Seventh avenues. Where they moved, real estate values depreciated between 15 and 20 percent. In 1911 Nail & Parker, an African-American real estate firm, bought ten apartment houses on the north side of 135th Street between Lenox and Seventh avenues and invited blacks to rent them. This event signaled the beginning of Harlem's transformation from a white to a black neighborhood.

In 1900 the majority of Manhattan blacks were engaged in domestic and personal services. Among males in other professions, there were 236 bookkeepers and accountants, 427 manufacturing workers, and 476

2.

draymen, hackmen, and teamsters. Of women, 418 were dressmakers, 67 nurses and midwives, and 103 seamstresses.

A disastrous race riot erupted in East St. Louis, Illinois, on July 2, 1917. In less than two years thousands of African-Americans, migrating from the South, had moved into that city. As cheap labor they were used to thwart attempts at union organization. Nearly two thousand blacks died, and six thousand were forced out of their homes. Reverberations were felt in black communities throughout the country, and demonstrations were held to focus attention on these events.

"On July 28, 1917 ten thousand New York Negroes silently marched down Fifth Avenue to the sound of muffled drums. The procession was headed by little children dressed in white, followed by the women in white, the men bringing up the rear. They carried banners. . . . This was the 'Silent Protest Parade,' organized by Negro leaders in Harlem, and one of the strangest and most impressive sights New York has witnessed. They marched in silence and they were watched in silence; but some of those who watched turned away with their eyes filled. . . .

"In view of the temper of the times, the Protest Parade was a courageous form of action to take."
JAMES WELDON JOHNSON, *BLACK MANHATTAN*

1. A side street between Lenox and Seventh Avenues around 1915; photograph by Brown Brothers.
2. Silent march of nearly ten thousand on Fifth Avenue led by Dr. W. E. B. Du Bois and James Weldon Johnson to protest the East St. Louis race riots, July 1917; NYPL/SC.

1.

2.

America and New York Enter the First World War

On April 2, 1917, President Woodrow Wilson called for a declaration of war against Germany. With a standing army of two hundred thousand men, the U.S. government initiated the draft of able-bodied men, making it possible for the nation to mobilize quickly. Patriotic fervor gripped everyone, and "Kill the Kaiser" became the call to arms. On June 5, between 7:00 A.M. and 7:00 P.M., nearly ten million men nationwide went to their local voting places to register for the draft. Virtually everyone went into the infantry.

Those drafted from New York represented a cross section of the city's ethnic mix including a considerable number of German-Americans.

1. The Twenty-second Coast Artillery as it marched past Fifth Avenue and Forty-eighth Street, August 30, 1917; photograph by Alice Austen, SIHS.
2. Recruitment drive for the Sixteenth Regiment at City Hall Park, 1917; OYL.
3. "Selected men local board for Division #184, City and State of New York," August 5, 1918; photograph by Frederick J. Weber, QBPL. Depicted are draftees primarily from Jamaica, Queens. They are Joseph Gallagher, Alfred M. Searing, Anthony Kraus, Vito Cippriano, Victor H. Josephson, Charles E. Friedall, James Fanan, Donato Coggiono, Hector Tosselli, Tony Schulteiss, Frank C. Erler, Joseph T. Dowgivilla, George Kubicke, John Neu, Clement O'Malley, John Hamerling, Joseph H. Miller, A. Xavier Weber, and John Carboni.

4. Preparing to depart for camp, August 5, 1918; photograph by Frederick J. Weber, QBPL. Depicted are draftees primarily from Jamaica, Queens. They are Robert D. Watkins, Charles Robinson, Edward N. Holling, Charles Walker, and Harry Cole.

"With their bands clamoring 'Over there! We'll be there, over there!' more than 25,000 men of the Twenty-seventh Division, U.S.A., formerly the National Guard, marched down Fifth Avenue, from 110th Street to Washington Square, today, passing in review before Gov. Whitman, Mayor Mitchel, and nearly 2,000,000 people, who cheered themselves hoarse as they bid farewell to the State's troops. Every available bit of space from which the spectacle might be viewed between the curbstones and the Avenue's serrated sky-line was jammed to its capacity. Flags and bunting waved in the breeze from nearly every window. The rain which had threatened during the forenoon began to fall mainly at two o'clock, flooding the streets and driving the crowd to doorways and stores for shelter. Then the sun came

out again and through it all the troops marched on.

"As a demonstration of military power, it was one of the most impressive scenes the city ever witnessed. Waves of olive-drab tipped with flashing bayonets, flowed down Fifth Avenue like the remorseless thrust of a river in full flood. For more than six hours the human stream swept down the asphalt channel, infantry, machine guns, artillery, engineers, signal and sanitary troops, clattering cavalry, wagon trains, pontoons, all the equipment of a miniature army."
NEW YORK EVENING POST, AUGUST 30, 1917

1.

The Victorious Troops Come Home

The entry of the United States into the war shifted the balance of power to the Allied forces. Following the 1918 Allied offensive on the western front, German resistance crumbled. Germany and Austria agreed to President Wilson's demand that their troops retreat to their own territories before an armistice could be signed. On November 11 fighting ceased with an Allied victory and a humiliating defeat for Germany. Millions of Europeans died in the fighting; there were 116,516 American fatalities, with thousands maimed or injured. Veterans hobbling on crutches became a common sight. New York welcomed its valiant soldiers with parades on Fifth Avenue.

1. Veterans of the seventy-seventh Division marching up Fifth Avenue on May 6, 1919; MA. The Victory Arch, at Fifth Avenue and Twenty-fourth Street, which can be seen in the background, was built in 1918 to honor the city's war dead. It was one of many such monuments erected throughout the city.
2. Governor Al Smith and other dignitaries reviewing the return of the "Harlem Hell Fighters" 369th Infantry on Fifth Avenue, March 5, 1919; CB. Continuing to march up Fifth Avenue, they were welcomed warmly when they arrived in Harlem.
3. Greeting a disabled veteran on the streets of Harlem, March 5, 1919; CB.

222

2.

3.

"The regiment, now the 369th Infantry, arrived back in New York on February 12, 1919. On February 17 they paraded up Fifth Avenue. New York had seen lots of soldiers marching off to war, but this was its first sight of marching veterans. The beautiful Victory Arch erected by the city at Madison Square as a part of the welcome to the returning troops was just nearing completion. . . . The parade had been given great publicity, and the city was anxious and curious to see soldiers back from the trenches. The newspapers had intimated that a good part of the celebration would be hearing the now famous Fifteenth band play jazz and seeing the Negro soldiers step to it. . . . Lieutenant Jim Europe walked sedately ahead, and Bandmaster Eugene Mikell had the great band alternate between two noble French military marches. And on the part of the men, there was no prancing, no showing of teeth, no swank; they marched with a steady stride, and from under their battered tin hats eyes that had looked straight at death were kept to the front."

JAMES WELDON JOHNSON, *BLACK MANHATTAN*

1.

Bustling Midtown Manhattan, Quiet Queens

Throughout the last quarter of the nineteeth century, Fifth Avenue above Thirty-fourth Street had been the city's most elegant residential neighborhood. When B. Altman & Company opened on the northeast corner of Fifth Avenue and Thirty-fourth Street in 1906, it signaled a change. Midtown Manhattan was becoming less residential and more commercial. This trend continued when such hotels as the St. Regis opened in 1904 at Fifth Avenue and Fifty-fifth Street and the Plaza in 1907 at Fifth Avenue and Fifty-ninth Street. In the 1920s and 1930s Fifth Avenue began to be lined with office towers as it became a new commercial and professional center where crowded sidewalks and congested avenues and side streets were commonplace.

When it was incorporated into Greater New York in 1898, the borough of Queens was a cluster of towns and villages. As both a bedroom community for Manhattan and an entity itself, it built residential, commercial, and industrial areas. During the 1920s, the population of Queens grew from 469,042 to 1,079,129; however, its population and physical density never approached those of Manhattan.

2.

"Ellen got off the bus at the corner of Fifth Avenue and Fifty-third Street. Rosy twilight was gushing out of the brilliant west, glittered in brass and nickel, on buttons, in people's eyes. All the windows on the east side of the street were aflame. As she stood with set teeth on the curb waiting to cross, a frail tendril of fragrance brushed her face. . . .

"The whistle blew, gears ground as cars started to pour out of the side streets, the crossing thronged with people. Ellen felt the lad brush against her as he crossed at her side. She shrank away. Through the smell of the arbutus she caught for a second the unwashed smell of his body, the smell of immigrants, of Ellis Island, of crowded tenements. Under all the nickelplated, goldplated streets enameled with May, uneasily she could feel the huddling smell, spreading in dark slow crouching masses like corruption oozing from broken sewers, like a mob. She walked briskly down the cross-street. She went in a door beside a small immaculately polished brass plate."

JOHN DOS PASSOS, MANHATTAN TRANSFER

1. Fifth Avenue above Forty-second Street, about 1929; OYL.
2. Intersection of Jamaica Avenue (Fulton Street) and 160th Street (Washington Street), 1917; photograph by Frederick J. Weber, QBPL.

1.

Jewish Immigrants, Doctors, and Philanthropists

With the outbreak of the First World War, the mass immigration of Jews from Eastern Europe to the United States was interrupted. After the war immigration of all groups was reduced to a trickle by the imposition of the quota laws. As a consequence of Eastern European immigration, the New York Jewish community had crystallized into three principal groups: the established German Jews and the first- and second-generation Eastern European Jews. Although they shared a sense of belonging to the same religious community, they lived separate lives geographically, economically, socially, and culturally. German Jews were in banking, law and medicine; Eastern European Jews were primarily in the men's and women's clothing industries as workers, craftsmen, and owners.

Prior to the war, embarrassed by the hordes of Eastern European Jews arriving in New York, Jacob H. Schiff, a successful investment banker and a leader of the German Jewish community, initiated the Galveston Plan. Rather than arrive in New York, Eastern European Jews landed in Galveston, Texas. From there they were sent to cities and small towns in the western states to "relieve the tremendous congestion in the seaboard cities." Despite the Galveston Plan, tens of thousands of Eastern European Jews continued to settle in New York.

1. The Freund family reunion, about 1920; YIVO.

2. Mount Sinai Hospital medical staff, about 1916; AJA. Predominantly German Jews, the senior medical staff members were distinguished for their intellectual caliber, cultural attainment, and sheer brilliance of scientific productivity.

3. Joint Distribution Committee meeting to discuss relief funds for European Jews affected by the ravages of war, 1918; NA. Among those attending were Cyrus Adler, Sholem Asch, Arthur Lehman, Jacob Schiff, and Felix Warburg.

4. Immigrants attending a citizenship class at the HIAS (Hebrew Immigrant Aid Society) building, 1920; YIVO.

"Ours was a middle-class existence, well to do, well behaved, complacent. When I was born, in the last month of 1886, our house was brownstone with a high stoop, on Ninety-fourth Street near Lexington Avenue. . . .

"My father, Robert Levy, born in Hesse-Cassel, Germany . . . was an importer of nettings and veilings, who climbed slowly but steadily to affluence in this country.

"To his family he was first and foremost a businessman, virtually a slave to his success in pursuit of security for his family. . . .

"Our father had the prejudice of many men of German-Jewish origin against Jews born 'east of Berlin.'"
IRMA LEVY LINDHEIM

"Despite the process of assimilation, the Jews will, for a long time to come, continue as a distinct group. This is inevitable because of the natural force of social cohesion. Jews are more likely to associate with other Jews than with Gentiles. The majority of Jewish boys are likely to keep company with and marry Jewish girls and thus group cohesion will continue and group traditions be perpetuated. . . . Even if centuries of assimilation in an atmosphere of tolerance were unbroken by waves of anti-Semitism, it would probably be at least eighty generations before the Jews would disappear as a distinguishable people upon the American scene."
MORRIS RAPHAEL COHEN, *A DREAMER'S JOURNEY*

1.

2.

3.

Italian Immigrants, Professionals, and Artisans

The First World War and 1920s immigration quotas sharply reduced Italian immigration to the United States. However, according to the 1930 census, there were 1,070,353 people of Italian descent living in New York City, accounting for 17 percent of the city's total population. Of that number, approximately 444,000 were foreign-born. As their fortunes improved, they moved out of Manhattan's Little Italy. They spread into other neighborhoods in Manhattan (East Harlem), Brooklyn (Red Hook, Greenpoint, Bedford, Stuyvesant Heights, Bensonhurst), the Bronx (Arthur Avenue), Queens, and Staten Island.

Although dedicated to their families and their neighborhoods, some Italian-Americans began to pursue higher education as a route to joining mainstream America. Some went into business and professions, while most second- and third-generation Italian-Americans tended to seek blue-collar rather than white-collar jobs. They worked in construction, manufacturing, and the utilities and were members of the fire, police, and sanitation departments. Within their neighborhoods they established restaurants, grocery stores, meat markets, and bakeries that maintained the traditions of their homeland.

1. *Italian emigrants aboard the* Principessa Mafalda, *about 1920; 3M.*
2. *Two Italian children at Ellis Island, 1919; CB.*
3. *"Italian child finds here first penny." Ellis Island, 1926; photograph by Lewis Hine, NYPL.*
4. *Husband and wife, about 1928; FM.*
5. *"An Italian craftsman working in bronze," 1930; photograph by Lewis Hine, NYPL.*

"The inside of our new American house, in 1925, was reassuringly Italian. There were the Italian smells from the kitchen (above all the aroma of coffee, which father bought fresh-roasted at De Rosa's on Mulberry Street). . . .

"Among the Italians I met who found life in America easy, profitable, and pleasurable, far easier, more profitable and pleasurable than in Italy, were the ditchdiggers, hotel and restaurant people, Sicilians, wheeler-dealers, the opera crowd and the aristocrats. . . .

"The ditchdiggers were all called 'Tony' (as Pullman porters were then called 'George'). In spite of what seemed to some Americans their miserable and pitiable living conditions, they made more money, were less oppressed, and worked fewer hours than back home. . . . They sent money home, produced flocks of children, ate amply and succulently, made their own wine, and became very portly as soon as possible. The lucky ones were buying houses and automobiles by easy payments.

"Hotel and restaurant people were in clover. . . . At the bottom of the ladder was the cheap one-family *trattoria*, where Mama cooked, Papa served, one always found homemade red wine served in coffee cups and homely advice on how to bear life's burden. At the top were northern Italians . . . who ran and sometimes owned some of the great 'French' restaurants and managed the big hotels."

LUIGI BARZINI, *O AMERICA!*

1.

When the Irish Ruled New York

To say that the Irish ruled New York City from the end of the nineteenth century through the 1920s would not be an exaggeration. As leaders of Tammany Hall and Democratic county executive committees they were in a position to influence Democratic politics and the city government, where there were tens of thousands of patronage jobs. The police, firefighters, and schoolteachers were mostly Irish. There had been an uninterrupted succession of predominantly Tammany Irish mayors from the turn of the century: George B. McClellan, William J. Gaynor (half Irish and an anti-Tammany Democrat), John Purroy Mitchel (a Fusion candidate who preferred to think of himself as a WASP), John F. Hylan, and Jimmy Walker. Al Smith, from the Lower East Side, had been elected governor and

was the unsuccessful 1928 Democratic presidential candidate. Irish Democratic party bosses ran virtual fiefdoms. In Manhattan they were Richard Croker and Charles Murphy. In the Bronx they were Ed Flynn and Charles Buckley. In Brooklyn it was Hugh McLaughlin.

After the First World War, Irish immigration to the United States dwindled. Although there were two hundred thousand Irish-born in New York in 1920, the majority were second and third generation. They overcame nineteenth- and early-twentieth-century derogatory stereotypes that had haunted their parents and relatives. They were becoming more middle class; they dominated the construction industry, joined the managerial class, and moved into the professions. More of them began to go to college.

2.

3.

4.

For decades George M. Cohan had been the undisputed Irish-American king of Broadway. A number of New York Irish cultural luminaries began to emerge in the 1920s. There was New York–born playwright Eugene O'Neill, who won a Pulitzer Prize in 1920 for *Beyond the Horizon* and in 1921 for *Anna Christie*. Although Irish Catholic F. Scott Fitzgerald's *Great Gatsby* was set in a community of wealthy New Yorkers outside the city, he had a dubious connection with his Irish roots. The same could be said of John O'Hara, whose fiction used New York as its backdrop.

The Irish lived in every section of the city. In Manhattan they were on both the Upper East Side and Upper West Side, in Washington Heights, and in Inwood. In Brooklyn, they were around the navy yard and in Greenpoint, Williamsburg, Prospect Park, Flatbush, Sunset Park, and Bay Ridge. In Queens they were in Long Island City, Astoria, Woodside, Sunnyside, and Rockaway Beach. In the Bronx they were in Mott Haven, Melrose, Highbridge, Fordham, and Kingsbridge.

1. Unveiling statue of Victor Herbert, Central Park Mall, 1927; CB. Born in Dublin, composer Victor Herbert raised light opera to a degree of sophistication that it had never before reached. An Irish patriot, he led the Friends of Irish Freedom.

2. First-grade class, St. Patricks's School, Kent Avenue, Brooklyn, 1917; MERCY.

3. Friends in front of 1923 Dodge at 68-09 38th Avenue, Woodside, Queens, 1926; LGWA. From left to right: Patrick Cooney, Daniel Traynor, Mary and Kathleen McGuire, and John Traynor.

4. Maria Rita Coakley Shannon with her niece Peggy Coakley in the backyard of her parents' home, 2701 Heath Avenue, Bronx, about 1929; EK.

1.

Marching for Irish Freedom

In 1916 the Friends of Irish Freedom, a mass organization supporting an independent Irish republic, was created, with composer Victor Herbert as its leader. It supported Sinn Fein, Ireland's new republican party, and its effort to obtain independence from Great Britain. A huge meeting was held at Carnegie Hall that year. By 1919 the organization counted more than 275,000 members nationwide.

At the Irish-American Convention of May 14, 1917, it was resolved to "urgently request the President and congress to demand that England make good her promises . . . by granting to Ireland full national independence" and "that she settle the Irish Question permanently and finally."

1. St. Patrick's Day Parade, 1919; MCNY. In 1918 women were for the first time included among the marchers. These women, from the St. Columcille (Chelsea) branch of the Friends of Irish Freedom, marched in the parade the following year.

1.

Flying for Women's Rights

Although a November 1915 statewide referendum on women's voting rights had been defeated, suffrage activists embarked on a second campaign that eventually in 1917 led to the passage of the women's suffrage amendment to the York State Constitution with New York City carrying the state. This momentum led to the passage in 1920 of the Nineteenth Amendment to the U.S. Constitution, providing women with the right to vote.

1. Suffragists assembled on Midland Beach, Staten Island, December 2, 1916; photograph by Gertrude Brugman, NYHS. Their sign reads "Women Want Liberty." In an effort to draw attention to the women's suffrage issue, a group of activist women planned to drop leaflets on President Wilson's yacht when it was moored in New York Harbor. He came to witness the new illumination of the Statue of Liberty. Mrs. Richberg Hornsby piloted the plane, which did not fulfill its heroic mission; however, the event was fully reported in the newspapers and accomplished its objective of publicizing the women's suffrage amendment.

WHEN LIFE IS VERY STRENUOUS AND SPIRITS ARE WAY DOWN
YOU'D BETTER GO TO POLLY'S IN LITTLE GREENWICH TOWN
FOR THERE THE CLANS ARE GATHERED – ITS THERE YOU'LL FIND 'EM ALL
THE ARTISTS AND THE WRITERS RANGED ALONG THE WALL.
MISS POLLY TAKES THE MONEY AND MIKE SAYS HE JUST CAN'T
WAIT ANY FASTER ON THE FOLKS IN POLLY'S RES-TAU-RANT.
J.T.B.

GREENWICH VILLAGE – NEW YORK

JESSIE TARBOX BEALS

1.

New York Bohemians

Throughout most of the nineteenth century a vital intellectual and cultural life flourished in New York; there were writers, painters, and sculptors who, although independent, looked toward Europe as a beacon. At the turn of the century, when Paris became the capital of the international avant-garde, it became both a magnet and a model for young American artists and writers who went to study and live there. Paris had a lifestyle they wanted to emulate. Promulgated by opera and theater, *la vie bohème* was interpreted by Americans as "the artist's life."

Seeing themselves as a new generation, bohemians rejected both the personal values represented by the Victorian family and the public culture of their parents. Greenwich Village became the locus of their "revolutionary" activities during the second and third decades of this century. With its picturesque configuration of older buildings, convoluted alleys, and low rents, it was a New York equivalent to Montmartre, Montparnasse, and the Latin Quarter. New styles were born, new magazines published, new plays written, and new dances performed. On occasion artists, playwrights, and dancers collaborated. Mabel Dodge held a Wednesday evening salon in her living room at 23 Fifth Avenue that might have rivaled Gertrude Stein's in Paris. Creating their own restaurants, bookstores, galleries, and theaters, the bohemians developed a sanctuary existing apart from the rest of New York. Greenwich Village was a place to

escape from the conventional bourgeois values of family, sex, and art. Some of the most radical, creative, and innovative people of this generation were associated with the Village. Among them were Max Eastman, Isadora Duncan, Emma Goldman, Edward Hopper, Gaston Lachaise, Walter Lippmann, Eugene O'Neill, John Reed, Edna St. Vincent Millay, and Alfred Stieglitz, Within its precincts anarchism, communism, feminism, and socialism were debated, encouraged and practiced.

To broadcast their nonconformity, the bohemians created their own distinctive clothing style. Women wore loose-fitting smocks of bright-colored fabrics, slouch hats, needlepoint aprons, peasant shawls, patterned stockings, flat sandals, flowing scarves, beads, Gypsy jewelry, and sometimes pants. Men wore oversize tweedy jackets and coats, work shirts, unusual ties and slouch hats.

1. *Polly's Restaurant, about 1916; photograph by Jesse Tarbox Beals, MCNY. Owned by anarchist Polly Holladay of Evanston, Illinois, it offered cheap meals and was staffed by radicals.*
2. *Washington Square Bookstore, about 1918; photograph by Jesse Tarbox Beals, MCNY.*
3. *Act I,* Hobohemia, *about 1918; MCNY. The so-called little theater movement, with informal programs and nonprofessional casts, flourished. Adapted from a Sinclair Lewis story, this short-lived play poked fun at anarchism, cubism, Freud, and feminism.*
4. *Marguerite and William Zorach, about 1916; PZ. Both studied painting in Paris and were leading figures of the emerging American avant-garde.*

1.

2.

An Established Chinese-American Community

Perhaps the most segregated of all New York ethnic communities, the Chinese remained apart. Chinatown in lower Manhattan, which evolved around the end of the nineteenth century, was their exclusive turf. With a static population hovering at around four thousand (the Chinese Exclusion Act of 1882 prohibited immigration from China.), they maintained a private world with its own language, economy, social structure, and institutions. As a consequence of the immigration restrictions, it became a very male-dominated society. In 1920, for every fifteen-year-old Chinese girl, there were sixteen boys. The Chinese were excluded from many occupations and had to seek employment in jobs where Caucasians did not compete. There are few New York Chinese families that do not have hand laundries and

restaurants as part of their heritage. Economic growth was financed internally. Those who wanted to go into business for themselves acquired the capital by means of a *hui*, a rotating credit association, an institution introduced from southern China. People from the same village or clan created a pool of capital; regularly they would have to compete for the right to use these funds. As a result, restaurants, gift shops, and other Chinese-owned enterprises came into being and flourished, creating a merchant elite. The New York Consolidated Benevolent Association served as an informal local government. It acted as a liaison with the outside American community, settled disputes between other Chinese organizations, and sponsored social welfare programs.

Although Chinese (Cantonese because

3.

most of New York's Chinese came from southern China) was spoken by the first, second, and often third generations, the New York Chinese Public School was created by the Chinese community to impart knowledge of Chinese traditions and teach the rudiments of the language. It operated on weekends and after school hours. (This school still exists.)

1. *A parade through Chinatown honoring the late Dr. Sun Yat-sen, founder and first president of the Republic of China, 1925; CB. The parade and memorial service were sponsored by the New York branch of Dr. Sun's political party, Kuomintang. Sixteen Chinese-American organizations, each headed by a band playing a funeral dirge, joined the march. A portrait of Dr. Sun was carried at the head of the procession. On the dark velvet-covered reviewing stand a single white rose, typifying the spirit of the patriot, was to be seen.*
2. *The Ging Hawk Club of the East Seventeenth Street YWCA performing* The Gift of the Gods, *a traditional Chinese play, 1934; CB.*
3. *Unidentified Chinese merchant family, about 1925; MCA. Christian missionaries*

influenced Chinese-Americans' assimilation in a number of ways: getting them to adopt the Christian faith, assisting in their learning English, and encouraging them to wear Western-style clothes. This was particularly evident in the merchant class.

1.

2.

4.

Harlem Transformed

With the outbreak of the First World War, immigration from Eastern and Southern Europe was interrupted, and the source of cheap labor terminated. The American industrial economy was expanding and needed workers. The black South was seen as a source. Recruiters were sent to the South to encourage rural blacks to migrate to jobs where they would make more money and find better working conditions.

On November 5, 1917, the *New York World* reported: "Since the first of last April, 118,000 Negroes have gone from the South to Pennsylvania, West Virginia, New York, New Jersey, Ohio, Indiana, Missouri, Illinois, Michigan and Connecticut to accept work. They went to take places vacated by foreign laborers who returned to Europe at the

outbreak of the Great War." For southern blacks, the North also offered the opportunity to escape the onerous effects of racism and segregation that had been codified in the South since the end of the Civil War. Beyond that there was the promise of educational opportunities for themselves and their children. When they arrived in New York, they were perceived as being different. On April 27, 1927, the *New York Times* said, "The new arrival from the South is . . . a seedy, collarless, slouching fellow wearing a battered old soft hat. Slow in motion, he is constantly buffeted by the swift black tides of the avenue that sweep past him."

Blacks came to Harlem not only from the rural South, but also from all across this country and from Jamaica in the British

5.

6.

7.

West Indies. Those who came from places other than the South were often bourgeois, professional, and educated. Dr. W. E. B. Du Bois called the educated middle class the "Talented Tenth," suggesting that they represented only 10 percent of the total black population. Together the blacks in New York transformed Harlem. The place was neither bourgeois northern black nor rural southern black, but a new amalgam that was distinctly Harlem.

1. *Seventh Avenue and 124th Street, about 1925; NYPL.*
2. *"Dinner party—Harlem socializes," 1927; photograph by James Van DerZee.*
3. *Apartment buildings on the north side of 135th Street between Lenox and Seventh avenues purchased in 1911 by Nail and Parker, about 1916; NYPL/SC.*
4. *Interior of a Harlem tenement, about 1916; photograph by Brown Brothers.*
5. *Madame C. J. Walker, who made a fortune selling hair products, about 1916; NYPL/SC.*
6. *Marcus Garvey, about 1918; photograph by James Van DerZee. A Jamaican who settled in Harlem in 1917, Garvey created a black nationalist movement that encouraged black pride and a return to Africa.*
7. *"Gay Northeasterners," strolling on*

Seventh Avenue, about 1929, NYPL/SC. From left to right: Edith Scott, Helen Corbin, and Rosie Swain.

1.

Harlem in the Twenties

By 1920 more than eighty thousand blacks lived in Harlem. The boundaries of black Harlem were roughly drawn from 110th Street on the south. On the east it was Lenox Avenue to 126th Street, then Lexington Avenue to the Harlem River and along the Harlem River north to 155th Street. On the west it was from Eighth Avenue and 116th Street along St. Nicholas Avenue to the Harlem River. At this time Harlem was not totally black; Jews still lived there, and Italians were in East Harlem.

When African-Americans moved into Harlem, they were not inheriting abandoned or deteriorating property. They moved into prime real estate, streets lined with spacious brownstones that had been built for middle-class whites in the 1880s and 1890s. There were four- and five-floor apartment buildings and some tenements. There were parks, opera houses, churches, and libraries, all of which had been built for middle-class whites. Harlem was one of the most desirable neighborhoods in Manhattan. However, the blacks who moved in were not immune from white real estate speculators. There were tales of landlords who had converted nine-room apartments that had rented for $40 into one-room lodgings each renting for $100 to $125 per month.

1. *Reverend Adam Clayton Powell, Sr., with a Sunday school class assembled outside the Abyssinian Baptist Church, 1925; photograph by James Van DerZee. Under Powell's leadership, a massive church was constructed on 138th Street between Lenox and Seventh avenues.*

2. *Members of the Alpha Phi Alpha fraternity basketball team, 1926, photograph by James Van DerZee.*

3. *Staff of the Dunbar National Bank, 1928; NYPL/SC. The bank was within the Dunbar Apartment complex on Seventh Avenue between 149th and 150th streets; both the bank and apartments received financial assistance from the Rockefeller family. Countee Cullen, Dr. W. E. B. Dubois, A. Philip Randolph, and Bill Robinson lived there.*

4. *Children's dance class, about 1928; photograph by Otis C. Butler, NYPL/SC.*

"It should be noted that Harlem was taken over without violence. In some of the large Northern cities where the same sort of expansion of the Negro population was going on, there was not only strong antagonism on the part of whites, but physical expression of it. In Chicago, Cleveland, and other cities houses bought and moved into by Negroes were bombed. In Chicago a church bought by a coloured congregation was badly damaged by bombs. In other cities several formerly white churches which had been taken over by coloured congregations were bombed. In Detroit, mobs undertook to evict Negroes from houses bought by them in white neighbourhoods."

JAMES WELDON JOHNSON, *BLACK MANHATTAN*

241

1.

Harlem Renaissance

On March 21, 1924, writer Alain Locke presided at a dinner at the Civic Club where black and white writers and cultural figures discussed emerging new black talent. The *New York Herald Tribune* in reporting on the event gave this new movement a name: It said that America was "on the edge of a Negro renaissance." What became known as the Harlem Renaissance was an amalgam of artists and writers who were active in Harlem in the 1920s. They debated literary tradition, folk culture, politics, and sex. Collectively they produced art and literature of great merit. Among the artists and writers associated with the Harlem Renaissance were Arna Bontemps, Countee Cullen, Aaron Douglas, Jessie Fauset, Langston Hughes, Zora Neale Hurston, Claude McKay, Wallace Thurman, and Gene Toomer. They

helped establish Harlem as the cultural capital of black America. Prior to the 1920s, black American culture had been defined only as rural folk culture. They demonstrated that there was an urban black culture equivalent to urban white culture.

1. Party in honor of Langston Hughes on the rooftop at 580 St. Nicholas Avenue, 1926; NYPL/SC. From left to right: Langston Hughes, Charles S. Johnson, E. Franklin Frazier, Rudolph Fisher, and Hubert T. Delany. When his book of poems was published by Alfred A. Knopf in 1926, Hughes was beginning to establish himself as America's premier black poet.

2. Countee Cullen, 1941, photograph by Carl Van Vechten; NYPL/SC. Cullen was a poet-novelist who graduated from New York University and received a master's degree from Harvard University.

3. Claude McKay, about 1925; NYPL/SC. The Jamaican-born McKay was recognized as an editor, a poet, and a novelist.

"These constitute a new generation not because of years only, but because of a new aesthetic and a new philosophy of life. They have all swung above the horizon in the last three years, and we can say without disparagement of the past that in that short space of time they have gained collectively from publishers, editors, critics and the general public more recognition than has ever before come to Negro creative artists in an entire working lifetime. First novels of unquestioned distinction, first acceptances by premier journals whose pages are the ambition of veteran craftsmen, international acclaim, the conquest for us of new provinces of art, the development for the first time among us of literary coteries and channels for the contact of creative minds, and most important of all, a spiritual quickening and racial leav-ening such as no generation has yet ever felt and known."

ALAIN LOCKE, SURVEY GRAPHIC, MARCH 1925

1.

2.

Harlem Clubs and Harlem Jazz

It was the Roaring Twenties; prosperity and Prohibition were curious handmaidens. The Harlem club scene was hot. It was a place for white people to be entertained by black folks. You could lose yourself on booze and possibly cocaine; you could do the Charleston and the black bottom and be entertained by some incredibly talented musicians, dancers, and comedians like Louis Armstrong, Cab Calloway, Florence Mills, Jelly Roll Morton, Bessie Smith, Snake Hips Tucker, and Ethel Waters. There was the Cotton Club, Connie's Inn, and Small's. No white visitor to New York would miss "going uptown." Of wider impact than the art and literature of the Harlem Renaissance was the music created in Harlem in the 1920s. Jazz was born in New Orleans and moved up the river to Chicago and Kansas City. James Reese Europe's Clef Club band had established jazz in New York in the previous decade. Harlem jazz in the twenties evolved into a big band sophisticated sound exemplified by Duke Ellington and Fletcher Henderson's compositions. Musicians performed uptown, but the music business was downtown. By the mid-twenties most dance bands were booked out of New York, most network radio programs emanated out of New York, and Tin Pan Alley was the acknowledged center of the music-publishing business. Harlem became synonymous with jazz, and jazz made Harlem an international symbol of black cultural achievement.

3.

4.

"Connie's, on Seventh Avenue and 132nd Street is the first white outpost on the uptown colored frontier, the first stop on the route of the downtown night clubbers. . . .

"Walk down one flight of stairs and you are in this rendezvous, so low-ceilinged as to be cavelike. . . .

"Around the ringside tables one sees many faces that have become familiar to both the Broadway and society journals . . . Jack Pickford, Mark Hellinger, Max Schuster, Gertrude Vanderbilt. . . . And, of course, Harry K. Thaw, without whose name no roster of night club customers would be complete.

"The Cotton Club, on Lenox Avenue at 142nd Street, is an upstairs edition of Connie's. The same type of high-priced orchestra, the same type of revue, the same type of customers. Possibly the Cotton Club gets a little the best of it in the matter of clientele. It would seem so, at any rate, even if one passed snap judgment merely on the luxuriousness of the cars that park around the building during the whoopee hours."
NEW YORK DAILY NEWS, NOVEMBER 1, 1929

1. Cotton Club program, 1925; NYPL/SC. The Cotton Club, like the other clubs, had a whites only policy. The whites were entertained by blacks, who could not be patrons themselves.
2. Cotton Club entertainers, undated; photograph by Vithana Studio, NYPL/SC.
3. Duke Ellington, 1929; FD. Big band leader and pianist, he was an acknowledged composer and arranger of genius.
4. Fletcher Henderson, 1926; NYPL/SC. In 1926 Henderson was a pianist, bandleader, composer, and arranger. He created a legendary band that was, in the opinion of many musicians, the finest band ever known. He often played in downtown clubs.

1.

2.

Jewish Stars of Stage, Screen, and Radio

Ethnic vaudeville and burlesque provided opportunities for Irish, Italian, and Jewish comedians to display their talents. The Yiddish theater, which flourished on the Lower East Side, served as a platform for Jewish talent. Florenz Ziegfeld's *Follies* was a showcase that projected other entertainers into stardom. Jewish performers, like Eddie Cantor, George Jessel, Al Jolson, and the Marx Brothers, began their careers on New York stages. Tin Pan Alley, the music publishing-business, was centered on Times Square. Although the motion-picture industry was born in New York, it moved to Hollywood at the end of the second decade of the twentieth century. Many Jewish performers, composers, and writers were "bi-

coastal." Taking the 20th Century Limited from Grand Central to Chicago and spending another two and a half days on a train to California, they were associated with films that were often adapted from New York stage successes or in which New York was the subject or setting. Network radio, centered in New York, blossomed at the end of the 1920s, giving some of these stars further opportunities to present themselves to nationwide audiences, which devoured their "ethnic fare."

3.

5.

1. *Crowds outside Warners Theater on Broadway, waiting to see Al Jolson in* The Jazz Singer, *1927; SI. In what was considered to be the first talking motion picture, Jolson appeared in blackface, a stage convention at the time. The son of a cantor, Jolson began his career in circuses, minstrel shows, and vaudeville. Hollywood found his exuberant style well suited to early talkies.*

2. *Al Jolson departing from Grand Central Station, probably for Hollywood, about 1927; MOMA/FS.*

3. *George Gershwin and Irving Berlin, about 1928; FD. Gershwin was one of the most outstanding musical talents of his generation whose career was terminated by his early death. Berlin, who wrote for both Broadway and Hollywood, created some of America's*

most popular music, including "Alexander's Ragtime Band" (1911) and "Easter Parade" (1948).

4. *Eddie Cantor greeted by Postal Telegraph boys wearing "popeye" masks on his return to New York from Hollywood, about 1933; MOMA/FS. Born on the Lower East Side, Cantor starred in the* Ziegfeld Follies *of 1917. A popular national figure, he had a regular weekly radio show, which evolved into a television program.*

5. *Maurice Schwartz, Celia Adler, and Lazar Freed appearing in the Yiddish Art Theatre's production of Sholem Aleichem's play* Stempenyu, *1929; MCNY. When Jacob Adler, the actor, and Jacob Gordin, the author, arrived in New York in the 1890s, Yiddish theater in America took on a new life.*

Maurice Schwartz's Yiddish Art Theatre stimulated a new burst of activity in the 1920s and 1930s.

1.

Ziegfeld Girls

Every age creates its own symbols of glamour. In the 1920s it was the Ziegfeld girls. They appeared in Florenz Ziegfeld's extravagant stage revues, the *Ziegfeld Follies*, designed "to glorify the American girl." They ran on Broadway from 1907 to 1925 and again in 1927 and 1931. Ziegfeld's *Follies* were a magnet for beautiful and talented women from across the country. More of them ended up in the chorus line than became stars. They were an extended family, some of whose members married rich and famous men, giving rise to the derogatory appellation "gold digger." Ziegfeld was an incredible talent scout and impresario. He discovered Fanny Brice singing in a burlesque house and offered her a job at seventy-five dollars a week. When she left the *Follies* stage after introducing "My Man," he gave her a check for twenty-five hundred dollars, saying, "You earned it." He transformed American stage productions by creating a style based on lavish sets, extravagant costumes, and complex routines that has been emulated for generations. He eventually moved to Hollywood to advise Samuel Goldwyn on movies based on the *Follies*.

"Allyn King, the featured beauty of the 'Follies of 1916,' is a Southern girl of 17. Miss King, who besides being lovely in face and figure, is a singer, dancer, and actress of talent, was born in Winston-Salem, N.C., and that town is naturally very proud of the winsome blond miss who has impressed New York at an age when most girls are still in the seminary. Miss King recently played the prima donna role of the 'Follies' for a week when Ina Claire was out of the cast, and her work won the commendation of Flo Ziegfeld and Ned Wayburn.

"She has the radiant charm of the typical well-bred Southern girl. Her father was a physician, who left his family well provided for. Bad investments swept the little fortune away, and at the age of 15 Miss Allyn went on the stage to support her mother and sis-

ter. She made a plucky fight of it, and her chance came last spring when a travelling showman saw and heard her in a New Haven cabaret and immediately informed Mr. Ziegfeld that he had made a 'find.'

"The impresario of the 'Follies' sent for Allyn and her charming mother—a big sister rather than a stage guardian—and immediately signed her as a feature of the 'Follies of 1916.' Her success has been instantaneous."

NEW YORK SUN, JULY 30, 1916

1. *"Telephone Girl," Ziegfeld Follies routine, undated; MCNY.*
2. *Sheet music cover for "The Girl of My Dreams," 1920; MCNY.*
3. *Lois Wills and Ruth Wadell, Follies girls, eating oysters, 1925; CB. At a single sitting the two devoured 204 oysters. They were judged winners of the Follies girls' oyster-eating contest.*

249

WE HOLD THE 18th AMENDMENT TO BE UNCONSTITUTIONAL

THE VOLSTEAD ACT
MUST BE REPEALED

"IF THIS BE TREASON
MAKE THE MOST OF IT"

1.

Prohibition

The Eighteenth Amendment to the U.S. Constitution went into effect on January 16, 1920, making it illegal to manufacture, sell, and transport all alcoholic beverages. With it came the National Prohibition Act (popularly called the Volstead Act after its author) by which the amendment was to be enforced. Although the law of the land, Prohibition was hardly a New York idea. Support for it came from the rural heartland of America, but it was never an enforceable law. Moonshining, smuggling, and speakeasies flourished. When a New York City member of Congress, Fiorello La Guardia, said that it would take a police force of 250,000 to enforce Prohibition in New York City and another 200,000 to police the police.

"Naturally enough, the speakeasy handles a fat slice of night trade. From the humble barroom with its sawdust-splashed floor to its high hat offspring with mirrored walls.

"The first named, modeled on saloon lines, smacks of pre-war days. It flaunts a bar, with footrail and cuspidors and, as of yore, contains a back room. The patronage is mainly masculine, the air reeks with tobacco smoke, and he who starts to get tough is promptly ejected by a pair of expert bouncers. All in all, a poor place to go looking for trouble.

"A second cousin, once removed, is the grocery or delicatessen store. With a room in the rear, where the 'goods' are delivered over the counter. As in the former, beer, gin, and whiskey are the favorite offerings, which are peddled at much the same rates.

2.

If the shop is Italian, as is often the case, 'red ink' is an added attraction.

"More common is the brand of parlour that fills a brownstone basement. A pair of dark and dingy rooms, where 'the stuff' is dispensed at tables. The walls are plastered with a spotty paper and no one speaks above a whisper. For this is serious drinking and Prohibition at its gloomiest. Here comes the lonely bibber to drown his mounting woes. In a dim and dismal corner, all by his little self. Here, too, his female counterpart. May they weep in each other's highballs. . . .

"Last and latest is the type de luxe. Filling a six-storey mansion and including, besides a Grade-A kitchen (under an ex-chef of a great hotel), two bars, a dance floor, ping-pong and backgammon rooms, a picture gallery, and a five-piece band. Where

cocktails fetch a dollar a throw and champagne twenty-five a quart. All done charmingly and with perfect manners, for in our western circles the de luxe speakeasy now fulfills the function of the home.

"Entrance to these haunts is effected originally through a friend. But a different friend for the different types; for each has its pet clientele. Thus, for one type, you must know a stockbroker, for another an advertising man. Again, a clubman may be the right person, a reporter, or indeed, a racketeer."

CHARLES SHAW, *NIGHTLIFE, VANITY FAIR'S INTIMATE GUIDE TO NEW YORK AFTER DARK*, 1933

1. *"Fifteen thousand, twenty-five hundred of them women, tramp New York streets in blistering heat to register their protest against the dry laws, July 4, 1921,"* photograph by Underwood and Underwood; MCNY.
2. *Federal Prohibition agents Izzy Einstein and Moe Smith with a still they captured in a cellar, 1925; CB. (Their legendary exploits were romanticized in a 1985 film starring Jackie Gleason and Art Carney.)*
3. *Advertisements for speakeasies and pure-grain alcohol, about 1925; all MCNY.*

251

1.

Yankees, Giants, and Dodgers

During the 1920s New York boasted of having three major-league baseball teams—the Yankees (American League) in the Bronx, the Giants (National League) in Manhattan, and the Dodgers (National League) in Brooklyn—and several minority teams in the Eastern Colored League: the Cuban Stars East, Bachrach Giants, and Lincoln Giants. The 1920s saw the birth of a new age for baseball; attendance broke all records, and the players became stars. Fueled by the rise of sportswriters and later radio broadcasts, baseball became, without question, the dominant pastime. More than any other person, the New York Yankees' Babe Ruth personified the new sports star; with his face seen everywhere, he was virtually deified.

"When the Babe stepped to the plate in that momentous eighth inning the score was deadlocked; Koenig was on third base, the result of a triple; one man was out and all was tense. It was the Babe's fourth trip to the plate during the afternoon, a base on balls and two singles resulting on his other visits.

"The first Zachary offering was a fast one for a called strike. The next was high. The Babe took a vicious swing at the third pitched ball and the bat connected with a crash that was audible in all parts of the stand. It was not necessary to follow the course of the ball. The boys in the bleachers indicated the route of the record homer. It dropped about half way to the top. Boys,

2.

3.

4.

No. 60 was some homer, a fitting wallop to top the Babe's record of 59 in 1921.

"While the crowd cheered and the Yankee players roared their greetings the Babe made his triumphant, almost regal tour of the paths. He jogged around slowly, touched each bag firmly and carefully, and when he imbedded his spikes in the rubber disk to record officially Homer 60, hats were tossed into the air, papers were torn up and thrown liberally and the spirit of celebration permeated the place. . . .

". . . Ruth's homer was a fitting climax to a game which will go down as the Babe's personal triumph."

JAMES S. CAROLAN, *NEW YORK TIMES*, OCTOBER 1, 1927

1. *Yankee Stadium on opening day, April 18, 1923; OYL. Called The House That Ruth Built, it was in the Bronx on the north bank of the Harlem River at 161st and River Avenue.*
2. *Mayor Jimmy Walker at the Polo Grounds throwing out the first ball of the season, 1932; MCNY. Built in 1890, the Polo Grounds was on the south bank of the Harlem River between 155th and 157th streets.*
3. *Ebbets Field, about 1925; CB. Home of the Brooklyn Dodgers, at Bedford Avenue and Montgomery Street in Flatbush (Crown Heights today), it opened in 1913 with twenty-four thousand grandstand seats.*
4. *Babe Ruth, 1927; photograph by Nickolas Muray, MOMA/PC. His averages that year*

were: batted .356, hit 60 home runs, scored 158 runs, had 138 bases on balls, had 417 total bases and 164 RBIs.

1.

2.

The Upper East Side

Bounded by Fifth Avenue on its eastern perimeter, Lexington Avenue on the west, Fifty-ninth Street on the south, and Ninety-sixth Street on the north, the Upper East Side became New York's premier neighborhood. When Fifth Avenue was lined with mansions at the turn of the century, it was a sanctuary for the rich. With Central Park as its front yard, this was an extremely desirable place to live. After the First World War the shortage of cheap domestic help and the attraction of apartment living left many of these mansions unoccupied, By 1931 forty-three apartment houses had been built on Fifth Avenue, radically transforming it from a series of mansard-roofed houses to an extended facade of high rises. In this era of apartment living, the spacious new Park Avenue apartments succeeded Fifth Avenue in their appeal and status. Brownstones built prior to the First World War and lining the side streets also housed former mansion dwellers. This area defined the way of life of upper-class New York society.

3.

1. *Looking north on Fifth Avenue with the
Pulitzer Fountain and Saint-Gaudens'
General Sherman in the foreground, 1925;
MCNY.*
2. *The ubiquitous doorman with his brass-
buttoned uniform and peaked cap at 480
Park Avenue, about 1930; CB. (Although they
were below Fifty-ninth Street, a series of
large apartment buildings on Park Avenue,
some with huge interior courtyards, were
considered part of the Upper East Side.)*
3. *Mr. and Mrs. F. Leonard Kellogg in
their upstairs drawing room at 118 East
Seventieth Street, about 1928; FLK. The
Kelloggs purchased the house, which had
been built in 1900–1901, in 1910. The Kelloggs
traced their lineage to a Scottish clan on the
male side and early Dutch settlers on the
female side.*

1.

Old New York Society

How does one define "Old Society?" Is it determined by family lineage (Dutch and British ancestry)? Is it determined by club membership (Union Club and Knickerbocker Club for men and Colony Club for women)? Is it by schools (Buckley and Browning for boys, Brearley and Spence for girls)? Is it by listing in the *Social Register*? Clearly those who can trace their ancestries back to the first Dutch and British settlers are Old Society. Among them are the Van Rensselaers, the Rhinelanders, and the Livingstons. Those who made fortunes in the early nineteenth century, like the Astors, Vanderbilts, and Whitneys, were seen as nouveaus by the Old Society. As had happened in previous generations, the Old Society married into the nouveaus to maintain their wealth. At the beginning of the twentieth century, the new fortunes were the Morgans and the Rockefellers. By the 1930s all these families were included under the umbrella of Old New York Society.

2.

3.

4.

"Comparatively few people know about real New York Society, for it refuses to allow its names to make news. These respectable families, tolerant of others though convinced of their own priority, lead traditional lives of culture much the same as those of the aristocracy of any other capital, if a little more conscientious. They are in no way especially typical of New York. They do not allow their lives to be arranged by the street. They live in their own houses, have their own possessions, their silver, linen-rooms and cellars. They go to church on Sunday, do charitable work, play bridge, listen to music, give dinner-parties and go to balls."

CECIL BEATON'S NEW YORK

1. Union Club members, 1928; UC. One of the oldest and most prestigious of the men's social clubs, the Union was founded in 1836. This photograph was taken at the Columbia University rowing clubhouse. In 1933 the club moved into its current home at 101 East Sixty-ninth Street. The numbers indicate members names: No. 3 is Warham Whitney, No. 10 is H. Gallatin Pell, No. 27 is Kiliaen Van Rensselaer, and No. 38 is John H. Bouvier, Jr.

2. Interior, Metropolitan Club, about 1925; NYHS. At Fifth Avenue and Sixtieth Street, the Metropolitan was founded in 1891 by Morgans, Vanderbilts, Hamiltons, Cromwells, Browns, Whitneys, and Roosevelts.

3. Buckley School class, about 1928; BS. Buckley has been one of the city's leading independent boys' schools since its founding

in 1913 by B. Lord Buckley. He believed in "an academically selective institution which emphasized scholarly achievement, pursuit of excellence and sound moral and ethical standards."

4. Mrs. Cornelius Vanderbilt Whitney with Lady Jane Duff, a niece of the earl of Lonsdale, arriving at the Metropolitan Opera for the first opera of the season, 1932; NYT.

1.

Touches of Elegance

In addition to Rolls-Royces, black-tie dinners, and white-tie functions, having a box at the Metropolitan Opera and riding on the Central Park bridle paths were two visible symbols of an elegant lifestyle that a New Yorker could attain in the thirties and forties. Participating in either, or both, was an indication that one had achieved a certain degree of wealth and possible social status. Although the opening of the Metropolitan Opera House on Broadway between Thirty-ninth and Fortieth Streets in 1883 (it was demolished in 1966, when the new opera house was built at Lincoln Center) might have been seen as an event of cultural importance, it became more a symbol of achievement for the new moneyed aristocracy benefiting from the spurt of economic growth that took place in the post–Civil

War period. Influenced by Western European models, these tycoons built opera houses and museums while acquiring the accoutrements of aristocratic culture, such as collections of paintings and sculpture and fine houses filled with sumptuous furnishings. Those who followed in their wake saw themselves as inheriting a mantle of wealth and sophistication. To go to the opera was seen as representing such hallmarks.

When Central Park opened to the public in 1859, horses and carriages were the principal means of transportation that populated the park's drives. When automobiles took over the city's streets, Central Park's bridle paths served several purposes. They provided a rural romantic intrusion in the urban landscape because horses were seen as belonging more to the country than to the

2.

city. They also provided the opportunity for those with country houses and horses a place to ride when they were in the city.

1. In the Metropolitan Opera foyer, 1943; photograph by Weegee, ICP.

2. Diamond Horseshoe at the Metropolitan Opera House, about 1940; photograph by Andreas Feininger, AF.

3. A protest on the bridle paths, 1936; CB. Ninety members of the "Early Bird Equestrians," a group of riders who objected to the rich monopolizing the Central Park Bridle Paths. Intentionally, they came dressed in a motley array of costumes.

1.

The New Middle Class: Jackson Heights, Grand Concourse, and Rockaway

Postwar prosperity transformed the economic and social structure of New York. First- and second-generation working-class immigrants began to move into the middle class. They no longer felt trapped in their ethnic ghettos; they could search for a better quality of life that was both comfortable and respectable in other neighborhoods. People moved to second-settlement neighborhoods because they wanted amenities, such as more living space, better plumbing, and improved air circulation. They exchanged tenements for modern elevator apartments and detached one- and two-family houses. They wanted to have a place where the whole family could sit down and eat at the same table. They were desirous of sending their children to better public schools. First

the Irish and Germans moved, then the Jews and Italians.

The geography and density of Manhattan encouraged dispersal to the other boroughs. Lower Manhattan, once one of the most densely populated areas in the world, was emptying out. Between 1910 and 1930 the percentage of New Yorkers living in Manhattan dropped from 49 percent to 27 percent. At the same time the population of the Bronx and Queens doubled.

In the Bronx there was the Grand Concourse, "the Park Avenue of the middle class," a broad tree-lined boulevard with spacious apartments stretching over four and half miles. Grand Concourse residents were "manufacturers and tradesmen, doctors, dentists, lawyers, engineers, school

Modern Garden Apartments

"Under Queensboro Corporation Management"

25 minutes from Manhattan

in

JACKSON HEIGHTS

New York City

BEAUTIFUL gardens and beautiful apartments are outstanding characteristics of Jackson Heights. Yet rentals are moderate. You now can enjoy a country environment, golf and tennis and all modern conveniences without paying a premium in rent. Jackson Heights is complete in itself. It has its own theatres, churches, shops, and schools. Visit Jackson Heights today.

7 rooms—3 baths from $190 to $300
6 rooms—2 baths from $160 to $220
5 rooms—2 baths from $125 to $150

Smaller suites if desired

THE QUEENSBORO CORPORATION

82nd St. (old 25th) and Polk Avenue
Jackson Heights Subway Station

JACKSON HEIGHTS, New York City

Jackson Heights office open Daily and Sunday until 8 P. M.

Subways, 5th Ave. Bus, Coach from Waldorf Astoria, Special Cadillac Express Service to Wall Street and Midtown Manhattan

Telephone: Newtown 6000

NEW YORK OFFICE: 14 E. 41st St., LEXington 2530

teachers, salesmen and minor executives."

In Queens there was Jackson Heights, a complex of cooperative apartment buildings with detached structures called garden apartments. There was a golf course, tennis courts, bowling alleys, children's playgrounds, and a community center. It was the epitome of civilized suburban living only "twenty minutes and a five-cent fare" from Manhattan. However, Queensborough Realty, the developer of Jackson Heights, would not rent to Catholics and Jews.

In Brooklyn there was Eastern Parkway with fine apartment buildings where many wealthy Jews lived and Flatbush with tree-lined streets and detached houses with roomy front porches, separated by lawns and privet hedges.

Rockaway, the "Irish Riviera," was originally a resort. Long Island Railroad trains made it possible for workingmen to join their families in the evenings or on weekends. It was not unusual for a Manhattan-based Irish family to give up its apartment for the summer, put its household furnishings in storage, and take a room and kitchen or a bungalow for the season. The Irish areas were Seaside and Hammels. Eventually the bungalows became year-round residences.

1. Cornelia and Sigmund Glatzer celebrating their twenty-fifth wedding anniversary at the Biltmore Hotel, 1926; DM. It was a grand affair with food and music. Mrs. Glatzer wore a sequined dress from Saks Fifth Avenue, and her daughter Daisy wore a dress that she made herself.
2. Advertisement for Jackson Heights garden apartments, about 1925; QBPL.
3. Bungalow colony, Rockaway, about 1928; QBPL.
4. Grand Concourse, Bronx, about 1924; BCHS.

1.

City College and Public Schools in the Bronx and Queens

CCNY (College of the City of New York), at Amsterdam Avenue and 138th Street, better known as City College, and the public school system became part of a network that provided quality education without the high costs associated with private schools, colleges, and universities. For many Eastern European Jews, going to City College became synonymous with escape from Lower East Side poverty. In the 1920s and 1930s, they accounted for four-fifths of the student body, which reached a high point of 32,030 in 1929.

After the First World War, City College became known for academic excellence and its successful basketball teams. Morris Raphael Cohen, the distinguished professor of philosophy at CCNY, said, "So long as Jews were shut up in their ghettos and

excluded from the universities they had no chance to make contributions to the life of science. But when ghetto gates were opened there were special factors which led the Jews to make extraordinary contributions to the development of modern science." The 92d Street YMHA's athletic director Nat Holman was CCNY's basketball coach. Reflecting, a team member said, "Our victories were important beyond the actuality of the score; immigrants or (mostly) sons of immigrants, we triumphed over the original settlers . . . became Americans, became winners, understood what it meant to belong, the way we never belonged as critics of society."

The public schools served dual purposes, depending on whether you were an established resident or an immigrant. The estab-

2.

3.

4.

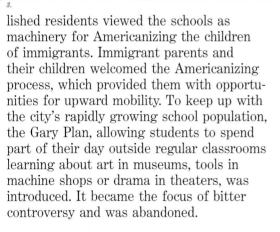

lished residents viewed the schools as
machinery for Americanizing the children
of immigrants. Immigrant parents and
their children welcomed the Americanizing
process, which provided them with opportunities for upward mobility. To keep up with
the city's rapidly growing school population,
the Gary Plan, allowing students to spend
part of their day outside regular classrooms
learning about art in museums, tools in
machine shops or drama in theaters, was
introduced. It became the focus of bitter
controversy and was abandoned.

1. City College campus, about 1925; MCNY.
2. Jamaica (Queens) High School class play
When a man proposes, about 1930; photograph by Frederick J. Weber, QBPL.
3. Jamaica High School girls' chorus line,
about 1925; QBPL.
4. Morris High School (Bronx) class photo,
1922; BCHS.

1.

2.

The Ruth Snyder Murder Trial

It was the O. J. Simpson trial of the twenties. Ruth Snyder, a housewife, had allegedly persuaded her lover, Henry Judd Gray, to help kill her husband. The Queens County Courthouse trial was tabloid delight. Coverage of it boosted the *Daily News* circulation by a million. A legion of reporters followed it; telegraph operators transmitted their stories. Theater impresario David Belasco went in clerical garb, saying that he attended "solely as a lover of drama." Movie stars sat in the courtroom. Tried by an all-male jury, Snyder and Gray were convicted and sentenced to die in the Sing Sing electric chair in January 1928. The *Daily News* managed to get a photograph of Snyder's electrocution; it appeared on the paper's front page.

1. Ruth Snyder with her mother and daughter, 1928; CB.
2. Ruth Snyder jury foreman William E. Young (carrying coat) leaving the Queens County Courthouse, 1927; CB.
3. New York City police making arrests after an opium raid in Chinatown, 1926; CB.
4. Mug shot of Louis "Lepke" Buchalter, 1939; NYPD. He was the principal architect of Murder Incorporated, which operated from 1936 to 1939. His cadre of Jewish and Italian killers traveled with black bags, each containing a knife, an ice pick, a rope, and a gun.
5. Mug shot of Lepke's principal sidekick, Jacob "Gurrah" Shapiro, 1939; NYPD.

3.

4.

5.

Cops and Gangsters

The Lower East Side germinated a generation of Jews who made incredible contributions to American cultural and economic life. The same conditions of hardship and deprivation also bred a coterie of criminals who terrorized the city for decades. Prohibition gave them the opportunity to organize a network that engaged in racketeering, prostitution, extortion, and murder. They infiltrated local industries and ran protection rackets. They gained control of Harlem's numbers games. Ambitious politicians like Thomas E. Dewey and William O'Dwyer made names for themselves prosecuting these gangsters.

Chinatown had its ambitious and honorable merchants and restaurant operators. It also had its underworld. Secret societies called *tongs* controlled gambling, prostitution, and opium. They often battled for turf in what became know as the tong wars of the 1920s. These did not cease until the mid-1930s, when federal officials threatened to deport the tong leaders.

1.

2.

The Stock Market Crash and the Depression

It was the "Roaring Twenties." The stock market was booming. Production was high. Consumer demand was high. Refrigerators, radios, plumbing fixtures, and automobiles were in demand. Unemployment was down; income was up. It could not have been better! There had been an extended bull market with what seemed to be endless windfall profits. The New York Stock Exchange's volume of transactions increased nearly five-fold during the decade. Otto Kahn, a partner in the firm of Kuhn, Loeb & Company, said that investors "were determined that every piece of paper should be worth tomorrow twice what it was today."

By 1928, the prices of stocks had soared beyond the point of safe return for thousands of investors. Stocks were being priced far above their real values and were being purchased with as little as 10 percent down payments with the rest being financed by brokers' loans. On October 29, 1929, the bottom dropped out of the market. Between late October and mid-November stocks lost 40 percent of their total value—a drop of thirty billion dollars in paper value. Economic malaise set in and lasted well into the next decade.

The fallout from the stock market crash affected everyone. Bankruptcies increased, factories curtailed production, and unemployment skyrocketed. The American dream had become a nightmare. Senator Robert Wagner of New York said, "We are in a life and death struggle with the forces of social and economic dissolution." By the spring of 1930 there were more than four million unemployed nationally. In 1935 unemploy-

266

3.

5.

ment reached a peak of fifteen million.

Both the Depression and restrictive quotas curtailed immigration. Few Europeans would choose a country without opportunities. Long lines of hopeless, humiliated men and women were evident throughout the city. There were soup kitchens for the hungry. Hoovervilles, shantytowns where the unemployed lived, were found from Central Park to Brooklyn. By 1933 about one-fourth of New York's work force was unemployed. For African-Americans it was worse: About 50 percent were out of work.

"We lived on 145th Street near Seventh Avenue. One day we were so hungry we could barely breathe. I started out the door. It was as cold as all-hell and I walked from 145th Street to 133rd down Seventh Avenue, going into every joint trying to find work."

BILLIE HOLIDAY, *DOWNBEAT*, NOVEMBER 1939

1. "The Goal," cartoon by Edmund Marcus, 1929; NYSE. This cartoon captures the mood of the times; everyone wanted to be part of the stock market.
2. "Black Tuesday," Wall Street on October 29, 1929; NYDN.
3. Unemployed men waiting in line at the Emergency Unemployment Relief registration office, Sixty-ninth Regiment Armory, Lexington Avenue and Twenty-fifth Street, 1931; OYL.
4. Hooverville in the middle of Central Park, about 1931; MCNY.
5. Unemployed men in Harlem waiting in line at the Emergency Unemployment Relief registration office, 1931; CB.

1.

The El and the Subway

The Interborough Rapid Transit (IRT) system began operating its subways in 1904. The IRT built a large system connecting Manhattan with the Bronx, Brooklyn, and Queens. Although an extensive elevated system predated the subways, New York's rapid transit system evolved as a combination of subways and independent elevated systems. Because the els were not competitive with subways and were regarded as noisy and ugly, they were abandoned gradually in Manhattan and some parts of the Bronx and Brooklyn. However, elevated tracks that had been built as parts of the subway systems remained. In 1923 the Brooklyn Rapid Transit (BRT) Company with its wide group of subways and elevated tracks in Brooklyn, Manhattan, and Queens was reorganized as the Brooklyn-

Manhattan Transit (BMT) Corporation. In 1921 Mayor John Hylan won approval to build the Independent (IND) subway system with most of its fifty-nine miles underground. The first IND routes opened in 1932, and the system was completed in 1940. Suffering from serious financial problems, both the IRT and BMT were acquired by the city of New York during the La Guardia administration. They were merged with the IND and operated by the Board of Transportation. (Essentially this is the system that operates today.)

1. BMT elevated terminal, Jamaica Avenue
at 168th Street, Queens, 1918; QBPL.
2. Subway passengers, 1938; photograph by
Walker Evans, MMA/WEA.
3. El station interior, Sixth and Ninth
avenue lines, downtown side, Columbus
Avenue and Seventy-second Street, 1936;
photograph by Berenice Abbott, MCNY.
4. Subway musician, 1938; photograph by
Walker Evans, MMA/WEA.
5. Subway passengers, 1938; photograph by
Walker Evans, MMA/WEA.

1.

Skyscraper Heaven

Although the Depression devastated the New York economy, by a curious contradiction it did not halt the construction of new office buildings, apartment buildings, and public structures. Given the city's economic plight, some of the commercial buildings, although completed, were not fully rented. Much of the present Manhattan skyline was built between 1929 and 1940; many projects were initiated during the economic boom of the twenties and completed in the thirties.

Here is a brief catalog. Office buildings: Empire State (1931), McGraw-Hill (1931), and Rockefeller Center (1932–1940); apartment buildings: San Remo (1930), Majestic (1930), Eldorado (1931), and River House (1931); others: New York Athletic Club (1930), Waldorf-Astoria Hotel (1931), New School for Social Research (1930), and Foley

Square Federal Courthouse (1936). Three main elements of the transportation infrastructure were built during this period: the Triborough Bridge (1936), the Lincoln Tunnel (1937), and the Queens-Midtown Tunnel (1940).

These construction projects were an expression of New York's dynamism and preeminence. The Empire State Building at a height of 1,250 feet was for two generations the world's tallest building. With most of the new construction in midtown Manhattan, what emerged was a new concept of urbanism in which independent buildings towering into the sky became self-contained worlds.

During the 1930s and 1940s Robert Moses built his empire, which left an indelible mark on the city's landscape. The consummate

2.

3.

"power broker," he managed to expand and maintain his authority over four decades and five mayoralties. A partial list of the many projects with which he was associated includes: Triborough Bridge, Bronx-Whitestone Bridge, Belt Parkway, Grand Central Parkway, Brooklyn-Queens Expressway, Gowanus Expressway, Van Wyck Expressway, numerous housing projects, Lincoln Center, Jacob Riis Park, 1939–1940 World's Fair, refurbishing of the city's parks, and development of new recreational facilities. His legacy is mixture of triumphs and disasters.

1. Midtown looking northeast, 1932; photograph by Gottscho-Schleiser, MCNY.
2. John D. Rockefeller, Jr., driving the final rivet at a ceremony celebrating the completion of Rockefeller Center, November 1, 1939; RC.
3. Plumbing up a column, the Empire State Bulding under construction, 1931; photograph by Lewis Hine, NYPL.

"When one approaches Manhattan Island, for instance, from the Staten Island Ferry or the Brooklyn Bridge, the great towers on the tip of the island sometimes look like the fairy stalagmites of an opened grotto; and from an occasional vantage point on the twentieth floor of an office building one may now and again recapture this impression. . . . What our critics have learned to admire in our great buildings is their photographs. . . . In an article chiefly devoted to praise of the skyscraper . . . the majority of the illustrations were taken from a point that the man on the street never reaches. In short, it is an architecture, not for men, but for angels and aviators!"

LEWIS MUMFORD, *STICKS AND STONES*

1.

On the Street

"There are those who consider that it is impossible to find any unity in the chaotic pattern of New York; or that, romantically enough, the emergence of unity would cancel its major charm. But the uneconomic and antisocial nature of many of the city's living ways demand a clear reorientation. The potential unity necessary to such reorientation already exists in the New Yorker's own concept of his city. In this shared consciousness—generated by a look, a grin, an anecdote as cabalistic to outsiders as the shop talk of mathematicians—the complex of the metropolis finds its organizing principle, deeper than civic pride and more basic than the domination of mass or power. To the degree that this principle, this wise geolatry, can be instrumented by the forms and processes appropriate to it, New York will emerge in greatness from the paradox of its confusions."

NEW YORK PANORAMA: THE BEST OF 1930S NEW YORK

2.

3.

1. Street scene, 1934; photograph by Walker
Evans, MMA/WEA.
2. Hot dog stand, West Street and North
Moore Street, 1936; photograph by Berenice
Abbott, MCNY.
3. Roast corn man, Orchard and Hester
streets, 1938; photograph by Berenice Abbott,
MCNY.

1.

3.

2.

4.

Incredible Marketplace

"In the field of retail trade, New York likewise occupies a predominant position among American cities. In 1935 its total retail sales amounted to $2,847,000,000, which was about eight percent of the national total. No other American city could show anything like this figure, the closest being Chicago with less than half the New York total. As a matter of fact, New York transacted more retail business in 1935 than did any state in the Union except the state in which it is situated; and this business was conducted in more stores (numbering 115,500) than were in operation in any state except New York and Pennsylvania. Employed in the retail and wholesale establishments of the city in 1935 were 522,908 persons, or 37,764 more than were employed in the city's industrial plants. Supervising this great army of wage-workers were 114,882 proprietors and firm members. Employees in the city's retail and wholesale establishments received an average of about $1,500 each for their labor in 1935, as against an average of about $1,200 paid to the city's factory workers."

NEW YORK PANORAMA: THE BEST OF 1930'S NEW YORK

1. A&P (Great Atlantic and Pacific Tea Company) at 246 Third Avenue, Manhattan, 1936; photograph by Berenice Abbott, NYPL.

2. Newstand, Third Avenue and Thirty-second Street, Manhattan, 1935; photograph by Berenice Abbott, NYPL.

3. Hardware store, 316 Bowery, 1938; photograph by Berenice Abbott, NYPL.

4. Tri-Borough Barber School, 264 Bowery, 1935; photograph by Berenice Abbott, MCNY.

5. Lyric Theatre, Third Avenue between Twelfth and Thirteenth streets, 1936; photograph by Berenice Abbott, MCNY.

6. Blossom Restaurant, 103 Bowery, 1935; photograph by Berenice Abbott, NYPL.

7. Whelan's drugstore, Eighth Avenue and Forty-fourth Street, 1936, photograph by Berenice Abbott, NYPL.

8. Rope store, South Street and James Slip, about 1936; photograph by Berenice Abbott, NYPL.

1.

2.

Ethnic Food

In a city where cultural assimilation had been a pattern for nearly three centuries, in the 1930s and 1940s, food stores and restaurants remained the most visible sign of ethnic identity. First- and second-generation immigrants of Eastern European Jewish and Italian origins preferred the foods their families had prepared and eaten for generations. Jewish, Italian, and what were called "ethnic neighborhoods" were studded with small specialized shops that sold these foods.

The 1939 *The WPA Guide to New York City* lists twenty-three categories of "foreign restaurants": Armenian, Austrian, Chinese, East Indian, English, French, French-Hungarian, French-Italian, German, Greek, Hungarian, Irish, Italian, Japanese, Jewish, Latin American, Mexican, Polish,

Russian, Spanish, Swiss, Syrian, and Turkish. These restaurants were no longer patronized exclusively by their constituent ethnic groups but were seen as interesting, inexpensive, and varied places to "eat out."

3.

4.

1. *Hanging pasta out to dry at the Atlantic Macaroni Company, Long Island City, 1943; photograph by Marjorie Collins, LC.*
2. *Bakery on First Avenue, 1943; photograph by Marjorie Collins, LC.*
3. *Chicken market, 55 Hester Street, 1937; photograph by Berenice Abbott, MCNY. Translation of the sign in Hebrew: "Strictly Kosher chicken market, fresh killed hourly."*
4. *De Martino's fish market, 1943; photograph by Gordon Parks, LC.*

1.

America's Major Industrial City

"In addition to being America's greatest commercial center, New York is also this country's major industrial city. More workers are paid more wages for producing more goods in more manufacturing establishments here than in any other American city—or indeed in any one of 43 states. In 1935 . . . 485,144 workers were employed in 26,061 factories scattered throughout the five boroughs of the city. . . . Only the states of New York, Pennsylvania, Michigan, Illinois and Ohio paid more wages to more factory workers, and produced manufactures of greater total value. . . . With reference to the United States as a whole, New York City factories employed six percent of all the workers, who were paid nearly eight percent of all the wages for manufacturing

eight percent by value of all the products of the country. . . .

"The preponderance in New York City of highly skilled workers engaged in the manufacture of high-quality articles is one of the primary reasons for its dominant position among American industrial cities. . . .

"Industrial establishments engaged in the fabrication of products that require large reduction in bulk or weight of raw material avoided Manhattan because of space and transport problems. . . .

" . . . of the city's 26,094 industrial establishments 18,694, or about 72 percent, were situated in Manhattan. Employed in these latter were 288,000, or about 59 percent, of the city's industrial wage-earners—an average of about 15 workers to each factory. . . .

"... Engaged in the manufacture of fur goods were more than 2,000 shops employing about 9,500 wage-earners. The value of their product exceeded $124,000,000, which was 86 percent of the value of all fur goods manufactured in the United States. There were 10,272 apparel and accessories plants (nearly triple the number of plants in the city's next most important industry), which employed an average of 187,334 workers and manufactured goods valued at $1,383,000,000, more than $675,000,000 of this sum being added in the process of manufacture.

"Next in importance with respect to the number of plants involved and value produced was the printing and publishing industry with 3,159 establishments, employing 49,783 wage-earners and turning out products valued at $490,357,000. . . .

"Of greater importance than the city's printing industry, from the point of view of value produced, and nearly equaling it in total number of plants in operation, was the foods and beverages industry."
NEW YORK'S PANORAMA: THE BEST OF 1930'S NEW YORK

1. Blacksmiths and drop forgers, Brooklyn Navy Yard, 1939; QBPL. The Brooklyn Navy Yard occupied a total of 197 acres, 118 on land. In 1938, it had ten thousand employees, one-third of whom were WPA (federally funded) employees. Founded in 1801, the yard was associated with early steamboats; the Fulton *was constructed here in 1814–1815 from the inventor's plans. The navy yard exerted a strong influence on Brooklyn's commercial and manufacturing economy. In the 1880s it helped make Brooklyn the nation's fourth-largest industrial city. During the First and Second World Wars, the Brooklyn Navy Yard launched some of the navy's major battleships and aircraft carriers.*

1.

Growth of Mass Consumption

The boom of the twenties fueled demand for new consumer products that became accepted as everyone's prerogative. Although residents of Manhattan might have found automobiles more of a nuisance than a necessity, those who lived in the other boroughs were increasingly dependent on them. As a consequence, automobile auxiliaries, such as new car showrooms, used car lots, service garages, and gas stations, became part of the urban landscape in most of the boroughs with the exception of Manhattan. Although ethnic foods continued to be popular among first-generation immigrants, their children were likely to embrace more American standardized, factory-made foods like bread, crackers, cookies, and infinite varieties of canned goods.

Industrial production transformed both the exterior landscape of the city and the interior landscape of the apartment and detached residential dwelling. All the new household appliances, like washing machines, refrigerators, and vacuum cleaners, were dependent on electrical power. Radios and telephones became family necessities. Like automobiles, these household appliances generated their own support structure in the form of salesrooms where they were purchased and stores and shops where they were serviced and repaired. A cadre of workers was required to maintain and operate these new facilities.

At the same time there was a modest shift in economic patterns. In addition to consumer products, there was the birth and expansion of professional services like lawyers, accountants, and bookkeepers.

Although industrial production was still the backbone of the American economy, consumer services were playing a more significant role.

1. Management and truck drivers at the National Biscuit Company factory, 172-02 Jamaica Avenue, Queens, 1932; QBPL.
2. Chevrolet automobile salesmen in front of their showroom, 139-17 Hillside Avenue, Queens, about 1938; QBPL.

1.

Transactions in the Financial Markets

Businesses were dependent on telephones and telegraphs for their daily transactions. In the 1920s, to make a telephone call, you had to reach an operator, give her the number, and wait for the other party to respond. To send a telegram, you followed the same procedure to reach the telegraph company. There an operator would take your message and relay it to a telegraph operator. There were two principal telegraph companies: Postal Telegraph and Western Union. Postal Telegraph had legions of uniformed bicycle messengers who raced through the streets delivering messages. Rotary dial telephones were introduced at a later date.

The quotation department of the New York Stock Exchange demonstrates how specific transactions were conducted. Clerks with headsets were in constant communica-

tion with the trading floor; they posted current bids and asked quotations on billboards. Member firms would call the operators for current quotations. The operators simply looked up at the boards for the latest quotes.

2.

3.

1. The quotation department at the New York Stock Exchange, 1931; NYSE. The people in this room provided current bids and asked quotations for stocks via direct wire to member firm offices.

2. Ticker tape delay indicator on the floor of the New York Stock Exchange, 1938; NYSE. All transactions were reported on the ticker tape. When the volume of transactions soared, it was customary to experience a delay in the tape report.

3. A Curb Exchange broker eating while he conducts his business over the phone, about 1920; NYSE.

1.

Easter in Harlem

In 1930 the *New York Herald Tribune* reported, "About fifty-five churches in Harlem have their own buildings while about seventy-five so-called 'churches' are small groups of sects meeting in storefronts or residences . . . some are pastored by primitive, but sincere cotton-field preachers, some by astute grasping charlatans preying on the ignorant and superstitious, some by religious fanatics with new and outlandish creeds."

The established Baptist and Methodist churches bought structures that had been built by the previous white residents. In 1923 the Abyssinian Baptist Church built its own impressive home on 138th Street in Harlem.

"The multiplicity of churches in Harlem, and in every other Negro community, is commonly accounted for by the innate and deep religious emotion of the race. Conceding the strength and depth of this emotion, there is also the vital fact that coloured churches provide their members with a great deal of enjoyment, aside from the joys of religion. Indeed, a Negro church is for its members much more besides a place to worship. It is a social centre, it is a club, it is an arena for the exercise of one's capabilities and powers, a world in which one may achieve self-realization and preferment. . . . Aside from any spiritual benefits derived, going to church means being dressed in one's best clothes. . . ."

JAMES WELDON JOHNSON, *BLACK MANHATTAN*

2.

3.

"The broad pavements of Seventh Avenue were colorful with promenaders. Brown babies in white carriages pushed by little black brothers wearing nice sailor suits. All the various and varying pigmentation of the human race were [sic] assembled there: dim brown, clear brown, rich brown, chestnut, copper, yellow, near-white, mahogany, and gleaming anthracite. Charming brown matrons, proud yellow matrons, dark nurse-maids. . . .

"And the elegant strutters in faultless spats; West Indians, carrying canes and wearing trousers of a different pattern from their coats and vests, drawing sharp comments from their Afro-Yank rivals."
CLAUDE MCKAY, *HOME TO HARLEM*

1. *Father Harrison, right, and Father Shelton Haile Bishop, left, greeting parishioners after Easter service at St. Phillip's Protestant Episcopal Church, about 1940; photograph by M. Smith, NYPL/SC.*
2. *Father Divine, 1939; NYDN. Throngs of people idolized this Baptist preacher, whose Peace Mission movement provided free meals for its members during the Depression.*
3. *Robert Day putting on roller skates, 1939; photograph by M. Smith, NYPL/SC.*

Harlem's Heroes

In a sense Harlem's heroes were also black America's heroes. If they didn't come from Harlem, they were adopted by Harlem. If they came from Harlem, so much the better. Throughout Harlem's history, musicians and entertainers have been heroes. In the 1920s Harlem's heroes were musicians, entertainers, artists, poets, and writers. In the 1930s and 1940s, they were still musicians and entertainers, but sports figures, personified by world heavyweight boxing champion Joe Louis, became more prominent. Originally from Detroit, Louis became an adopted Harlem citizen and opened a restaurant and bar in the 1940s.

"Throngs estimated by the police at 100,000 persons swarmed into the streets of Harlem last night to celebrate the victory that made Joe Louis world champion. With fishhorns and cowbells, drums and rattles, the crowd began a demonstration said by observers to be without parallel in the history of the Negro neighborhood. Persons who did not join the marching and dancing on the pavements and the sidewalks took part in the festivity by shouting from their windows. Others ripped telephone books and newspapers to shreds, showering the pieces into the air in the fashion of confetti. Nearly 1,000 policemen stood guard over the celebrants, intervening at times to keep traffic moving. The crowd was too good-humored, patrolmen said, to require other supervision.

"Two drums and a yellow, white and green

3.

4.

5.

banner described as the flag of Abbyssinia [*sic*] formed the nucleus of a parade that drew an estimated 10,000 marchers. Lenox Avenue witnessed a similar demonstration. . . . White persons caught in the jam were not molested, as far as the police could learn, but were the subject of much joshing, a favorite form of greeting for white men being 'Howdy, Mr. Braddock.'"
NEW YORK TIMES, JUNE 22, 1937

1. *Joe Louis, the Brown Bomber, walking along a Harlem street with his bride, Marva Trotter, 1935; CB. They were married the previous night a few hours before his knockout victory over Max Baer.*
2. *Bill "Bojangles" Robinson marching along Lenox Avenue in an Elks parade, 1939; CB. Thousands of Black Elks and Daughter Elks from all parts of the country arrived in Harlem to participate in the fortieth annual convention of the Improved Benevolent Order of Elks of the World.*
3. *Black Yankees, 1939; photograph by M. Smith, NYPL/SC. Three New York minority teams belonged to the Negro National League at this time: Black Yankees, Brooklyn Eagles, and New York Cubans.*
4. *W. C. Handy, composer of the "St. Louis Blues," and his wife watching a Negro*

National League game, about 1939; photograph by M. Smith, NYPL/SC. Handy moved to New York in 1918 and established a music-publishing company specializing in the work of black musicians.
5. *Lieutenant Hubert Julian, seated in the cockpit of his plane as he prepared for his transatlantic flight to Rome, 1928; CB. A daredevil, he parachuted into Harlem. As a result of joining the Ethiopian Air Force in its battle to resist Mussolini's invasion, he acquired the nickname Black Eagle.*

S. M. PURA Iᴬ CON SU CORTE DE HONOR EN LA CORONACION EL SABADO 9 DE MAYO - 1931. NEW YORK CITY.

PHOTO BY R. Castilla NYC.

1.

A Latino Presence

According to the 1890 census, there were 5,994 people from the Caribbean, Mexico, Central America, South America, and Spain (1,421) residing in New York. Cubans, Puerto Ricans, and Spaniards were the predominant groups. By 1920 the number had reached 41,094, and by 1930 it was 110,223, with Puerto Ricans accounting for 40.7 percent of the total. The increased migration of Puerto Ricans to New York was stimulated by the granting of U.S. citizenship to Puerto Ricans in 1917.

In the 1920s and 1930s, distinct Latino neighborhoods emerged in Manhattan: East Harlem (El Barrio), Chelsea, and parts of the Lower East Side. In Brooklyn Latinos lived in Red Hook, in Williamsburg, and near the navy yard. In the Bronx they were scattered. They coexisted with other immi-grant groups like Jews and Italians, with whom they shared surrounding territories. In contrast with turn-of-the-century Latino immigrants who came with education and commercial experience, those arriving in the 1920s and 1930s were skilled or semi-skilled factory workers, artisans, white-collar workers, and service-sector employees.

1. *Pura Belpre with her court of honor at a coronation ceremony, 1931; CEP. Such events were often held for community fund-raising. Belpre was the first Puerto Rican librarian in the New York Public Library system. In 1929 she was transferred to a branch on 115th Street in East Harlem, where she implemented Spanish-language programs and developed her specialty, the art of story-telling for children.*

2. *Joaquin Colon and family, about 1930; CEP. Joaquin, the brother of Jesus, a prominent left-wing political activist, was involved in conventional community activities.*

3. *Puerto Rican League picnic at Hecksher Park in Brooklyn, 1934; CEP.*

4. *Justo A. Marti, about 1920; CEP. In 1944 he opened the Carlton Photo Shop at the corner of Flatbush Avenue and Prospect Place in Brooklyn. His photographs, which documented the artistic, cultural, economic, and political life of the Latino community, appeared in its newspapers over an extended period of time.*

1.

The La Guardia Years

Although the son of an Austrian Jewish mother and an Italian father, Fiorello La Guardia always identified with his Italian-American heritage. In 1916 he was the first Italian-American elected to Congress representing a working-class district in lower Manhattan. By following La Guardia's career, you can witness the power shift among immigrant political groups. The Irish in Tammany Hall had dominated New York City politics for generations. Although a Republican, La Guardia earned the epithets of "liberal, progressive, and socialist." During the height of the Depression, in 1933 he ran for mayor as a Fusion candidate and was elected. He completely reorganized and modernized the city's governmental structure by eliminating the fiefdoms that had been created during the Tammany years.

His rise to political power was based on his own personal magnetism as a sort of Everyman with whom many people could identify; his mayoralty also reflected a substantial maturation within the Italian-American community.

In 1930 there were 1,070,355 (15.44 percent of the total population) first- and second-generation Italians living in New York City. There were 269,702 in Manhattan, 487,344 in Brooklyn, 165,004 in the Bronx, 127,381 in Queens, and 29,924 on Staten Island. Second- and third-generation Italian-Americans had clearly moved out of the manual laborer straitjackets of their parents and grandparents. A 1931 study conducted by the Educational Bureau of the Casa Italiana at Columbia University compiled a list of the occupations of bridegrooms. In

2.

order of numerical importance, they were: laborers, chauffeurs, barbers, tailors, shoemakers, clerks, painters, mechanics, salesmen, bakers, plasterers, carpenters, cooks, pressers, butchers, ice dealers, waiters, printers, bricklayers, electricians, cabinetmakers, upholsterers, grocers, fruit dealers, laundry workers, restaurant workers, auto mechanics, stonecutters, and masons. This survey neglected to query Italian women, who were the most numerous workers in the garment industry.

Italians also became more prominent in the labor movement, principally in the International Ladies Garment Workers Union and the Longshoremen's Union. Beyond this, more Italians joined the professions as doctors, lawyers, teachers, college professors, and business administrators. Along with

their own movement more into the American mainstream, La Guardia's mayoralty contributed to a long-delayed sense of group pride among Italian-Americans.

1. Mayor Fiorello La Guardia being driven to a fire in Woodside, Queens, 1939; MA.
2. Sunday dinner at the Martinetti home in the Bronx, 1939; photograph by Marjorie Collins, LC. Mr. Martinetti was a restaurant owner.

1.

The 1939–1940 World's Fair

As the nation continued to struggle to revive what had been the bouyant economy of the twenties, the 1939–1940 New York World's Fair emerged as both a local and national symbol of a resurgent nation. It was the biggest, costliest, most ambitious, and most flamboyant international exposition ever held. It cost more than $150,000,000 and occupied a 1,216-acre site in Flushing Meadow, Queens. There were fifteen hundred exhibitors representing thirty-three American states and fifty-five foreign countries occupying three hundred structures. Its visual symbols, the seven-hundred-foot-tall Trylon and two-hundred-foot-diameter Perisphere, rising from what had been a Queens dump, projected optimism. "The World of Tomorrow," with subtexts of the wonders of technology and the

blessings of democracy, was its theme. Some of the exhibits were America at Home, Aviation, Christian Science, Coca-a-Cola, Democracity, Court of Peace, Electric Farm, Firestone, Food, Ford, France, Gas Wonderland, General Electric, General Motors, Lagoon of Nations, Masterpieces of Art, Railroads, Science Education, Town of Tomorrow, and World of Fashion. There was an amusement park and scores of restaurants serving American and foreign food.

General Motors' Futurama, designed by Norman Bel Geddes, was the fair's most popular attraction. Despite a one-hour wait, it was seen by 5,100,000 people in one year. Each visitor, seated in an armchair provided with a sound narration, traveled on a conveyor above a scale model depicting the American landscape of 1960. Laced with

2.

3.

4.

superhighways, it was an anthem to the automobile that borrowed heavily from Le Corbusier's drawings for "Une ville contemporaine" exhibited at the Salon d'Automne in Paris in 1922.

The fair ran for almost two years, opening on April 30, 1939, and closing on October 26, 1940. A tribute to science and technology as well as consumerism, it attracted a total of 44,931,681 visitors, many of whom were not New Yorkers. The fair demonstrated that New York, as a city, was a relatively new American concept: a tourist destination.

1. View of the world's fair, Flushing, Queens, 1939; OYL.
2. National Cash Register exhibition, "the world's largest cash register," 1939; OYL.
3. Interior of the Transportation Building with a simulated rocketport demonstration, 1939; OYL.
4. Mrs. Sally Bloom and her son, Jack H. Bloom, 1939; JHB.

1.

2.

New York Kids: 1930s–1940s

What was it like to grow up in New York in the 1930s and 1940s? Were New York kids different from kids in other parts of the country? Were they smarter, more grown up, more sophisticated? The answer to both of these last questions is a resounding yes. New York kids were different. They were more bookish and more animated; they were street-wise and independent. Did they see themselves apart from most Americans? Again the answer is yes. Available to them was a variety of choices: plays, concerts, and museum programs tailored to young audiences.

AMERICAN MUSEUM OF NATURAL HISTORY CHILDREN'S PROGRAMS
The museum had programs directed to school class groups, such as its Platoon Program, which attracted 67,932 children in 1944, and others that were available to families. These included: May 1941, music program in the Africa Hall; June 1942, "Around the World Summer Cruise"; July 1943, East Indian dancers; August 1943, Hawaiian dancers; November 1943, East Indian dancers; 1945, Tommy Dorsey's dance group; March 1948, Swiss dance group; December 1948, "The Animal's Christmas Dinner" exhibit; 1948 and 1949, "Boy's and Girl's Book Fair."

NEW YORK PHILHARMONIC CHILDREN'S CONCERTS

The Philharmonic had regular children's programs from the 1940s. The program on February 19, 1940, was typical. With Rudolph Ganz conducting, there were three soloists: J. Amans, S. Bellinson, and S. Richart. The program included: Mozart's Overture to *The Marriage of Figaro*, Johann Adolph Hasse's Concerto, Flute in D Major, Percy Grainger's "Walking Tune," Felix Mendelssohn's Scherzo from *Midsummer Night's Dream*, Gabriel Pierre's "Cydalise," a sing-along, "Frère Jacques," and Georges Bizet's "Berceuse," "The Top," and "Galop."

MUSEUM OF MODERN ART CHILDREN'S PROGRAM

The Museum of Modern Art's Department of Education pioneered in children's art programming. It arranged special exhibits and conducted art classes such as these: November 4–11, 1940, "Designing a Stage Setting"; November 11–December 23, 1940, "Student Work from Fourteen High Schools"; July 15–28, 1941, "Abstract Painting: Shapes of Things"; August 12–25, 1941, "Lettering and Arrangement in Poster Design"; March 11–May10, 1942, "Children's Festival of Modern Art"; June 2–July 9, 1942, "Understanding Modern Art"; and December 6, 1944–January 7, 1945, "Children's Holiday Circus of Modern Art."

1. *Ballet class recital, Jamaica, Queens, about 1935; photograph by Frederick H. Weber, QBPL.*
2. *Paula Sarnoff and Dick Baer waiting to go to New Jersey, 1933; PSO.*
3. *Church is out, Harlem, about 1939; NYPL/SC.*
4. *Classroom at P.S. 33, 1942; photograph by Morris Engel, CP.*
5. *Kids in the movies, about 1940; photograph by Weegee (infrared), ICP.*

Harlem in the 1940s

"Harlem is the queen of black belts, drawing Aframericans together into a vast humming hive. They have swarmed in from the different states, from the islands of the Caribbean and from Africa. And they still are coming in spite of the grim misery that lurks behind the inviting façades. Overcrowded tenements, the harsh Northern climate and unemployment do not daunt them. Harlem remains the magnet.

"Harlem is more than the Negro capital of the nation. It is the Negro capital of the world. And as New York is the most glorious experiment on earth of different races and divers groups of humanity struggling and scrambling to live together, so Harlem is the most interesting sample of black humanity marching along with white humanity. Sometimes it lags behind, but

nevertheless it is impelled and carried along by the irresistible strength of the movement of the white world.

"Like a flock of luxuriant, large-lipped orchids, spreading over the side of a towering rock, the color of African life has boldly splashed itself upon the north end of Manhattan. From the nucleus of a comparatively few years ago, it has grown like an expansive tropical garden, springing naturally from the Northern soil. . . .

"Holding the handle of Manhattan, this special African-American area is like no other in New York. It lacks the oppressive drabness of the East Side. It is more comparable to Chinatown, which, although it has slum features, does not exude the atmosphere of the slums. Harlem is like the glorified servant quarters of a vast estate. It

3.

5.

7.

4.

6.

8.

has that appearance, perhaps, because the majority of Aframericans are domestics, who live in imitation of their white employers, although on a lower level. The distinction of Harlem is unlike the huddle of European minorities in New York. The essential quality of the latter is the magic of foreign languages and particular national traits which are emphasized in everyday living. But as Aframericans express themselves in the common American idiom and have shed all the externals of African traits, the distinguishing characteristic of Harlem lies in the varied features and the African color of its residents.

"Perhaps it is easier for the eye to appreciate Harlem than for the heart to understand. Harlem is noisy and its noises strike the eye as loudly as they do the ear.

Because the district is congested, the street corners and bars provide an outlet as forums and clubs. Children swarm in the streets, although the new playgrounds are full of them. . . .

"Visually, Harlem creates the impression of a mass of people all existing on the same plane. Even the natives are generally unaware of the prestige of their own notables."

CLAUDE MCKAY, *HARLEM: NEGRO METROPOLIS*

1. *Portrait, about 1938; Aaron Siskind.*
2. *Interior of Harlem apartment, about 1940; photograph by Aaron Siskind.*
3. *Smoking, about 1945; photograph by Helen Levitt.*
4. *Sidewalk portrait, about 1945; photograph by Helen Levitt.*
5. *Policeman, 1943; photograph by Gordon Parks, LC.*
6. *A woman and her dog, 1943; photograph by Gordon Parks, LC.*
7. *Garveyite, 1943; photograph by Gordon Parks, LC.*
8. *Street vendor, 1943; photograph by Gordon Parks, LC.*

1.

Billie, Ben, Hamp, and the Savoy

Although born in Baltimore, Billie Holiday lived in Harlem in her youth and identified with it throughout her career. In 1935 she became famous overnight as a result of a series of records she made with pianist Teddy Wilson. Known for the sheer beauty of her voice, she went on to become one of the most widely recognized singers of her generation. *Downbeat* said of her first solo concert that it "was an event to go down in jazz history. Unsurpassed in her own field as a great and individual song stylist, and long a favorite in jazz circles, the turnout at Town Hall was far beyond expectations." Drugs, unfortunately, began to play a larger and more destructive role in her life. Lionel Hampton, one of the all-time greats of jazz, whether on the vibraphone, drums, or piano, displayed remarkable agility. With

Benny Goodman's band from 1936 to 1940, he left to form his own band.

Ben Webster, one of the most influential tenor saxophone players of his day, was at one time or another a member of some of the major bands of the day: Fletcher Henderson, Cab Calloway, and Duke Ellington.

When the Savoy Ballroom opened on Lenox Avenue between 140th and 141st streets in 1926, it was described as "the world's most beautiful ballroom." A vast, cavernous space accommodating crowds of nearly five thousand, it was the home of the big band battles and the lindy hoppers.

2.

3.

1. Singer Billie Holiday with, left to right, Ben Webster (tenor sax), Ram Ramirez (piano), and Johnny Russell (tenor sax), in an alley behind the Apollo Theatre, 1935; FD.
2. Dancing at the Savoy, 1935; photograph by Aaron Siskind.
3. Lionel Hampton in a zoot suit, 1942; CB.

"The much heralded Battle of Swing between Chick Webb's and Count Basie's bands took place Sunday night, January 16, at the Savoy Ballroom. . . . Applause for both bands was tremendous and it was difficult to determine which band was the more popular.

"Nevertheless, the ballot taken showed Chick Webb's band well in the lead over Basie's, and Ella Fitzgerald well out in front over Billie Holiday and James Rushing. The battle took place after Benny Goodman's concert at Carnegie Hall, and many of Benny Goodman's band, including Gene Krupa, Lionel Hampton, Jimmie Mundy, Hymie Scherzer and others were present. Mildred Bailey, Red Norvo, Teddy Hill, Willie Bryant, Eddy Duchin, Duke Ellington and Ivie Anderson were also on hand.

". . . Both bands played magnificently, with Basie having a particular appeal for the dancers, and Webb consistently stealing the show on the drums. Ella Fitzgerald caused a sensation with her rendition of "Loch Lomond" and Bille Holiday thrilled her fans with "My Man."
DOWNBEAT, FEBRUARY 1938

1.

1943 Harlem Riots

On the evening of August 1, 1943, a new phenomenon, the urban riot accompanied by extensive looting, erupted in Harlem. It was sparked by the rumor that a black solider had been shot by the police. The trouble began when the police raided a dingy hotel. A policeman attempted to arrest a thirty-three-year-old woman for disorderly conduct. A crowd began to collect. The policeman claimed that a black military policeman had attacked him. As the soldier ran from the scene, the policeman shot him in the back. Other policemen arrived on the scene and took the injured man to Sydenham Hospital.

". . . The Harlem grapevine spread with amazing swiftness the news that a Negro soldier had been shot and was at the hospital. Within an hour a crowd of 3,000 persons had gathered in front of the hospital, while another crowd of almost 1,000 went to the West 123rd Street Station apparently under the impression that the soldier had been taken there. . . .

". . . A wild outbreak of riot and pillage swept the streets of Harlem last night and during the hours of darkness today, and it was not until long after daylight that police were able to restore a semblance of order. Four men were killed in the mob violence and looting, which was suppressed in one section, only to break out in another. Forty policemen and 155 civilians were listed by police as injured, and many more casualties

2.   3.

of the wild and lawless night received minor injuries. A crowd of Negroes at 9 A.M. today overturned an automobile parked on Lenox Avenue between 136th and 137th Streets and set fire to it. . . .

". . . Men and women with bleeding and bruised heads and bodies crowded the emergency wards of Harlem hospitals, where physicians and Red Cross workers, called in for emergency duty, were almost overwhelmed by work. . . . Before daylight the business section of Harlem was a litter of broken glass and merchandise which looters had pulled from windows and had dropped on the sidewalk and in gutters when police came along. . . .

". . . Mayor La Guardia was notified as soon as the trouble began developing, and he drove to the West 123rd Street Station.

The crowd booed him when he appealed to them to go home, and they jeered contingents of police who soon began arriving from other parts of the city.

". . . At 7:50 A.M. the situation was still so bad that Mayor LaGuardia broadcast an emergency message to the city saying that 'shame has come to our city and sorrow to a great number of our decent, law-abiding citizens residing in Harlem.'"

NEW YORK POST, AUGUST 2, 1943

1. One of many overturned cars that were set on fire during the evening of August 1, 1943; CB.
2. Three Harlem boys, aged twelve, thirteen, and fourteen, wearing tuxedos they took from a looted clothing store, August 1, 1943; CB.
3. An injured man being led away by a policeman, August 1, 1943; CB.

1.

Summer in the City

"The two moments when New York seems most desirable, when the splendor falls all round about and the city looks like a girl with leaves in her hair, are just as you are leaving and must say goodbye, and just as you return and can say hello. We had one such moment of infatuation not long ago on a warm, airless evening in town, before taking leave of these shores to try another city and another country for a while. There seemed to be a green tree overhanging our head as we sat in exhaustion. All day the fans had sung in offices, the air-conditioners had blown their clammy breath into the rooms, and the brutal sounds of demolition had stung the ear—from buildings that were being knocked down by the destroyers who have no sense of the past. Above our tree, dimly visible in squares of light, the city rose in air. From an open window above us, a whiff of perfume or bath powder drifted down startlingly in the heavy night, somebody having taken a tub to escape the heat. On the tips of some of the branches, a few semiprecious stars settled themselves to rest. There was nothing about the occasion that distinguished it from many another city evening, nothing in particular that we can point to to corroborate our emotion. Yet we somehow tasted New York on our tongue in a great, overpowering draught, and felt that to sail away from so intoxicating a place would be unbearable, even for a brief spell."
E. B. WHITE, *WRITINGS FROM THE NEW YORKER, 1927–1976*

2.

1. Astoria public swimming pool, with Hell
Gate railroad bridge in the background,
1940; MA.
2. The beach at Coney Island at four o'clock
in the afternoon on July 28, 1940; photograph
by Weegee, ICP.

1.

New Year's Eve and Times Square

Celebrating New Year's Eve in New York could be either an immensely private or public affair. For those who preferred to be private, there were parties at home or in private rooms in hotels and restaurants. For those who preferred a public place, there was Times Square.

To celebrate completion of the new Times Tower in 1906, Adolph Ochs, publisher of the *New York Times*, arranged to have an illuminated ball drop from the top of the building at midnight on New Year's Eve. In what became an annual event, crowds filled the bars, restaurants, and theaters in the surrounding area. As midnight approached, tens of thousands blanketed the sidewalks and streets abutting Times Square, making the whole area seem like the inside of a

jammed subway car. At the stroke of midnight the ball dropped, and the crowd's jubilation was expressed in a cacophony of whistles, horns, and rattles that could be heard for blocks.

TIMES SQUARE JAMMED

"As the white globe atop of the Times Building descended from the top of its staff and the figures, 1937, pushed slowly into sight, police mounts shied at the terrific din of horns, cowbells, whistles, the roars and screams from human throats and the wailing of thousands of motor-car horns.

"Perfectly synchronized with the dropping of the white globe and the white figures announcing the new year was THE NEW YORK TIMES bulletin board.

"More than 1,600 policemen on foot and on horseback, were helpless in their attempt to keep the crowds on the sidewalks. The lines broke, shouting men and women pushed their way into the middle of the Square and brought every vehicle to a standstill. It was a long time before traffic could move again. . . .

"Police officials, straining to keep the celebrants within bounds, were unable to estimate with any degree of accuracy the actual size of the pleasure seekers in the theatrical zone. They gauged it at from 400,000 up. . . .

"Spending was prodigious. Night clubs, theatres, motion picture theatres, restaurants and hotels entertained the largest crowds in their history, and at top prices. . . .

"It was a better-dressed crowd than Times Square has seen at any New Year's celebration since 1929. There were high hats and ermine in unusual numbers."
NEW YORK TIMES, JANUARY 1, 1937

1. The Di Costanzos celebrate New Year's Eve in their family-owned restaurant on Mulberry Street in Manhattan's Little Italy, 1942; photograph by Marjory Collins, LC. At the right is a Gypsy friend who came to join the festivities and dances to entertain them.
2. Crowd in Times Square waiting for the ball to drop, New Year's Eve, 1936; NYDN.
3. Horn blowing and bell ringing in Times Square, New Year's Eve, 1940; CB.

1.

Emigré Intellectuals and Artists

When Adolf Hitler came to power in Germany on January 30, 1933, the National Socialist party initiated policies of racial and political persecution directed toward "non-Aryans" and all those who held views politically and philosophically opposed to the views of the party. In addition to Jews, who were specifically targeted, the Nazis attacked artists, museum directors and curators, art historians, critics, writers, editors, publishers, actors, film directors, theater directors, musicians, and university professors who might or might not have been Jewish. There was no toleration of any idea, point of view, or artistic style that questioned Nazi authority—hardly a climate in which creativity could flourish. Shortly

thereafter a trickle of intellectuals and artists began to leave Germany. Some went to Great Britain and France; others came to New York and Los Angeles. As conditions in Germany worsened, with the fall of France and German occupation of most of the European continent, the dimensions of the exodus increased.

When the New School for Social Research created the University in Exile in 1933, there was a haven in New York. During the next decade Alvin Johnson, founder of the New School invited over ninety intellectuals from Germany, Austria, and France to teach. Among them were Hannah Arendt, Rudolf Arnheim, Hanns Eisler, Erich Fromm, Otto Klemperer, Claude Lévi-Strauss, Erwin Pis-

2.

cator, and Wilhelm Reich. Although some of them did not remain in New York after the end of the Second World War, they made an indelible contribution to New York's cultural life.

The magnitude of the intellectual migration was equaled by the arrival of many major artists seeking refuge in New York. *Art News'* April 1942 issue described this major artistic migration as "the largest, we are told, since the fall of Constantinople." Among the artists were painters, sculptors, and printmakers of diverse styles who had established themselves as leaders of the avant-garde in France, Germany, Great Britain, and the Netherlands. Along with them came a group of art dealers who

transformed the New York art market from one that passively sold the work of living artists to one that actively promoted artists and their work.

1. Faculty of the University in Exile, New School for Social Research, 1933; NYT. From left to right, seated: Emil Lederer, Alvin Johnson, Frieda Wunderlich, Karl Brandt; standing: Hans Speier, Max Wertheimer, Arthur Feiler, Eduard Heimann, Gerhard Colm, and E. von Hornbostel.

2. Photograph taken on the occasion of the Pierre Matisse Gallery's exhibition "Artists in Exile," 1942; photograph by George Platt Lynes, SI. Front row, from left to right: Matta, Ossip Zadkine, Yves Tanguy, Max Ernst, Marc Chagall, and Fernand Léger. Back row: André Breton, Piet Mondrian, André Masson, Amédée Ozenfant, Jacques Lipchitz, Pavel Tchelitchew, Kurt Seligmann, and Eugene Berman.

1.

Communists, Socialists, Nazis, and Anti-Semites

Throughout the late nineteenth century and during the first half of the twentieth century, New York had been a center for trade union activity. Although some of the unions preferred not to be associated with any political parties, it was an inescapable fact that labor organizers also became political activists. The Socialist party developed a large following among Eastern European Jewish immigrants, particularly those in the International Ladies Garment Workers Union. After the October 1917 revolution in Russia and the subsequent creation of the Communist International in 1919, a split developed in the American Socialist Party between those who believed in a nonrevolutionary path and those who supported workers' revolutions throughout the world. Some trade unions supported the Communists, and

others were hostile. The ILGWU fought Communists within its ranks. First- and second-generation working-class Jews living in Brooklyn and the Bronx found themselves bitterly divided between the Communists and Socialists.

With the rise of fascism in Europe in the 1930s, there were German-Americans who identified with Hitler and Italian-Americans who supported Mussolini. One of the most visible groups in New York City and adjacent areas in New Jersey and Long Island was the German American Bund. Its members marched with the Nazi swastika flag and gave the Nazi salute. On October 30, 1937, a contingent of the Bund marched along East Eighty-sixth Street through Yorkville, Manhattan's German stronghold, with Nazi flags amid American flags.

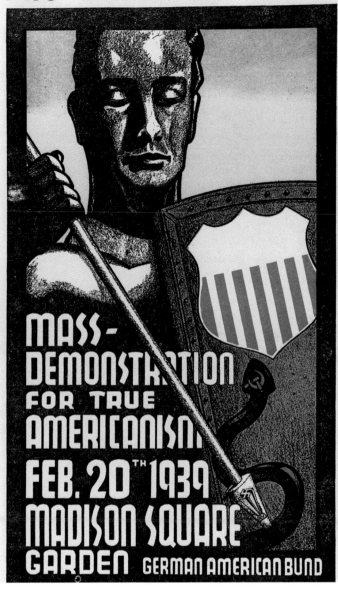

Perhaps the Bund's activities were the most visible forms of anti-Semitism; however, there were other lingering pockets of xenophobia to be found within the city. The Jewish community mobilized. In 1933 an estimated one hundred thousand people, both Jews and non-Jews, marched through Manhattan to Madison Square Garden, where a rally was held, to protest the policies of Nazi Germany.

1. May Day, 1937; PWW. In Europe, May Day became the traditional day on which to demonstrate working-class solidarity. It was adopted in this country, and New York hosted the nation's largest May Day parades. Banners carried by contingents within the parade demonstrated the issues that were their concerns at the time.
2. Election campaign literature, Rockaway Beach, Queens, 1932; AJHS.
3. Outside German American Bund rally in Madison Square Garden, 1939, WW. A contingent of fifteen hundred police was on duty to restrain anti-Bund demonstrators.
4. Announcement of German American Bund rally at Madison Square Garden, 1939; AJHS.

1.

World War II

The Japanese bombed Pearl Harbor on December 7, 1941. Within hours President Franklin Delano Roosevelt declared war on Japan and its allies, Germany and Italy. Although the United States had been supporting Great Britain and its allies in Europe, no American troops had been involved. America was in the war, and there was full-scale mobilization on the home front. New York, with its sizable industrial base, became a major supplier to the war effort. The Brooklyn Navy Yard also played a prominent role. To meet new demands, the navy yard expanded from some forty acres to a complex of three hundred buildings covering almost three hundred acres. Between 1941 and 1945 navy yard workers repaired more than 5,000 ships, converted more than

250 for wartime use, and built 3 battleships and 4 aircraft carriers.

During the war the U.S. government's Fair Employment Practices Commission was established. The pressure for increased war production brought some benefits to the African-American community. In June 1942 the *New York Age* reported that some employers were now willing to hire black workers. It stated that Brooklyn manufacturers and supermarket chains had expressed interest in hiring blacks.

2.

3.

"Declaring that 'heads of government respond only to pressure' and that 'Negroes must fight for what they get,' A. Philip Randolph, international president of the Brotherhood of Sleeping Car Porters and national director of the March on Washington Movement, was the principal speaker at the Movement' s second New York mass meeting Friday night. . . . Mr. Randolph traced the history of the March on Washington Movement, its conferences with Mayor La Guardia and Mrs. Roosevelt which led up to the march being called off after a second conference, in which President Roosevelt and important members of the Cabinet met with a group of Negro leaders and discussed issues, which resulted in the President's Executive Order 8802 and the cre-

ation of the FEPC. . . . Randolph declared that 'the March on Washington Movement has learned that the Federal Government itself has become the carrier of the germ of race discrimination and segregation' and that 'the Government and the President will respond to pressure and that the organization of the Negro masses can exercise pressure.'"

NEW YORK AGE, SEPTEMBER 19, 1942

1. Pearl Harbor Day, December 7, 1941; photograph by Weegee, ICP.
2. Celebrating the departure of Italian-American soldiers, Brooklyn, 1942; LC.
3. Anti-Japanese demonstration; photograph by Weegee, ICP.

1.

Victory in Europe and Asia

After nearly four years of active American participation in Europe and Asia, the Second World War ended in two separate events. The Russians captured Berlin on May 2, 1945. The German government capitulated on May 7, and V-E Day was celebrated on May 8. In Asia the United States dropped two atomic bombs on Japan. The first was on Hiroshima on August 6, and the second on Nagasaki on August 9. The Japanese capitulated on August 14, and V-J Day was celebrated that day.

The war was over, and the troops began to come home. New York had been a port of embarkation for troops going to Europe. It was a port of arrival for their return.

1. The subway rush hour came to a standstill as the report of Hitler's death was received on May 1, 1945; WW.

2. V-J Day, Times Square, August 14, 1945; photograph by Alfred Eisenstaedt, TL.

3. U.S. troops returning from Europe pack the decks of the British luxury liner turned troopship Queen Mary as it steams into New York Harbor with some fourteen thousand troops aboard, June 20, 1945; WW.

2.

3.

SEETHING CITY HAILS VICTORY

"The great news of Japanese surrender hit New York just after 7 o'clock last night, and almost instantly it transformed five boroughs full of 7,500,000 people into a roaring, writhing spectacle of elation that completely overshadowed the big V-E Day show.

"The worst war in history, the war that killed or wounded 908,098 Americans since the enemy struck Pearl Harbor 1,346 days ago, was over.

"The people of New York dashed into the streets. Millions of voices roared out the news. Even as they roared, they were drowned out by the shrilling of sirens and the pealing of church bells. Factory and boat whistles took up the chorus that spelled the end of war and the beginning of peace.

"Times Square, the mecca of the extroverts and the nucleus of every big spontaneous demonstration in the world's biggest city, was ready and waiting with a crowd of half a million who boiled over with a frenetic madness the moment the announcement came.

"From the instant when the illuminated moving news sign on the Times Building flashed the Japanese surrender, the Times Square throng began to grow as people poured into it from all sides to join in the leaping and shouting and horn blowing and kissing that demonstrated the utterly uncurbed joy of the people.

"In less than an hour the Times Square crowd was doubled to about a million strong, and in an hour after that the hard-pressed police estimated that two million yelling, milling celebrants of peace were jammed into the area bounded by Ninth and Sixth Avenues and Fortieth and Fifty-third Streets.

"On through the evening, the great and wild demonstration swept on, and it continued almost unabated past midnight and into the morning hours of today. But despite its dizzy tempo, there was little disorder and few arrests, and no serious injuries were reported."

NEW YORK HERALD TRIBUNE, AUGUST 15, 1945

313

With the end of the Second World War in 1945, America became the world's dominant power. Six years of war and occupation left Europe in shambles. The horrors of the concentration camps were revealed, refugees flooded the continent and displaced person camps temporarily housed millions. War refugees and Holocaust survivors made their way to New York. Out of this chaos the United Nations was born and New York was selected as its permanent headquarters.

America's wartime alliance with the Soviet Union deteriorated into a battle of titans—the Cold War. Europe was divided into two spheres of influence—East and West. When America learned that the Soviets, too, had developed an atom bomb, there was a rush to create an even more deadly means of mass destruction, the hydrogen bomb. Bomb shelters were designated in public buildings and family shelters were built in backyards.

Outer space was another arena of competition. When the Soviets launched the Sputnik in 1957, they established their leadership. American prestige was restored five years later when John Glenn orbited the earth three times in a Mercury space capsule. In 1969, Americans walked on the moon.

After the war, the American economy began a period of sustained growth that lasted almost thirty years, with the gross national product increasing nearly 300 percent. This prosperity lead to the suburbanization of the New York metropolitan area. Automobiles made everywhere accessible. Subdivisions were developed on Staten Island and in Nassau, Rockland, and Westchester counties as well as in parts of New Jersey.

From supreme commander of Allied forces in Europe, Dwight Eisenhower became president of Columbia University and later president of the United States. During his two-term presidency, conservatism and caution prevailed. He believed that American prosperity was based on rugged individualism and self-reliance, on business enterprise and on minimizing the role of government as it affected citizens and commerce. During the Eisenhower administration, Senator Joseph McCarthy of Wisconsin accelerated his campaign of anticommunist vilification. His tactics caused concern in New York's left-liberal political community. Finally discredited, McCarthy's influence waned.

A dramatic shift took place in the 1960s. Two forces, the Civil Rights Movement and the anti-Vietnam War Movement contributed to a renewed sense of social justice. Under the leadership of Dr. Martin Luther King, Jr., blacks throughout the South organized in an effort to overcome the vestiges of post-Civil War Jim Crow racism. Sparked by college students who saw the futility of American military involvement in Southeast Asia, there were demonstrations and marches throughout the country. New York was an active center for protest. A student uprising at Columbia University in April and May 1968 focused on three issues: dissatisfaction with the war in Vietnam, civil rights and community relations affecting Harlem, and the grievances of Black students.

Although Dr. Martin Luther King, Jr., was able to mobilize blacks in the south and some northern cities, Malcolm X emerged as the leader of his own Muslim sect. First as a member of the Nation of Islam and later proselytizing with his own philosophy, he galvanized the dissatisfaction felt by many blacks living in urban areas. An agonizing issue, police brutality, served as the fuse that ignited riots in Harlem in 1964. A white police lieutenant shot and killed a fifteen-year-old black high school student. Following the assassination of King in 1968, riots erupted across the country with Harlem and sections of Brooklyn participating. Although the acknowledged causes of these riots, racism and poverty, never disappeared, an increasing number of African-Americans were able to obtain an education, become professionals, and join the ranks of the middle class.

Tumultuous as the 1960s might have been, this decade germinated and developed many ideas and modes of behavior that have since become accepted American mores. Hippie-youth culture helped to sever traditional ties to lingering Victorian social standards and sexual practices. The 1969 street scene in the East Village informed the world that new lifestyles existed. Many in the white middle class embraced drugs. Women's liberation gained mass support, Gays and lesbians experienced new freedoms. This generation of Americans was being emulated around the world with New York as its stage.

One of New York's most distressed moments occurred in the 1970s when the city government's fiscal crisis became a paramount issue. New York City was on the

Chapter Five
Global City: After 1946
The World Comes to New York

verge of bankruptcy. The crisis was finally resolved by cuts in public service and federal loan guarantees and the city returned to normalcy. With the exception of another stock market crash in October 1987, the city's fortunes seem to have been ascending.

Although signs of wealth are apparent on the streets, in restaurants, in stores, and most of all in real estate ads, New York is not a paradise. The gap between rich and poor is widening. Economic and social problems persist. High unemployment, especially among young blacks and Latinos, and the visibility of the homeless demonstrate the contradiction in capitalism between wealth, poverty, and opportunity. Drugs, crime, rape and gangs exist. Fires occur, water mains break and civil unrest occasionally disrupts the peace.

With the end of the Cold War, the threat of mutually assured destruction evaporated. Perhaps a prosperous national economy and the globalization of commerce and industry, have contributed to a view of the city's future, which, at the moment, is clearly more optimistic than it has been for generations.

There are many factors that contribute to the city's economic surge—people being among the most important. Not since the end of the nineteenth century has New York experienced such an influx of new immigrants, cultures, and languages. At that time, it was people from Eastern and Southern Europe; they were resented by the old immigrants from Northern and Western Europe. It is a recurring story. The current old immigrants look down on the recent new immigrants.

The newest New Yorkers come from the Caribbean, Latin America, Asia, Africa, and the Middle East. Hundreds of thousands of Puerto Ricans arrived in the 1950s. In the 1980s and 1990s people from around the world have flocked to New York. In the 1995–1996 school year, the Board of Education reported students coming from 193 different countries. Between 1990 and 1994, a total of 562,988 new immigrants settled in New York City with 428,346 coming from (in descending order): Dominican Republic, Former Soviet Union, China, Jamaica, Guyana, Poland, Phillipines, Haiti, India, Ireland, Columbia, Korea, United Kingdom, Peru, El Salvador, Vietnam, Mexico, Iran, Canada, and Cuba.

What is the magnetism of New York? Today, it has the same appeal that it has had since the seventeenth century. New York is a place where immigrants believe that they can find a better life and where they can be successful. If not themselves, their children will have an education and a better life. There are many stories. A man from India who learned auto mechanics in Germany came to New York via Mexico. Shepherded across the California border by a "coyote," a professional immigrant smuggler, he was advised by a compatriot at the Los Angeles airport to take a flight to LaGuardia to avoid INS detection. Having arrived in Brooklyn, he went to work repairing taxis. Today, he is co-owner of a garage and is married with two children; he and his wife own their home.

The new immigrants come as professionals and laborers. A Japanese real estate executive says that New York is the only place outside of Tokyo where he feels at home. A Mexican woman with two children shares a three-room tenement with another family; she believes it is better to raise her children in New York than her native state of Puebla. A Russian-Jewish space scientist drives a Brooklyn limo. A Ghanain is the controller of a major health institution. Stock brokers from London and restauranteurs from France and Italy have made fortunes.

In the era of the global economy New York has emerged as the paradigm of global cities There are many definitions. Some say that global cities are primarily financial centers. French post modernist philosophers describe global cities as places that have more in common with each other than they do with their hinterlands. Today, New York, London, Paris, Hong Kong, and Tokyo are considered to be global cities. Because New York is multi-cultural, multi-religious, and multi-racial, it may be the model of the future.

Machiavelli said that the greatness of Rome was due to the constant influx of new people. Starting with Native Americans whose footpath became Broadway, New York's people, wave after wave of immigrants over the last four centuries, have made New York the world's most exciting city.

p. 316: Western Electric telephone, about 1960; AC.
Below: Total New York website, 1997; AC.
Preceding pages: New York 1986, photograph by Robert Cameron.

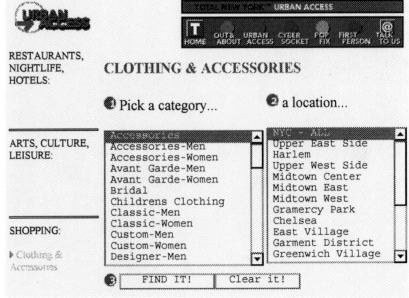

1.

Holocaust Survivors

On November 24, 1933, Rabbi Stephen S. Wise said, "Germany is a torture chamber for the Jewish people. The tragedy of the Jew lies in the two-fold purpose of the new rulers of the German Reich—to exterminate on the one hand and, in the meantime, to denigrate on the other." Clearly Rabbi Wise and other leaders of the Jewish community could see the handwriting on the wall. In the following years there were reports of German "execution factories," where tens of thousands of Jews and others were being systematically murdered. When American troops liberated the Buchenwald concentration camp on April 11, 1945, there was confirmed evidence of Hitler's organized destruction of European Jewry.

After liberation of the concentration camps, European Jews who survived were sent to displaced persons camps. From there many went to Israel, and others came to the United States. Between May 1945 and December 1952, a total of 137,450 Jewish DPs arrived in the United States. By 1952 a total of 85,128 of them had settled in the New York metropolitan area.

1. *SS* Marine Flasher *arriving in New York Harbor with Jewish survivors, May 20, 1946; HIAS. This was one of the first ships to arrive with refugees following President Harry Truman's directive of December 22, 1945, allowing immigration at prewar levels. About two thousand arrived per month under the sponsorship of the United Service for New Americans, a member agency of the United Jewish Appeal.*
2. *Daughter greeting her refugee mother, about 1949; PHW.*
3. *Displaced persons at the pier, 1951; photograph by Ernst Haas.*

KATZ FAMILY REUNITED

"No more separations are expected in the Katz family. They were kept apart long enough in Europe, by concentration camps and forced labor battalions. Now those who remain—their parents were killed in Czechoslovakia—will stick together under the same roof in Brooklyn.

"On May 20, 1946, Aaron, Israel, Irene and Frieda Katz, ranging in age from 20 to 24 years, arrived here on the steamship *Marine Flasher* to rejoin their brother Sam, who came to this country in 1938. In the year which has passed since then, the girls have married, a baby has been born, but the family unit has remained intact.

"'We were separated so long, now we want to be together,' Sam Katz a furrier at 352 Seventh Avenue, said today. 'For six years, I didn't even know whether they were alive or not.'

"'The girls were married within two weeks after their arrival in New York. Their fiances came on the same ship, refugees also.

"'Their husbands are from Romania and one served in a labor camp with one of my brothers,' Katz explained. 'They're carrying on their trade in a textile factory, one of my brothers is a furrier, the other a baker.

"'When my sisters were married, they lived in furnished rooms at first. Then I bought a house at 146 Keap street in Brooklyn, and we moved together.'"
NEW YORK SUN, MAY 17, 1947

319

1.

Central Park West

The skyscraper had captured New York's imagination. The idea of working and living in buildings that towered above the street was becoming accepted. During the 1930s builders and developers responded by building a series of apartment houses along Central Park West that defined its character and echoed some of the tall new buildings in the midtown business district. Among them were the Beresford, the Century, the El Dorado, the Majestic, and the San Remo. While the Depression lasted, these buildings were not fully rented.

The nation experienced a period of economic growth immediately following the end of the Second World War. Second-generation immigrant families that participated in that growth and those who could afford it chose to live in the spacious apartments on Central Park West.

2.

"It was one of the many charms of the El Dorado that it faced Central Park. Here on the seventeenth floor there was no one to peer in on her nakedness but the birds of the air. This fact, even more than the spacious view of the green park and the skyscrapers, gave Marjorie a sense of luxury each day when she awoke. She had enjoyed the freedom from prying eyes for less than a year. Marjorie loved everything about the El Dorado, even the name, 'El Dorado' was perfectly suited to an apartment building on Central Park West. It had a fine foreign sound to it. There were two categories of foreignness in Marjorie's outlook: high foreign, like French restaurants, British riding clothes, and the name El Dorado; and low

foreign, like her parents. By moving to the El Dorado on Central Park West her parents had done much, Marjorie believed, to make up for their immigrant origin. She was grateful to them for this, and proud of them."

HERMAN WOUK, *MARJORIE MORNINGSTAR*

1. *Central Park West, 1932; photograph by Gottscho-Schleisner, LC. (Although this photograph was taken prior to the first years of this chapter, the physical conditions that it depicts hardly changed.)*
2. *The Sarnoff and Ganz families in their Central Park West apartment, about 1948; PSO.*

1.

The Garment District

With the growth of mass-produced ready-to-wear clothing, sweatshop production was replaced by factory production. As a result, unions like the International Ladies Garment Workers Union and the Amalgamated Clothing Workers Union enlarged their memberships, becoming forces in the garment industry.

By the 1920s clothing manufacturing had moved uptown from tenements on the Lower East Side and lofts on lower Broadway. New buildings constructed in the West Thirties and Forties between Sixth and Eighth avenues were planned for industrial use with substantial floor space and large elevators. Women's clothing manufacturing was concentrated here; other apparel-related fac-

tories and wholesale businesses bordered the area. There was men's clothing around Twenty-third Street and the contiguous fur district between Twenty-fifth and Thirty-first streets, with other specialties sprinkled along side streets. Certain buildings housed both showrooms and factories for one specific industry: children's clothes, lingerie, and accessories (handbags, belts, neckwear, jewelry, millinery). By 1931 the Garment District was the largest concentration of apparel manufacturing in the world. Immediately after World War II, as the nation became more fashion-conscious, the garment center prospered, becoming the source of wealth for a generation of Jewish families.

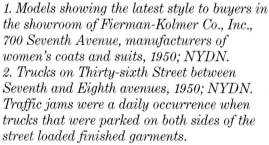

1. Models showing the latest style to buyers in the showroom of Fierman-Kolmer Co., Inc., 700 Seventh Avenue, manufacturers of women's coats and suits, 1950; NYDN.

2. Trucks on Thirty-sixth Street between Seventh and Eighth avenues, 1950; NYDN. Traffic jams were a daily occurrence when trucks that were parked on both sides of the street loaded finished garments.

3. Matchbook from Lou G. Siegel's kosher restaurant in the Garment District, undated; PS.

4. Sewing machine operators in the work-rooms of Cohen and Drimmer at 501 Seventh Avenue, manufacturers of junior and misses dresses; NYDN. Although unionized and working under more humane conditions than their Lower East Side predecessors, garment workers still spent their days huddled over sewing machines.

1.

A Population of Two Million Jews in 1950

In 1950 the population of New York City was 7,116,441. Of that number nearly 2,000,000 were Jews. The Jewish population of New York constituted nearly 40 percent of the total Jewish population in the United States. The newborn state of Israel was a common focus for many Jews, and the continuation of communal Jewish life was hardly questioned.

Jews, mostly immigrants and the children of immigrants, shared in America's postwar prosperity. Those in business and the professions benefited from an expanding national economy that demanded more consumer goods and services. Within the Jewish community the hierarchy remained frozen. Sephardic Jews with colonial ancestors and German Jews with nineteenth-century accomplishments in their backgrounds were at the top. At this point Eastern European Jews far outnumbered all others, dominating the New York Jewish image because of their numbers and growing influence. From this sense of strength emerged a new New York Jewish style, not one steeped in old country lore but one that totally embraced the American way of life, accepting its obsession with material well-being. Lavish weddings and bar mitzvahs were symbols of this new prosperity.

BAR MITZVAH

RECEPTION OF

Stanley Babit

AT THE

APERION MANOR

September 10, 1949

1. *Ramaz High School prom, 1950; JHB. From left to right: Stanley Beinenfeld, Evelyn Seelenfreund, Jack H Bloom, and Raiselle Sorscher.*
2. *The wedding of Stanley and Shirley Levine, Brooklyn, 1951; EW. The couple were Holocaust survivors from Ruthenia in Czechoslovakia.*
3. *Bar mitzvah invitation, 1949; PS.*
4. *Jack H Bloom, dancing with Froma Inselbuch, at his bar mitzvah, 1945; JHB.*

"This lunch stemmed from an old-country synagogue custom called a kiddush, or wine-blessing. The parents of a bar-mitzva boy were obliged by long tradition to serve wine to all worshippers. In the United States the custom had evolved—as they say elephants have evolved from one-celled creatures—into a noonday feast hardly less imposing than the main banquet after sundown. Wine-blessing played little or no part in it, though it was still called a kiddush.

"The caterers had given the old folkway modern form and variety. There was a five-hundred-dollar kiddush, a thousand-dollar one, and so forth. Mrs. Morgenstern had been miserably tempted by Lowenstein's famous twelve-hundred-dollar extravaganza, which included whole boiled salmons in jelly, a cascade of raspberry soda on a terraced frame of snow, and a Star of David in solid ice bordered by blue neon. But the father, panic-stricken by the mounting expense, had frozen at the thousand-dollar kiddush. The Morgensterns did not have enough friends and relatives at the temple to eat up the food, but that was no problem. On many another Sabbath there might be only four or five rows of worshippers, lonesome in a barren stretch of purple cushions and brown wood; but when a bar-mitzva was scheduled the house of God was seldom less than full, Marjorie had noticed the same phenomenon in the old synagogues of the Bronx."
HERMAN WOUK, *MARJORIE MORNINGSTAR*

1.

Little Italy in the Fifties and Sixties

At the turn of the century Little Italy, the area of Manhattan bounded by Houston Street on the north and Canal Street on the south with the Bowery as an eastern border and Mulberry Street on the west, was the center of the Italian immigrant population. As second and third generations prospered, some moved out to Brooklyn, the Bronx, Queens, and Staten Island while others went to Nassau, Rockland, Suffolk, and Westchester counties. In 1930 there were 1,070,355 Italians living in New York City; by 1960 the number had dropped to 858,601.

Although the buildings remained unchanged, by the mid-1950s, Little Italy had been transformed into a less congested residential area supporting a number of restaurants and food stores that maintained some continuity with the past. First organized in 1926,

the San Gennaro Festival, held annually on Mulberry Street, sounds a nostalgic note. Originally a religious celebration, it has evolved into a gastronomic event at which Italian specialties are consumed by people of every ethnic origin.

1. *Nuns outside Old St. Patrick's on Mulberry Street, 1955; photograph by Leonard Freed/MAGNUM.*
2. *Groups of men and women congregating on Mulberry Street, 1955; photograph by Leonard Freed/MAGNUM.*

1.

Conformity, Complacency, Conservatism, and Contradiction

America in the 1950s was a nation trapped in complacency, conformity, and conservatism. The postwar economic boom encouraged complacency. Conformity triumphed in food and clothes without style. Cocktail parties were minitheaters of social interaction. Conservatism was the essence of politics. Dwight Eisenhower was president, and Richard Nixon his vice president. It was the period of the cold war with the atomic nightmare haunting everyone. Senator Joe McCarthy, searching for Communists behind every door, manipulated the media. Television arrived in full force and started to consume people's lives. Cities began to be abandoned for suburbs, which gobbled up the agricultural landscape. America was not a monolith; there were contradictions. There

was Elvis, there was James Dean, and there was Marilyn Monroe.

Where was New York in the midst of all this? It was as conformist as it ever could be and perhaps as conservative as it ever had been. As a marketplace for thought, New York, underneath all this, generated some new ideas. Rachel Carson's *Silent Spring* created a tidal wave of environmental consciousness that still engulfs us. Columbia University was the breeding ground of the beat poets. Although part of America, New York might have been steering its own course.

2.

3.

1. *Edward R. Murrow in his CBS studio, 1957; photograph by Elliott Erwitt, MAGNUM. The legendary television journalist and commentator started in radio and made the transition to television. His* See It Now *television series set standards for documentaries and contributed to the fall of Senator Joe McCarthy.*

2. *James Dean in Times Square, 1956; photograph by Dennis Stock, MAGNUM. His life, which ended in tragedy, was the personification of the fifties malaise. In his most famous film,* Rebel Without a Cause, *he played a sensitive adolescent fighting a world of conformity.*

3. *Marilyn Monroe on the streets of New York, 1956; photograph by Elliott Erwitt, MAGNUM. Although identified more with*

Hollywood than New York, she was married to New York playwright Arthur Miller for a short time.

1.

Jackie, Bird, Dizzie, and Beauties

To some extent the African-American community shared in America's post–Second World War transformations. Some things improved, and some stayed the same. There was a little more prosperity, and there were new city, state, and federal agencies empowered to eliminate discrimination in employment and housing. Probably the most evident change occurred when Branch Rickey, president of the Brooklyn Dodgers, signed a contract with second baseman Jackie Robinson. When he joined the Dodgers on the field in 1947, Jackie Robinson became the first African-American to play in the major leagues. There were Dodgers who refused to play with him and requested transfers. The breakthrough served to open doors for blacks in other situations.

On the national horizon, changes were also taking place. A historic U.S. Supreme Court decision in 1954 eliminated segregation in public schools, and in 1957 Congress passed the first civil rights act affecting black voting rights since 1875. Changes were slow to take effect in the South. In 1957 Governor Orval Faubus of Arkansas fought the desegregration of Little Rock's Central High School. Federal troops were sent to keep order and enforce the law.

1. Two-and-a-half-year-old Jackie Robinson, Jr., with his father at Ebbets Field, 1949; CB. In 1947, Robinson's first season, total attendance at Dodger games broke all National League records, with 1,807,526 fans at Ebbets Field and 1,863,542 on the road. Robinson's batting average was .297, and he led the league with twenty-nine stolen bases. With him on their team, the Dodgers won the National League pennant, defeating the St. Louis Cardinals.

2. Charlie ("Bird") Parker cutting his birthday cake at Birdland while Dizzy Gillespie looks on approvingly, about 1947; NYPL/SC. One of the greatest musical innovators of his generation, alto saxaphonist Charlie Parker abandoned jazz for bop. Trumpeter and bandleader Dizzy Gillespie was the personification of bop.

3. Harlem Shriners' beauty contest, 1951; photograph by Burt Glinn, MAGNUM.

1.

2.

Success, Prosperity, and Poverty

Poverty and prosperity coexist as unhappy partners in the black community. From time to time success might be available to some and prosperity might embrace others, but poverty never disappears. The black middle class and impoverished blacks live in two different worlds even though they might share the same neighborhood.

"When John Creary left his apartment building shortly before eight o'clock on Saturday morning, the insulated quadrangle of the Dunbar Apartments was silent and empty. The buildings are arranged so that tenants enter the interior quadrangle and then walk through an archway into the surrounding streets. It is a brief ritual of passage from a symbolic stockade that is determined to withstand the ravages of Harlem. The Dunbar families are twice surrounded—by the ghetto around them and the city around the ghetto. . . . [T]he struggle for respectability and acceptance . . . is often lonely, always strenuous."

EDWARD WAKIN, *AT THE EDGE OF HARLEM*

3.

4.

"The way the Man has us, he has us wanting to kill one another. Dog eat dog, amongst us! He has us, like we're so hungry up here, he has us up so tight! Like his rent is due, my rent is due. It's Friday. The Man wants sixty-five dollars, If you are three days over, or don't have the money; like that, he wants to give you a dispossess! Take you to court! The courts won't go along with you, they say get the money or get out! Yet they don't tell you how to get the money, you understand? They say get the money and pay the Man, but they don't say how to get it. Now, if you use illegal means to obey his ruling to try to get it—which he's not going to let you do— . . . he will put you in jail— Man, age 31."

KENNETH B. CLARK, *DARK GHETTO*

1. Louis Armstrong with kids on the steps of his home at 34-56 107th Street, Corona, Queens, about 1965; LAA. Trumpeter, singer, composer, and bandleader, Louis Armstrong has been described as a genius comparable to the greatest names in the history of music. From 1942, although traveling to the far corners of the globe, Louis always loved to return to his home in Queens. Count Basie, Ella Fitzgerald, and Jackie Robinson all made their homes in St. Albans, Queens.
2. Bedford-Stuyvesant, Brooklyn, 1961; photograph by Leonard Freed, MAGNUM.
3. Harlem hard-core poverty, 1966; photograph by John Launois, BS.
4. Bedford-Stuyvesant, Brooklyn, 1961; photograph by Leonard Freed, MAGNUM.

1.

Puerto Ricans and Native Americans

Puerto Ricans and Native Americans have something in common: Both have had long histories as citizens of the United States. However, they are often seen and treated as being apart from the mainstream of American society.

In 1940 there were 61,463 Puerto Ricans living in New York. By 1960 there were 612,574. Deteriorating economic conditions in Puerto Rico created this tenfold increase in two decades. In Puerto Rico, a surge in population growth, accompanied by agricultural and manufacturing failures, induced hundreds of thousands to leave and seek a better life on the mainland, principally in and around New York City. As citizens Puerto Ricans did not experience the quotas or other restrictions placed on foreign immigrants.

The Puerto Ricans who came before 1945 were generally middle-class, educated professionals and businesspeople. Those who came after 1945 from both urban and rural areas in Puerto Rico were mostly impoverished, unemployed, underemployed, with no advanced education, and possessing minimal skills.

Although Native Americans were the first inhabitants of the New York City area, they have had an intermittent presence. Upstate tribes began moving into New York City during the nineteenth century. Men found work as laborers, factory workers and as longshoremen; women were seamstresses, cleaning women, and domestic servants. When the construction boom swept the city at the turn of the century, members of the Mohawk tribe came to the city and played a

2.

major role in bridge and skyscraper construction. They became known and sought after for their ability to work on office towers and bridges in high places of extreme danger.

These new Native American residents established a colony in the North Gowanus section of Brooklyn bounded by Court Street on the west, Schermerhorn Street on the north, Fourth Avenue on the east and Warren Street on the south.

The 1990 federal census reported 27,531 Indians living here. The American Indian Community House in Lower Manhattan now serves as a community cultural center while the Smithsonian's Museum of the American Indian in the Old Customs House provides a venue for exhibitions and programs that

interpret Native American culture and history for general audiences.

1. *Puerto Rican family arriving by ship in New York, 1947; CP.*
2. *Native Americans marching down Fifth Avenue, 1952; CB. Although Native Americans had long been relegated to reservations managed by the U.S. Bureau of Indian Affairs, growing numbers of them wanted to reform this situation. Some changes were made. In March 1968 President Lyndon Johnson sent Congress a special message on Native American affairs. He advocated for them, "An opportunity to remain in their homelands, if they choose, without surrendering their dignity; an opportunity to move to the towns and cities of America, if they choose, equipped with skills to live in equality and dignity."*

1.

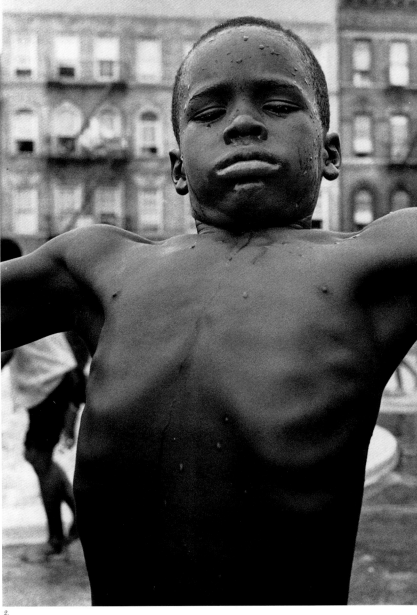

2.

The Rising Tide

LETTER TO MY NEPHEW ON THE ONE
HUNDREDTH ANNIVERSARY OF
EMANCIPATION

"Now, my dear namesake, these innocent
and well-meaning people, your countrymen,
have caused you to be born under conditions
not very far removed from those described
for us by Charles Dickens in the London of
more than a hundred years ago. (I hear the
chorus of innocents screaming: 'No! This is
not true! How *bitter* you are!'—but I am
writing this letter to *you* to try to tell you
something about how to handle *them*, for
most of them do not yet really know that
you exist. I *know* the condition under which
you were born, for I was there. Your countrymen were *not* there, and haven't made it
yet. Your grandmother was also there. . . .
She isn't hard to find. Your countrymen

don't know that *she* exists either, though
she has been working for them all their
lives. . . .

"This innocent country set you down in a
ghetto in which, in fact, it intended that you
should perish. Let me spell out precisely
what I mean by that, for the heart of the
matter is here, and the root of my dispute
with my country. You were born where you
were born and faced the future that you
faced because you were black and *for no
other reason.* The limits of your ambition
were, thus, expected to be set forever. You
were born into a society which spelled out
with brutal clarity, and in as many ways as
possible, that you were a worthless human
being. You were not expected to aspire to
excellence: you were expected to make
peace with mediocrity. Wherever you have

336

3.

4.

turned, James, in your short time on this earth, you have been told where you could go and what you could do (and *how* you could do it) and where you could live and whom you could marry. I know your country-men do not agree with me about this, and I hear them saying, 'You exaggerate.' . . . Take no one's word for anything, including mine. . . . Please try to be clear, dear James, through the storm which rises about your youthful head today, about the reality which lies behind the words *acceptance* and *inte-gration*. There is no no reason for you to try to become like white people and there is no basis for their impertinent assumption that *they* must accept *you*. The really terrible thing, old buddy, is that *you* must accept *them* . . . and accept them with love. For these innocent people have no other hope.

They are, in effect, still trapped in a history which they do not understand; and until they understand it, they cannot be released from it. They have had to believe for many years, and innumerable reasons, that black men are inferior to white men. . . . [T]he black man has functioned in the white man's world as a fixed star, as an immovable pil-lar: and as he moves out of his place, heav-ens and earth are shaken to their founda-tions."
JAMES BALDWIN, *THE FIRE NEXT TIME*

1. Malcolm X, 1959; NYPL/SC. In the pan-theon of black heroes, Malcolm X holds an exalted position, not only because he was a martyr but because he was an inspiration.
2. In a Harlem public swimming pool, 1961; photograph by Leonard Freed, MAGNUM.
3. Congressman Adam Clayton Powell, Jr., about 1965; NYPL/SC. Elected in 1941, Powell was the first black member of the New York City Council, and in 1944 he became the first black congressman from New York.
4. Demonstration, 1962; photograph by Bruce Davidson, MAGNUM.

1.

2.

The Explosions

July 16, 1964: An off-duty police lieutenant, Thomas Gilligan, shot and killed a fifteen-year-old black youth, James Powell, in the street opposite the Robert F. Wagner, Jr., High School on East 76th Street when Powell allegedly threatened the officer with a knife. About three hundred teenagers, mostly black, pelted policemen with bottles and cans.

July 18, 1964: Following a rally at Seventh Avenue and 125th Street to denounce the shooting of James Powell, a riot that engulfed an eight-block area in Harlem between Eighth and Lenox avenues and 123d and 127th streets.

July 19, 1964: A second day of rioting in Harlem. Groups roamed the streets, attacking journalists and others. Police in steel helmets were showered with bottles and bricks thrown from the tops of buildings.

February 21, 1965: Malcolm X was shot to death inside the Audubon Ballroom.

April 4, 1968: Violence erupted in Harlem and in Bedford-Stuyvesant, Brooklyn, after the news of Dr. Martin Luther King Jr.'s assassination was announced. There were numerous incidents of rock throwing, looting, and arson.

3.

The Young Lords

The Young Lords party, a Puerto Rican revolutionary political organization, was formed in New York during the summer of 1969 by a group of Puerto Rican college students who felt that they wanted to connect with the people they had left behind in the ghetto. Their thirteen-point program said that they were "fighting for the liberation of all oppressed people," Self-determination for all Latinos, equality for women, community control of institutions, and opposition to the war in Vietnam were some of their issues. The Young Lords engaged in street actions and organized school breakfast programs.

1. Mayor John Lindsay walking the streets of Bedford-Stuyvesant following the announcement of Dr. Martin Luther King Jr.'s assassination, 1968; NYDN.
2. Police and rioters in Harlem, 1963; CB.
3. Young Lords holding a press conference after they liberated a church in East Harlem, 1970; photograph by Charles Gatewood, MAGNUM. (Felipe Luciano, director of communications, Young Lords party, center, in front of microphones, today is a network television journalist.)

339

1.

The Peace Movement and the Women's Movement

Throughout the country the sixties were a period of turmoil and fundamental change. There was the civil rights movement in the South, student rebellions in Berkeley, hippies in San Francisco, and the uproar at the Chicago Democratic National Convention. New York had its equivalents. Students occupied faculty offices at Columbia University to demonstrate their dissatisfaction with CIA recruiting, ROTC training, and construction of a new gym in Morningside Park, on the edge of Harlem, from which neighboring black residents would be excluded. Some members of black and Latino communities were in rebellion. Segments of the white middle class were supportive of black and Latino issues; however, many found their focus in the peace movement and the women's movement.

As U.S. involvement in the war in Vietnam escalated, dissatisfaction at home grew. Liberals, artists, intellectuals, and students created coalitions that organized an ongoing sequence of massive parades down Fifth Avenue, venting their distaste for the government's failed adventure in Southeast Asia.

Dormant since the suffragists had won women's right to vote, the women's movement came to life again. First there were books that questioned women's role in contemporary society, and then there were demonstrations that coalesced around gender issues, discrimination in the workplace, and abortion.

2.

"While we cannot support any war, the war in Vietnam has become a classic example of the unjust war. It is a war which has seen villages reduced to ashes, rice paddies defoliated, prisoners and suspects tortured, innocents and non-combatants killed by the thousands. These crimes are committed in behalf of a series of dictatorships the very support of which is contrary to all American ideals. The leader of the present regime has described Hitler as his number one hero. Each of the many Saigon governments has ignored the rights which we as Americans hold to be self-evident. . . ."
PEACE MOVEMENT HANDBILL

"The feminine mystique says that the highest value and the only commitment for women is [sic] in the fulfillment of their femininity. It says that the great mistake of Western culture, through most of its history, has been the undervaluation of this femininity. It says this femininity is so mysterious and intuitive and close to the creation and origin of life that man-made science may never be able to understand it. But however special and different, it is in no way inferior to the nature of man; it may even in certain respects be superior. The mistake, says the mystique, the root of women's troubles in the past is that women envied men."
BETTY FRIEDAN, *THE FEMININE MYSTIQUE*

1. Peace demonstration on Fifth Avenue, 1968; WW. Over a period of years there were numerous peace marches down Fifth Avenue; the numbers swelled year by year until there were nearly a hundred thousand demonstrators.
2. ERA demonstration, 1977; CB. Betty Friedan and Gloria Steinem are signing a giant telegram to President Carter supporting the Equal Rights Amendment.

1.

The Sixties

Fresh winds were blowing all across America in the 1960s; there was evidence of a new cultural awakening in which conventions of the past were wilting while the energy of another generation was creating a new lifestyle that embodied both personal freedom and social commitment.

Although Central Park was hardly Haight-Ashbury, Parks Commissioner Tom Hoving allowed it to become a theater of opportunity for New Yorkers who wanted to experiment with the future. He brought artists, poets, and musicians into the parks to create events; he encouraged bike riding and picnicking. He made the parks open, accessible, and desirable to everyone.

1. Be-In, Sheep Meadow, Central Park, March 26, 1967; photograph by Barton Silverman, NYT/PARKS. The event was announced as an opportunity for people to come together and react spontaneously. Some people joined hands; others danced or made music.
2. Parks Commissioner Tom Hoving adding to the 105-yard canvas stretched around Central Park at Seventy-ninth Street and Fifth Avenue, May 15, 1966; PARKS. Organized by artist Phyllis Yampolsky, this was one of the first of what came to be known as Hoving Happenings.
3. Poet Allen Ginsberg reading in Washington Square Park, 1966; photograph by Jack Manning, NYT and PARKS.
4. Love-In, Central Park, 1967; photograph by Ben Fernandez.

2.

4.

3.

5.

5. Abe Schoener in the playground at Fifth
Avenue and Eighty-fifth Street, 1967; photograph by Allon Schoener.

1.

2.

Becoming an International Art Capital

Until the mid-1950s New York had been a provincial outpost for Western European culture and looked to London, Paris, or Rome for inspiration. Although Hitler's occupation of Europe devastated cultural life on the Continent, Paris appeared to have recovered its primacy, seeming central with the birth of existentialism and flourishing activity by artists with established prewar reputations.

In the wake of the Second World War, New York emerged as the world's undisputed global capital. Construction of the United Nations headquarters and the city's growth as a world financial center confirmed the magnitude of New York's new international political and economic importance. New York was no longer borrowing ideas and styles but was generating them without

mimicry. Within the next few years a new pantheon of artists, choreographers, composers, conductors, dancers, poets, and writers emerged: James Baldwin, George Balanchine, Leonard Bernstein, John Cage, Merce Cunningham, Allen Ginsberg, Jasper Johns, Norman Mailer, Jackson Pollock, Jerome Robbins, Mark Rothko, and Andy Warhol. It seemed as if there were collusion among collectors, critics, and curators, who, like the world of fashion, created a new style every year: abstract expressionism, pop, op, minimalism, and the list goes on. The Hamptons became the scene for successful artists and literati. SoHo replaced the Village and Vermont became exurbia.

4.

6.

NEW YORK VERSUS PARIS

"We all know what happened to International School of Paris painting at some time in between 1935 and 1945; it ceased to exist.

"We know how it happened; the evidence is plain in literally thousands of pictures by hundreds of very gifted, intelligent artists.

"Up to World War II, masters had succeeded masters, Isms chased Isms, in a brilliant evolution of at least a century's duration.

"And by the mid-1930's, there seemed no reason to believe that Paris's continuity would not continue forever. If there had been drab moments now and then, there was also a superb confidence in the inevitable reappearance of masters—as punctual as sunshine in Burgundy.

"The content of New York School painting, like the content of its ancestral School of Paris art, was and continues to be revolutionary, subversive, radically against the Establishment and practically everything that the Powers-that-Be stand for and do. . . .

" . . . One of the most remarkable accomplishments of New York painting has been its simultaneous renewal and defiance of the past. With its radical assumption that anything can become art and that the artist can do anything, the painters proceeded to drag past art up into the present. Willem de Kooning has called this 'reinventing the harpsichord.'"

THOMAS HESS, *A TALE OF TWO CITIES*

1. Andy Warhol with members of his so-called Velvet Underground, Viva on left and Ultra Violet on right, 1968; photograph by Sam Falk, NYT.
2. Living Theatre lobby, 1962; photograph by Fred McDarrah. Led by Julian Beck and his wife, Judith Malina, the Living Theatre presented controversial avant-garde plays.
3. Painter Mark Rothko, 1964; photograph by Hans Namuth.
4. Composer-conductor Leonard Bernstein in rehearsal at Avery Fisher Hall, 1977; CB.
5. Writer James Baldwin in his apartment, 1963; CB.
6. Writer Norman Mailer campaigning for mayor on a platform of making New York City the fifty-first state, 1969; CB.

1.

2.

3.

Manhattan and the Other Boroughs

In the minds of some New Yorkers, there is Manhattan and there are the boroughs. Residents of the boroughs often say they are going to the city, when they are planning to go to Manhattan. With disdain, Manhattanites talk about the bridge and tunnel crowd, which includes people from New Jersey. Greater New York came into being in 1898 as an amalgamation of five boroughs. At that time Brooklyn had long been an independent city, Queens was a cluster of towns and villages, the Bronx seemed like an extension of Manhattan, and Staten Island was an island unto itself. Despite consolidation, each borough retained its individuality and a fierce sense of civic pride.

Different lifestyles evolved outside Manhattan. Although they could hardly be called suburban in comparison with other American cities, New York's boroughs have fewer apartment buildings and more individual detached houses than are to be found in Manhattan. Automobiles, anathema to Manhattanites, are a necessity for outer borough residents. Life in the outer boroughs never moves at Manhattan's frenetic pace. All five boroughs share two things: pockets of wealth and poverty and a multiplicity of ethnic neighborhoods.

346

4.

5.

6.

1. *Shoveling snow, Carroll Gardens, Cobble Hill, Brooklyn, 1989; CB.*
2. *Sitting around, Staten Island, 1980; photograph by Bill Aron.*
3. *Watching television, Brooklyn, 1991; photograph by Ethel Wolvovitz.*
4. *Single-family houses in Queens, 1970; photograph by Bob Adelman.*
5. *Apartment buildings in Queens, about 1970; photograph by Bob Adelman.*
6. *Backyard grill in Queens, about 1970; photograph by Bob Adelman.*

1.

Taxi Drivers

Before the automobile, there was the hansom cab with a horse and driver. Gas-powered taxis hit the streets of New York in 1907 and have been one of its most prominent features ever since. By 1909 there were six major fleets employing hundreds of drivers and thousands of independent owner-drivers. When the police took control of licensing in 1923, there were 16,000 cabs. During the Depression the number went up to 75,000 drivers operating 19,000 cabs. In 1937 the medallion system was introduced; 13,566 were issued at ten dollars each. In the 1960s the number of medallion cabs dropped to 11,300. The city ordered all medallion cabs to be painted yellow in 1967; at the time about 10 percent of the drivers were women. The limited number of medallions and the refusal of some

drivers to take their patrons to minority neighborhoods (despite a law requiring them to do so) gave rise to so-called gypsy cabs serving these areas. In the 1970s there were approximately 13,000 gypsy cabdrivers. Limousine services offering transportation to the airports and in outlying neighborhoods grew in number. A 1992 Taxi and Limousine Commission survey found that among applicants for licenses, there were 42.8 percent from South Asia, 11.2 percent from Africa, 7.6 percent from the Caribbean, 7 percent from the Middle East, and 6.8 percent from Russia while 10.5 had been born in the United States. Pakistanis, who already spoke English, accounted for the high percentage from South Asia.

A TAXI DRIVER SPEAKS OUT

"Out of towners are cheap. Here in New York City you have an awful lot of people working on tips. The cab drivers, the waiters, the porters, the doormen—all working on tips. If they don't get a tip they don't go home with a good salary. Hey and when a person's got a family to support and a person doesn't tip him it hurts. And the thing is these out of towners are so used to where they live they don't tip. Or if they do put a tip they undertip the people.

"Only the blue collar workers overtip. They're the best tippers around. No matter what nationality they are. Women on the other hand are split half and half. . . .

"When it comes to people who live on Fifth Avenue, Eastend Avenue, Park Avenue, and Westend Avenue—let's be prac-

tical about it. They've got a doorman to tip, any nightclub they walk into there's always someone putting their hands out. How much could they tip? What I don't like about them is that the guy that opens the door for them, they hand him a buck and the cab driver—all they hand him is a quarter. This gets me. I did more of a service than the guy that just walked over and opened the door for them. That's the only thing I got against those people. In my opinion they overtip the wrong people."

CHARLES VIDICH, *THE NEW YORK CAB DRIVER AND HIS FARE*

1. Cabdrivers at the Brooklyn entrance of the Brooklyn-Battery Tunnel, 1989; NYDN. Three thousand of them are on their way to Manhattan to protest a fifteen-cent fare increase, which they consider insufficient to cover higher fuel costs.
2. Owner-driver Lobal Rathour with one of the few remaining Checker cabs, 1982; CB.
3. Driver Kevin Clement waiting on East Forty-first Street for someone to repair his flat, 1987; NYDN. Most fleet cabs don't carry spares because they cut down on trunk space.

1.

Kennedy and Wagner Campaigning

After his brother's assassination, U.S. Attorney General Robert Kennedy resigned from office and in 1964 moved to an apartment at United Nations Plaza. Although he had not lived in New York City since 1929, he launched a campaign for the U.S. Senate and was elected that year. In March 1968 he entered the race for the Democratic presidential nomination. He was assassinated while campaigning in California,

Robert F. Wagner, son of the Democratic U.S. Senator with the same name, served three terms as mayor of New York City. Elected for the first time in 1953, he prided himself in representing interests of the common man and appointed blacks and Puerto Ricans to senior municipal positions.

1. Democratic senatorial candidate Robert Kennedy with Mayor Robert F. Wagner, Jr., campaigning in Little Italy, 1964; CB.
2. Republican gubernatorial candidate Nelson Rockefeller campaigning for his first term in lower Manhattan, 1958; CB. In his entourage were senatorial candidate Kenneth Keating, candidate for lieutenant governor Malcolm Wilson, candidate for attorney general Louis Lefkowitz and candidate for comptroller James Lundy.
3. Representative Herman Badillo campaigning in his district, 1976; CB.

2.

3.

Rockefeller and Badillo Campaigning

Following an active career in the federal government under both Democratic and Republican presidents, Nelson Rockefeller ran for governor of New York in 1958 on the Republican ticket and was elected. A popular governor, he was reelected three times. As a leader of the moderate wing of the Republican party, he launched several unsuccessful campaigns for the presidency. In 1974 he became President Gerald Ford's vice president.

In 1966 Democrat Herman Badillo became the first Puerto Rican borough president of the Bronx, and in 1971 he was elected to the U.S. House of Representatives. He ran unsuccessfully for mayor twice and later became a deputy mayor.

1.

2.

A Population of One Million Jews

By 1996 the number of Jews in New York City had declined to 1,048,900, with 379,000 in Brooklyn, 314,500 in Manhattan, 83,700 in the Bronx, 238,000 in Queens, and 33,700 on Staten Island. While fewer in New York City, they account for 1,420,000 in the metropolitan area. A considerable number moved to the suburbs in the fifties; now there are 203,000 in Nassau, 98,000 in Suffolk, and 92,000 in Westchester counties. There are those who say that Jews have been completely assimilated into American society and that anti-Semitism no longer exists; however, the Anti-Defamation League still records numerous incidents of blatant anti-Semitism. Tombstones have been desecrated and synagogues burned. Even before the dissolution of the Soviet Union tens of thousands of Soviet Jews

transformed Brooklyn's Brighton Beach into their own colony. Some Jews say that intermarriage means an end to the Jewish community while others see it in more positive terms. There are those who believe that a return to Orthodoxy is the only solution, and there are those who see the need for more liberalism. There is no unanimity; however, there is cohesion, a sense of every individual's belonging to a larger entity.

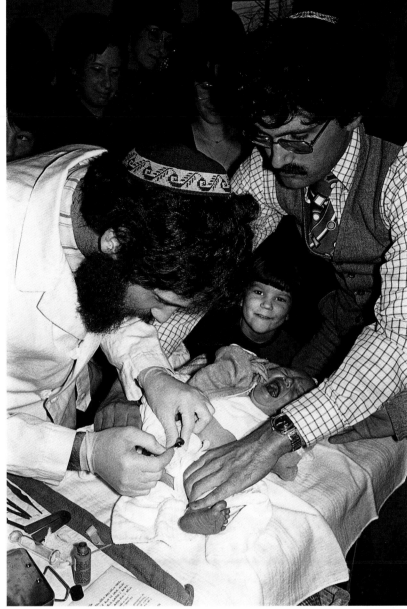

ON BEING JEWISH

"As a child growing up on Manhattan's East Side, I lived among Jewish WASPs. My father, an only child, had changed his name from Cohen to Cowan when he was twenty-one. He was so guarded about his youth that he never let my brother or sisters or me meet any of his father's relatives. I always thought of myself as a Cowan—the Welsh word for stonecutter—not a Cohen—a member of the Jewish priestly caste. My family celebrated Christmas and always gathered for an Easter dinner of ham and sweet potatoes. . . . I barely knew what a Passover seder was. I didn't know anyone who practiced archaic customs such as keeping kosher or lighting candles on Friday night. Neither my parents nor I ever mentioned the possibility of a bar mitzvah. In

1965, I fell in love with Rachel Brown, a New England Protestant whose ancestors came here in the seventeenth century. It didn't matter the least bit to her—or to me—that we were an interfaith marriage.

"Now, at forty-two, I care more about Jewish holidays I'd never heard of back then. . . . In 1980, fifteen years after we were married, Rachel converted to Judaism, and is now program director of Ansche Chesed, a neighborhood synagogue we are trying to revitalize. Our family lights Friday night candles and neither Rachel nor I work [sic] on the Sabbath. . . . I am not alone. Indeed, I believe my story. . . . is the story of much of my generation, Jew and gentile alike."

PAUL COWAN, *AN ORPHAN IN HISTORY*

1. Demonstration at the United Nations to oppose resolution equating Zionism with racism, 1979; photograph by Leonard Freed, MAGNUM.
2. Reunion of members of the Staroselsky family, Soviet émigrés, at Kennedy International Airport, 1990; NEW.
3. Bat miztvah, 1980; photograph by Bill Aron. This ceremony, an adaptation of the bar mitzvah for boys, is performed for girls when they reach the age of twelve.
4. Wedding, 1979; photograph by Bill Aron. Richard Siegel, one of the authors of The First Jewish Catalog, is swept up in dancing at this wedding.
5. Bris, 1977; photograph by Bill Aron. The traditional circumcision takes place eight days after Jewish boys are born.

353

1.

The Hasidic Jews of Brooklyn

Because the men dress with black hats and flowing black coats suggesting a bygone era, the Hasidim, a branch of Orthodox Jewry, are one of the most easily identifiable religious groups to be seen in New York. With Eastern European origins, there are two principal Hasidic groups based in Brooklyn, the Lubavitcher of Polish origin found in Crown Heights, and the Satmar from Hungary, in Williamsburg. The word hasidim means "disciples" and both these groups have a religious leader called a rebbe or rabbi. A Hasid can be a disciple of God only through the mediation of his rebbe. The Lubavitcher Hasidim are considered the more liberal of the two; they actively recruit disciples and can be seen beside their vans parked at curbside, passing out literature in various parts of the city. The Satmar rebbe

Joel Teitelbaum's followers have a more conservative approach. They prefer to create an enclave of Jews completely insulated from the twentieth century. They do not permit any secular education or any contact with other Jews.

The Lubavitcher Jews believe that America is fertile ground for their movement's desire to convert more Jews to Hasidism. The late Lubavitcher rebbe Menachem Mendel Schneerson had a regular cable TV program.

With headquarters in Brooklyn, both groups have an estimated one hundred thousand followers in New York and more throughout the country.

1. *Followers of the Lubavitcher rebbe Menachem Mendel Schneerson listening to their spiritual leader, 1976; photograph by Leonard Freed, MAGNUM.*
2. *Hasidic students on the steps of their yeshiva (school), 1975; photograph by Leonard Freed, MAGNUM.*
3. *School bus with Hasidic children, 1975; photograph by Leonard Freed, MAGNUM.*
4. *Children from a Hasidic school in a Brooklyn park, 1975; photograph by Leonard Freed, MAGNUM.*

THE REBBE SPEAKS

"The Jewish people began with one family, that of our father Avraham, and ever since then the Jewish family has been the foundation of our people. In the family, too, each member is a separate individual, with a particular function and purpose in life assigned to him and her by Hashgocho Protis. Unless there is unity in the family, there can be no unity of the Jewish people. How is family unity achieved? In the same way as mentioned above: When all members of the family accept the *One Torah* from *One G-d* in such a way that the Torah and Mitzvos are the only essential thing, and all other things are merely secondary, and have a significance only insofar as they are related to the essence—then there is true unity in the family.

"In attaining this family unity—bearing in mind also that Jewish families are the component parts of the Jewish people, hence the basis of the unity of Klal Yisroel, as mentioned above—the Jewish mother and daughter have a most important part, being the *Akeres haBayis*, as has been underscored on previous occasions.

"Needless to say, the said unity must be a constant one, without interruptions; this is to say, it must be expressed not only on certain days of the year, on certain hours of the day, but in every day of the year and in every hour of the day."
MENACHEM MENDEL SCHNEERSON, BROOKLYN, 1971

1.

A Population of Seven Hundred Thousand Italians

In 1990 there were about 700,000 Italian-Americans living in New York City, nearly 10 percent of the total population, Brooklyn has the largest number of Italian residents; Manhattan the least. The Bronx, Queens, and Staten Island all have sizeable Italian-American communities. Like Jews, a considerable number of second- and third-generation Italians moved to the suburbs of Long Island, Westchester, and New Jersey. Manhattan's Little Italy remains an echo of the old immigrant neighborhoods with Mulberry Street's door-to-door restaurants and a few residents. Italians now account for only 10 percent of the area's population; Chinese are 51 percent, and Latinos make up the rest. For seven days every September, Mulberry Street becomes a throbbing sea of food and amusement vendors for the

Feast of San Gennaro. Turn-of-the-century immigrants who could afford to abandon Manhattan's first settlement, Little Italy, moved uptown to East Harlem and Arthur Avenue in the Bronx. In 1930 there were 27,500 in the Arthur Avenue area. Like Mulberry Street today, it has clusters of restaurants and shops with few residents. Brooklyn's Bensonhurst boasts New York's largest concentration of Italians. First- and second-generation families have made Eighteenth Avenue, lined with food stores, meat markets, cafés, bakeries, and pizza parlors, a nostalgic reminiscence of ethnic New York in the thirties and forties. Smaller enclaves like Carroll Gardens in Brooklyn are a reminder of the sizable Red Hook Italian settlement. In the 1890s, Italians began to move to Corona, Queens,

2.

where they built one- and two-family houses surrounded by gardens. They first moved to Staten Island's Rosebank in the 1880s. Newer, more suburban neighborhoods have evolved from the earlier ones. In Rosebank is the Garibaldi-Meucci Memorial Museum dedicated to the liberator of Italy, Giuseppe Garibaldi. While in exile, Garibaldi came to Staten Island in 1850 and lived there intermittently for three years with Antonio Meucci, the disputed inventor of the telephone.

1. Neighbors, Bensonhurst, Brooklyn, 1986; photograph by Ethel Wolvovitz.
2. Friends: Michael Farella on left, John Polzella on right (unidentified man in center), Arthur Avenue, Bronx, 1986; photograph by Ethel Wovlovitz.

1.

"One Percent of One Percent"

The Mafia is the stigma of all Italian-Americans. No matter who they are or where they come from, America's fascination with the Mafia hangs over their heads. The Mafia does exist; however, there are serious questions to be raised by the exaggerated, often officially endorsed view that one ethnic group, the Italian-Americans, is fully responsible for every event associated with organized crime in the United States. In 1987 the crime-fighting U.S. Attorney Rudolph Giuliani said, "My father was the first one to tell me that the Mafia existed and that I should not be ashamed of it. It is a very small percentage of the Italian-Americans, less than one percent of one percent."

KILLERS

"Murder was the only way everybody stayed in line. It was the ultimate weapon. Nobody was immune. You got out of line, you got whacked. Everybody knew the rules, but still people got out of line and people kept getting whacked. . . . It didn't take anything for these guys to kill you. They liked it. They would sit around drinking booze and talk about their favorite hits. . . . They liked to relive the moment while repeating how miserable the guy was. . . . Guys would get into arguments with each other and before you knew it one of them was dead. They were shooting each other all the time. Shooting people was a normal thing for them. It was no big deal."

NICHOLAS PILEGGI, *WISE GUY*

2.

THE ORIGIN OF THE WORD "MAFIA"
"Not all the societies clung to or cherished by the immigrants had American roots. Some were brought with the immigrants. Among all the societies or associations brought over to or created in nineteenth-century America, the most infamous, most mythologized and most onerous for Italian Americans then and now is whatever is meant by 'the Mafia.'

"More nonsense continues to be written about this alleged secret society than about any other group. Immense anguish has been caused to millions of upright and honorable Americans with Italian heritage and surnames by the myths, stereotypes and assumptions concerning the Mafia and 'organized crime.' Otherwise sensible and savvy Americans with Italian surnames have

allowed themselves to look foolish denying the existence of American gangsters with Italian surnames (they exist) or denying that criminal organizations exist, among others, that are dominated or controlled by such gangsters. . . .

"There is evidence for the existence and meaning of the words *mafia* and *mafiusu*, and this evidence is found in the extraordinary work of the pioneer and founder of the study of folklore in Italy, Giuseppe Pitré. . . . Pitré devotes a substantial essay to the meaning of mafia and allied concepts including *omertà*, the code of secrecy and self-reliance that bound the poor together in their common abhorrence of civil authority."
A. BARTLETT GIAMATTI, INTRODUCTION TO
ALLON SCHOENER, *THE ITALIAN AMERICANS*

1. Funeral of reputed Brooklyn Mafia boss Joe Gallo, 1972; CB. His wife and daughter can be seen in the background.
2. The body of reputed Mafia boss Carmine Galente being removed from Joe and Mary's restaurant in Brooklyn, where he and an associate, Nino Capella, were shot, 1979; CB.

1.

Italian Festivals

Cities in Italy have religious festivals dedicated to their patron saints. Many of these festivals involve not only celebrations of food, music, and dancing but feats of incredible endurance restricted to men. When the tide of Italian immigrants from southern Italy and Sicily landed in New York at the turn of the century, they brought their saints and festivals with them. Many of these festivals persist and have become the reason for younger generations to return to the neighborhoods of their parents and grandparents, where an Italian parish remains as a symbol of the past.

The Feast of San Gennaro, celebrating the patron saint of Naples, occupies Mulberry Street in Manhattan's Little Italy every September. The Feast of St. Anthony on Sullivan Street is a reminder of the once-flourishing Italian community in Greenwich Village. The Feast of Our Lady of Mount Carmel is celebrated between July 6 and 17 in three neighborhoods: East Harlem, Little Italy, and the Bronx. The Feast of St. Rosalia takes place in Bensonhurst at the end of August. Williamsburg's feast dedicated to Our Lady of Mount Carmel and St. Paulinus occurs in July. St. Paulinus, the bishop of Nola, is commemorated with a huge tower, the *giglio*, carried a short distance through the streets of Williamsburg. The tradition of carrying the *giglio* is "dedicated to the sacred penance for those souls in purgatory and the remission of sins of the living."

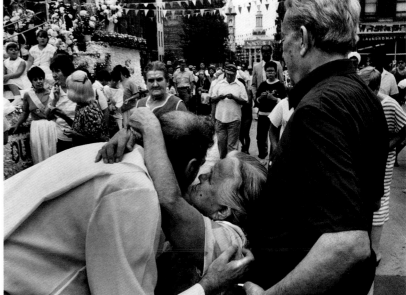

1. Carrying the statue of St. Anthony, Feast of St. Anthony, the Bronx, 1995; photograph by Ethel Wolvovitz.

2. Training for the giglio, Williamsburg, 1986; photograph by Ethel Wolvovitz. The five-story giglio is seen in the background. Only adult males lift this statue; however, boys participate in training sessions, lifting a much smaller statue.

3. Celebrating after the giglio lift has been completed and the statue has been carried its prescribed distance, Williamsburg, 1986; photograph by Ethel Wolvovitz.

4. Elderly woman embracing a priest, Our Lady of Mount Carmel Festival, East 116th Street, Manhattan, 1986; photograph by Ethel Wolvovitz.

1.

Gays and Lesbians

To be gay or lesbian before the late 1960s required maintaining a double life. New York had a history of gay and lesbian communities that centered at the turn of the century on the Bowery, later at Greenwich Village bars, and during Prohibition in Harlem jazz clubs and speakeaseys. Gay black social clubs organized some of the city's largest drag (transvestite) balls in Harlem at the Savoy Ballroom and Rockland Palace. A subculture known mostly to members, it expanded to other parts of the city: East Side, West Side, Times Square, Brooklyn Heights, and Jackson Heights in Queens.

As the gay community expanded, it found itself under attack by the police, politicians, and governmental agencies. During the 1950s men were often arrested on the charge of "homosexual activity." There was

a definite sense of harassment that could have been both spontaneous and organized. Although the police continued to raid gay bars, their June 1969 raid on the Stonewall Inn, on Christopher Street in Greenwich Village, backfired and turned into a riot.

From this point on the gay and lesbian movement gained momentum. Gays and lesbians marched openly at public demonstrations. The New York City Lesbian and Gay Community Services Center on West Thirteenth Street in Greenwich Village opened in 1984.

A gay rights bill was finally passed in 1986. Although the gay community seemed to have won one battle, it started to lose another, AIDS. Again activists began to demonstrate and petition to gain support and develop knowledge and understanding

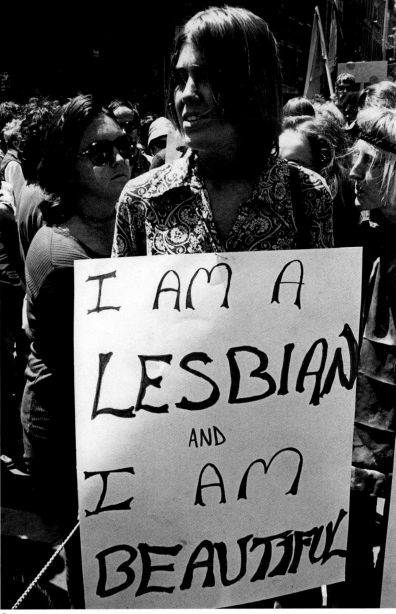

of the disease. The AIDS crisis continues to haunt all members of the gay community.

Like gay men, lesbian women had always been on the New York scene. During its heyday, liberal, experimental Greenwich Village provided a haven for lesbians. In the twenties black lesbians to be found in Harlem clubs and at rent parties. By the 1950s bars openly catering to a lesbian clientele proliferated in Greenwich Village. Like gay men, lesbian women were subject to police harassment. There were police raids on lesbian bars, and the Women's House of Detention at Sixth Avenue and Eighth Street became the symbol of women arrested on "morals charges." (An embarassment to city officials, it was closed in the 1970s.) What might have been the last police raid on a lesbian club occurred in

1964. Forty-three women were arrested at Mary Angela's on Seventh Avenue South in the Village. The judge dismissed the case when the arresting detective could not identify the women who had allegedly been dancing together. In the wake of the 1969 incident at the Stonewall Inn, lesbians also began to organize and to develop both political and economic support for their cause.

1. Gay rights demonstration, 1979; photograph by Harvey Stein.
2. Gay rights demonstration on the steps of St. Patrick's Cathedral, 1979; photograph by Harvey Stein.
3. Lesbian rights demonstration, about 1979; photograph by Harvey Stein.

1.

Celebrating Thanksgiving and Christmas

Since the Macy's Thanksgiving Day parade became a television staple, for three hours on this holiday morning, New York's image is burnished with "family values." For most people outside New York, their view of the city as violent, cruel, and dangerous is conditioned by the endless number of cop shows using the city as a backdrop. But on Thanksgiving Day, Broadway becomes Main Street America with New Yorkers serving as smiling, innocent hosts.

For New Yorkers themselves, it is another experience. Those who want to brave the rain and cold go bundled up with their kids. On a warm day, there are fewer hassles. Then there are those who know someone who has an apartment or office along the parade route; they can watch it with detachment as their kids run loose.

The parade of sixteen to eighteen floats has a history. In 1925 a Santa Claus float was accompanied by twenty-five female Macy's employees dressed in fur-trimmed parkas as snow babies. The 1955 parade featured the world's largest birthday cake on the Birthday to Tootsieland float; it had a large candle resembling a giant Tootsie Roll with real flames sprouting from an orifice fueled by an acetylene torch. Every year some new floats catering to contemporary tastes are added and old ones are retired. In the 1980s the parades featured the Cabbage Patch Kids float, the Rainbow Brite float, the Care Bears float, the Masters of the Universe float, the Statue of Liberty float, and the Disney Celebration float.

Built in Hoboken, New Jersey, of papier-mâché and coated with fiberglass to protect

2.

it from the elements, the average float lasts two years. To get the floats through the Lincoln Tunnel, they are designed with folding components that can be reduced to the height and width of the tunnel. On Thanksgiving Day one tube of the Lincoln Tunnel is closed at 1:00 A.M. for the exclusive use of the float convoy. It moves to an assembly point on the Upper West Side where the balloons are inflated. Later the floats are joined by high school bands from all across the country, and by celebrities who have included Sid Caesar, Imogene Coca, Eddie Fisher, Benny Goodman, Bob Hope, Danny Kaye, Groucho Marx, Ginger Rogers, and the Radio City Music Hall Rockettes. At 9:00 A.M. the parade begins and moves downtown along Broadway, arriving at Thirty-fourth Street about two hours later.

1. The 68th Annual Thanksgiving Day Parade with the Cat in the Hat and Woody Woodpecker balloons, 1994; WW. This was the first appearance for the Dr. Seuss character and the thirteenth for Woody. An estimated audience of forty-eight million watched it on television.
2. Santas in Times Square, 1977; photograph by Harvey Stein.

Mermaid Parade and Wigstock

New York is festival city. During every month of the year, in every borough, there are ethnic, religious, and American holiday celebrations that range from parades and marches to boat flotillas and fireworks. The streets, the rivers, the harbors, and the sky are animated because of people's desire to celebrate whatever seems to be important to a particular group.

Although planned by and for New York City residents, these festivals attract people from surrounding regions and distant locations. Because they can't experience the kind of street theater that is so much a part of New York life, nonresidents come to New York to be part of a crowd with which they can identify.

1. Mermaid Parade at Coney Island, 1996; photograph by Ethel Wolvovitz. An event originated by artists who wanted to celebrate Coney Island and ocean mythology. Groups in fanciful costumes of mermaids and other sea creatures fill the streets every June.
2. Wigstock, 1996; photograph by Ethel Wolvovitz. An annual Labor Day weekend event taking place in the heart of the gay community on Christopher Street and other locations like Tompkins Square Park in Manhattan, Wigstock is specifically designed for men in drag. Wearing a wig is essential for participation.

1.

3.

2.

4.

West Indian Carnival, Virgin of Guadalupe, Steuben Day, and Greek Independence Day

1. West Indian Day Carnival, Eastern Parkway, Brooklyn, 1991; photograph by Eli Reed, MAGNUM. Scheduled on Labor Day with a hundred steel drum bands and costumed dancers, it is estimated to attract three million people. This is New York's most popular festival.

2. Virgin of Guadalupe Festival, 1988; BHS. Sponsored by All Saints Catholic Church on Throop Street in the Williamsburg section of Brooklyn. As evidence of the increased size of the Mexican community, the miraculous appearance of this saint is celebrated here as it is in Mexico.

3. A gaggle of geese for the Steuben Day parade on Fifth Avenue, 1985; NYDN. Some forty thousand Americans of German descent participated in this event.

4. Greek Independence Day parade on Fifth Avenue, 1988; NEWS. Commemorating Greek independence from Turkish occupation in 1831, this parade brings together some two hundred Greek-American civic, political, and religious organizations.

1.

2.

The Newest Immigrants

REMAKING THE CITY

"Today, 'new immigrants' are once more transforming the city's population, its neighborhoods and the fabric of urban life. Since the removal of restrictive quotas from the national immigration laws in 1965, steady increases in the number of legally admitted immigrants have enabled nearly 900,000 immigrants, most from the Caribbean, Latin America and Asia to gain permanent status in the U.S. each year. One-fourth of these 'new immigrants' entered the U.S. through New York City and one-sixth chose to reside here. Like their predecessors a century ago, they too are redefining what it means to be a New Yorker and an American.

"Since 1965, well over two million new immigrants have settled in the city, includ-ing one million during the decade of the 1980's alone. These new New Yorkers have reversed the decades-long decline in the city's population and have strongly affected the city's neighborhoods, cultural fabric and economy. According to the 1990 Census, almost thirty percent of the city's population was foreign-born, a ratio beginning to approach the turn of the century (40 percent). Indeed, if we count island-born Puerto Ricans, who are U.S. citizens, as immigrants from a non-English-speaking culture, today's figure would be even closer to that of the turn of the century.

"As it did a century ago, New York thus serves as a living experiment on how other cities and the nation will respond to its new residents. How New York City includes its new immigrants in its economic, cultural and

3.

political fabric will determine whether the city will make as much progress between now and 2020 as it did between 1890 and the 1930's when the previous immigrant generation—and indeed the city itself—came of economic, cultural and political age."
JOHN MOLLENKOFF, NEW NEW YORKERS EXHIBITION, MUNICIPAL ART SOCIETY, 1993

1. Part of the long line outside the Immigration and Naturalization Service office at 26 Federal Plaza, in lower Manhattan, where these immigrants have gone to replace their green cards, 1993; NEW.
2. Illegal aliens being processed at the Immigration and Naturalization office at Seventh Avenue and Twenty-fourth Street in Manhattan, NEW.
3. Being sworn in as American citizens, 1991; NEW.

1.

Latinos and Latinas

New York's Latino population, including people from Puerto Rico, Colombia, Mexico, Brazil, Cuba, Peru, El Salvador, Ecuador, and other countries in Latin America, Central America, and the Caribbean, increased by 135.5 percent between 1960 (757,231) and 1990 (1,783,511).

Today Puerto Ricans remain the largest Spanish-speaking people. Following them are immigrants from the Dominican Republic. Although statisticians might group them together, they view themselves as separate and distinct nationalities.

Since the turn of the century there has been a Puerto Rican presence in New York. By 1930 Puerto Ricans accounted for 40.7 percent of the Latino population of 110,223. In the wake of the mass exodus from the island between 1945 and 1970, the Puerto

Rican population grew to 811,843. As a result of their considerable numbers, Puerto Ricans built a political base in the Democratic party and found jobs in the city bureaucracy. As early as 1959 people from Cuba, the Dominican Republic, Colombia, Ecuador, Peru, and other countries in Central and South America began arriving. Political refugees fleeing Castro's regime were the first large group. Dominicans started to come in sizable numbers after their 1965 civil war. Then Colombians, Ecuadorans, Peruvians, Salvadorans, and others came in substantial numbers. In contrast with the Puerto Ricans, who arrived earlier, the new Latino immigrants were generally urban and educated, had more skills, and came from middle-class business or professional backgrounds. The proportion

2.

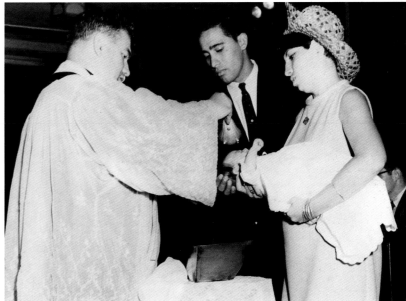

4.

3.

5.

of people with middle class backgrounds varied from country to country. Immigrants from Cuba, Argentina, Chile, and Uruguay tended to be more middle class than the Colombians, Dominicans, Hondurans, or Mexicans. Geographically their neighborhoods are widespread: Dominicans are in Manhattan's Upper West Side and Washington Heights and Cubans in Astoria and Elmhurst in Queens. Colombians, Ecuadorans, Peruvians, and groups from other countries established themselves in a number of Queens neighborhoods: Jackson Heights, Woodside, Elmhurst, East Elmhurst, and Corona. The newest arrivals, the Mexicans, have enclaves in Brooklyn and Manhattan's Lower East Side.

Among the prominent elected Latino officials are Bronx Borough President Fernando Ferrer, Bronx Congressman Jose Serrano, Nydia Velasquez representing sections of the Lower East Side, Brooklyn, and Queens in Congress, City Councilman Guillermo Linares representing Washington Heights, and former City Councilman Antonio Pagan.

1. Celebrating Mexican Independence Day in Van Cortlandt Park, 1991; NEW.
2. Beauty queens, about 1980; CEP. Three separate queens, representing Latin Americans, Cuban-Americans, and Mexican Americans, were designated at this event. The need to have three separate queens illustrates that Latinos do not view themselves as a monolithic community.
3. Puerto Rican Day Parade, Lexington Avenue and East Eighty-sixth Street, 1980; photograph by Charles Gatewood.
4. Baptism, about 1960; CEP. The Catholic Church maintains a continuing influence in the Latino community.
5. Botanica, Sunset Park, Brooklyn, 1989; BHS.

371

1.

2.

New New Yorkers

New York is a cauldron that has been nourished by successive waves of immigration. According to the 1990 census, people of color have for the first time become the majority of New York's population: Non-Latino blacks make up 25.2 percent, Latino groups are 24.4 percent, Asians 6.7 percent and whites (including foreign-born non-Latino whites) 43.7 percent. Demographic projections indicate that the growth of New York's nonwhite and Latino population will continue to accelerate.

WHERE NEW IMMIGRANTS LIVE

"Irish immigrants are concentrated in the white ethnic parts of the Northern Bronx, West Central Queens and Southwest Brooklyn. According to the 1990 Census, there were 10,710 post-1965 Irish immigrants in New York City.

"Indians live widely dispersed in what is called Asian Queens and are not highly concentrated in ethnic enclaves as some other groups tend to do. According to the 1990 Census, there were 41,734 Post-1965 Indian immigrants in the city.

"Haitians are a relatively small group in New York's new immigrant complex. According to the 1990 Census, there were 66,178 post-1965 Haitian immigrants. They have settled along the western edge of Flatbush in Brooklyn, Southeastern Queens

3.

5.

4.

6.

and on The Upper West Side of Manhattan.

"Although dispersed throughout the city, Korean concentrations can be found in Flushing, Elmhurst and Bayside Queens. According to the 1990 Census, there were 56,308 post-1965 Korean immigrants living in New York City.

"Chinese immigrants reside in the Chinatown area of Manhattan, Sunset Park in Brooklyn and the Elmhurst and Flushing sections of Queens. According to the 1990 census, there were 100,535 post-1965 immigrants from mainland China."

JOHN MOLLENKOPF, NEW NEW YORKERS EXHIBITION, MUNIPICAL ART SOCIETY, 1993

1. The Keane family of Bellerose, Queens, 1993, photograph by Linda Rosier. Holding green cards, James and Theresa Keane describe themselves as "Irish residents in the U.S.A."

2. Mrs. Kusam Mohan, standing in front of the newly restored Hindu temple in Flushing, Queens, 1979; NEW.

3. Marie Lily Cerat and her daughter Taina of Flatbush, Brooklyn, demonstrating for Haitian independence, 1993; photograph by Donna De Cesare.

4. Koreans Dong Koo Lee and his wife, Hyun Sook Lee, inside their fruit and vegetable market on Second Avenue in Manhattan, 1990; NEW.

5. Mrs. Yee with her daughter, working in a Chinese-operated clothing factory in Sunset

Park, Brooklyn, 1993; photograph by Ethel Wolvovitz.

6. Both the proprietor and his friend standing behind the counter at the Oriental Pastry and Grocery on Atlantic Avenue, Brooklyn, are Syrians, 1986; NEW. There was a dramatic increase in the size of the Arab community in the post-1965 immigration period. Although still concentrated in their old neighborhoods like Atlantic Avenue in Brooklyn, they have moved into Sunset Park and Bay Ridge in Brooklyn and Astoria in Queens.

373

1.

Ethnic Food

Among New Yorkers the appellation "ethnic food" hardly means anything special because everyday food has become ethnic. There was a time when bagels were Jewish and burritos were Mexican. No longer! Everyone's food has become everyone else's food. New Yorkers can eat knishes and empanadas at the same meal without thinking that there is anything unusual about it.

With more than 150 nationalities residing in New York, there are at least that many cuisines. Such food can be found on the street, in cafés, and in restaurants. Food is the one piece of cultural baggage most easily transported; wherever new immigrants decide to settle, restaurants, bakeries, and food stores crop up to define their turf and the ethnicity of the area. They provide new immigrants with the familiar foods from

homelands, making New York seem less foreign to them. This is an oft-repeated story. Perhaps it began with the Dutch and British because they had to cook something and did not get all their food ideas from the Native Americans. However strong their legacy may be in many areas, food is not one of them.

Ethnic food appeared in New York when the Chinese, Greeks, Italians, and Jews began arriving in the late nineteenth century. Street food, principally the territory of the Greeks, Jews, and Italians, was a companion to tenement life. Over the ensuing decades, street food became a New York staple. Whenever ethnic groups have street fairs and festivals, there is a legion of ethnic food vendors who belong to the particular celebrating group. They offer hot dogs,

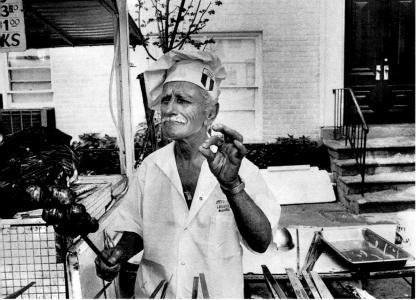

knishes, felafel, pizza, calzone, zeppole, sausage and onions, heroes, burritos, empanadas, tacos, cuchifritos, jerk chicken, chicken satay, fried rice, gyros, and kebabs, and the list goes on. Their annual convention is the mid-May Ninth Avenue International Festival of Food. Stretching from Thirty-seventh Street to Fifty-seventh Street, it attracts a half million people.

1. *Ninth Avenue International Festival of Food, 1979; photograph by Harvey Stein.*
2. *Nathan's Famous, Coney Island, Brooklyn, 1966; CB. Founded in 1916 by Nathan Handwerker, it has become a Brooklyn icon. Nathan's is the world's largest hot dog stand. In 1991 it served more than one million hot dogs.*
3. *Italian food vendor, 1987; photograph by Ethel Wolvovitz, EW.*
4. *Shopkeeper Arun Chettiar in his Indian food store, Elmhurst, Queens, 1990; NEW.*

1.

2.

The Streets and Sidewalks of New York

In America, where the automobile dominates the landscape, New York is an anomaly; it's a pedestrians' city. People walk of necessity more than desire. They walk to and from the subway, to and from their homes and offices, to and from stores, and to and from their cars if they can afford to own or rent them. They even develop calluses on the soles of their feet from walking so much. Zero Mostel once complained: "After a week in the country, my feet hurt from walking on the grass."

The streets belong to taxis, cars, buses, trucks, and bicycles. They never belong to pedestrians. The streets and sidewalks of New York are an urban theater where one sees everything: affection, beauty, wealth, poverty, joy, stress, youth, aging, work, play, and mostly diversity. There is no other place in the world where one sees so many different types of people wearing stylish, ordinary, conservative, and outlandish clothes representing a broad spectrum of ethnic groups and economic strata. They mix but never blend.

1. *Essex Street, Lower East Side, 1990; photograph by Bruce Davidson, MAGNUM.*
2. *All dressed up, Harlem, 1977; photograph by Anthony Barboza.*
3. *Hoops, Brooklyn, 1996; photograph by Martin Dixon.*
4. *On upper Broadway, 1973; photograph by Harvey Stein.*
5. *Bicycle messenger, 1994; photograph by Bill Cunningham, FG.*

1.

The West Village

Basking in the tradition of America's first bohemia, the West Village (Greenwich Village) retains the aura of a bygone era on its side streets lined with handsome nineteenth-century three- and four-story brownstones, many of which retain outdoor staircases and spacious backyards. It is residential on the cross streets, teeming with traffic on the avenues, and all over dotted with cozy restaurants and fascinating shops.

Although it encompasses the campuses of New York University and the New School, the Village no longer is the exclusive domain of artists, intellectuals and literati. With colonies in SoHo, TriBeCa, the Upper West Side, the East Village, Brooklyn Heights, and Park Slope, they are dispersed throughout the city. In the evening and on weekends, it's a different place. It is crowded with tourists and partygoers, few of whom live in the Village.

The East Village

The East Village used to be called the Lower East Side and sometimes still is. In the 1960s hippies, artists, poets, and intellectuals began to move into the area primarily because it was one of the least inexpensive neighborhoods in Manhattan. They changed its name to the East Village. Low-income people continued to surround the newcomers, who supported bookstores, theaters, film centers, bars, and restaurants throughout the area. Perhaps fashionable, with the appeal of grunge, the East Village became a mythical magnet for America's rebellious youth. Recently it has become more gentrified, attracting a contingent of young professionals who have contributed to another revitalization of the neighborhood.

1. The dance floor at Life, a club on Bleecker Street, 1997; photograph by Nancy Siesel, NYT. With a capacity of eleven hundred, this club attracts a primarily young, affluent crowd.
2. 3. 4. 5. Portraits taken with the facade of Cooper Union in the background, 1997; all photographs by Matt Harnett.

379

1.

A Turbulent Town: Riots, Demonstrations, and Fires

Life in New York is never calm. It is a city of tensions and calamities. One of the most fractious events in recent history pitted the Brooklyn African-American and Crown Heights Hasidic Jewish communities against each other. In August 1991, with a long history that has fluctuated between effective black-Jewish cooperation and bitter conflict, the two groups, the black mayor, and the police found themselves locked in a no-win situation. Gavin Cato, a seven-year-old black from Guyana, was killed by a car driven by a Hasidic Jew. Shortly after the accident Yankel Rosenbaum, a twenty-nine-year-old Hasidic Jewish seminary student from Australia, was stabbed and died of his wounds. Blacks and Jews took to the streets of Crown Heights screaming and taunting each other, throwing rocks, bottles, and insults.

Crown Heights became a virtual war zone. In the midst of this, the police were accused of showing favoritism toward the Hasidic Jews and the mayor was accused of inaction. A seventeen-year-old black high school student, Lemerick Nelson, Jr., was charged with Rosenbaum's murder; he was tried and found not guilty. Another Hasidic Jew, Jusef Litah, admitted that he had driven the car; he was later acquitted of homicide by a Brooklyn grand jury. Nelson was retried in a federal court and found guilty. Tensions between the two groups persist.

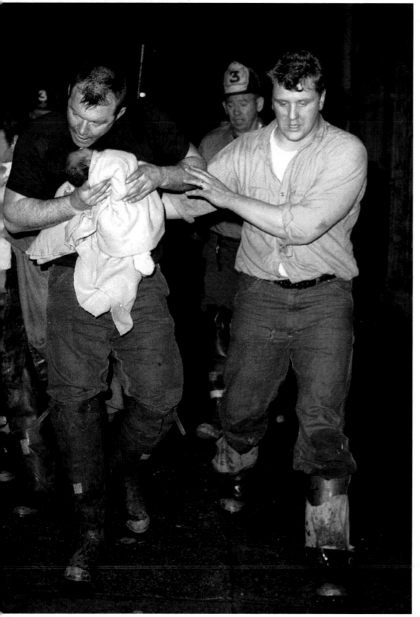

1. Led by Reverend Al Sharpton and flanked by police, black protesters march down Eastern Parkway in the heart of the Crown Heights Hasidic Jewish community, 1991; photograph by Keith Meyers, NYT.
2. Saving the baby, 1982; NYDN. Firemen are providing mouth-to-mouth resuscitation.
3. A demonstrator who refused to stop blocking traffic is being removed, 1978; photograph by Leonard Freed, MAGNUM.
4. The police line breaks up after the passing by of a foreign dignitary, 1978; photograph by Leonard Freed, MAGNUM.

It's a tough job being a police officer or a firefighter in New York; however, there are many men and women who dedicate themselves to the task. In fact, there are families whose members have been on the police force or in the fire department for generations. In 1996 there were 37,745 members of the police, 5,655 of whom were women, 5,138 African-Americans, 6,405 Latinos, and 509 Asians. In 1997 there were 11,033 firefighters, 38 of whom were women, operating from 222 firehouses. Being a police officer or firefighter is a dangerous occupation. In 1996 six police officers died in the line of duty. Between 1994 and 1997, eleven firefighters died in action.

Community attitudes toward the police, who are charged with maintaining public order, have fluctuated from positive to negative. When the crime rate drops, they are held in high esteem. Both corruption and brutality are issues that have haunted the police since the department's founding. Various mayors have appointed investigative commissions. In the 1970s the Knapp Commission dealt with corruption; the Mollen Commission submitted its report on police brutality in 1993. Similar problems don't haunt firefighters. They aren't called to action unless there is an emergency, and it is their job to be saviors.

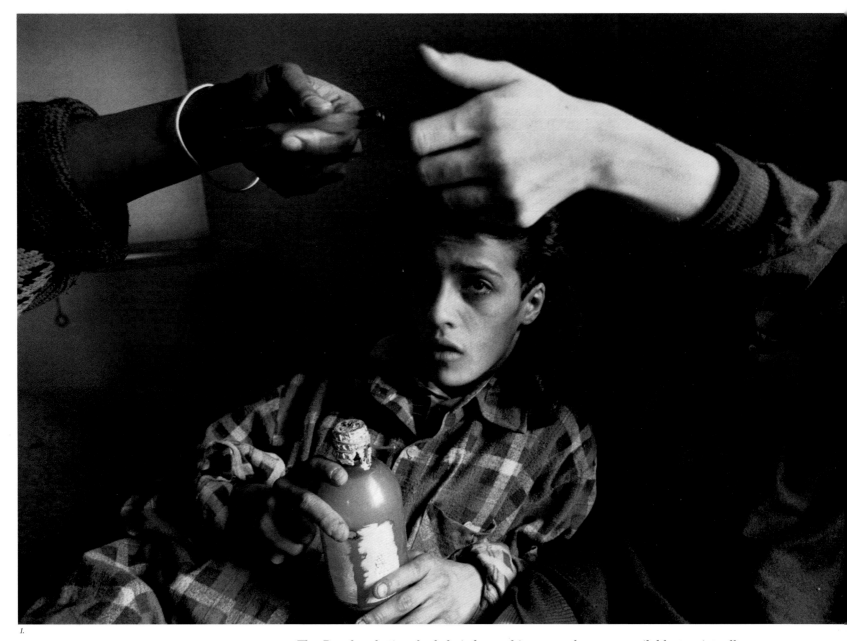

1.

The Drug Epidemic

The Dutch colonists had their long, thin white clay pipes for smoking tobacco. In 1836 Philip Hone boasted that his wine cellar contained 672 gallons of Madeira and sherry. In 1896 Stephen Crane described how the scourge of British imperialism, opium, was available in Chinatown. During the 1920s, Prohibition hardly daunted New York's appetite for alcohol. There was a time when drug use was considered recreational. Marijuana, cocaine, heroin, and opium were around but had a small following. Jazz musicians and their groupies had access to them. There was not much interference from the police or federal authorities because the number of drug users was relatively insignificant.

The epidemic hit in the 1960s. Everything changed; drugs invaded the ghettos and became available to virtually everyone, including kids. What might have been considered a nuisance before blossomed into an enormous social problem affecting a considerable portion of the population. By the mid-1980s crack, the most devastating of all, had invaded the city. At this time its impact was felt in a number of ways. Automobile driver fatalities increased by 3.4 percent. Of drivers under forty-five years of age who died in automobile accidents, 25 percent had used cocaine within forty-eight hours prior to death. Of suicides occurring during 1984, 20 percent had used cocaine shortly before death. Those who killed themselves with firearms were twice as likely to have used cocaine before death as those who killed themselves by other means. By 1990 more than forty thousand children were reported

to be in foster care with approximately 90 percent of them born to drug-using mothers.

New York leads the nation in the number of people addicted to hard drugs. Although social and economic boundaries do not limit drug use, the worst addiction problems can be found in impoverished neighborhoods. Many of the people involved in drug use and the drug trade come from socially troubled and economically disadvantaged areas. Despite the risks involved, selling drugs is seen as an attractive option in neighborhoods where there is little hope for employment, quality housing, satisfactory education, or social mobility. Where there is life with no future, drugs become a viable option. Drugs and crime are handmaidens. A 1997 United States Justice Department report indicated that the worst of the crack

epidemic seemed to be over. There were dramatic decreases in the percentages of newly arrested criminals who tested positive for crack, particularly among arrestees under the age of sixteen. The report further indicated that there was a correlation between the decline in New York City's crime rate and the reduced consumption of crack.

1. Crack users, Red Hook, Brooklyn, 1988; photograph by Eugene Richards, MAGNUM.
2. "War on crack," East Harlem (El Barrio). 1986; WW. A menagerie of dolls was placed in tenement windows by two neighborhood men wanting to draw attention to the war on crack.
3. A drug deal in progress, Red Hook, Brooklyn, 1988; photograph by Eugene Richards, MAGNUM. Although this transaction is taking place in a housing project hallway, during the height of the epidemic scenes such as this were common on street corners.
4. Police discovering a man dead from a drug overdose, 1978; photograph by Leonard Freed, MAGNUM.

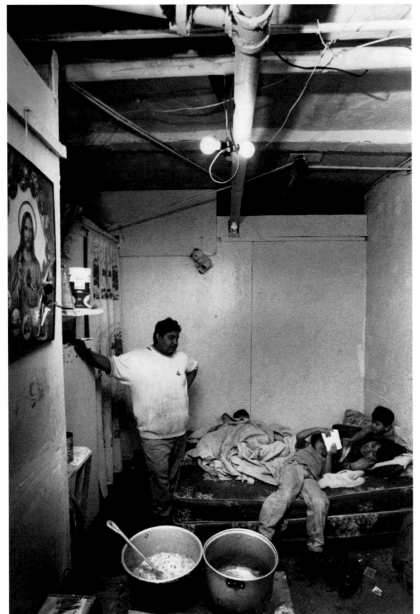

"How the Other Half Lives" Today

In 1890 the Danish immigrant, photographer, and social commentator Jacob Riis published *How the Other Half Lives*, a searing documentation of New York's tenement dwellers, including those on the Lower East Side, one of the most densely populated areas in the world. Through his books, reporting, and photographs, Riis drew attention to the miserable lives of the city's poor. Private charities, like the Five Points Mission and Children's Aid Society, sought to ameliorate their plight. Settlement houses with similar objectives sprang up on the Lower East Side. Although poverty hardly disappeared, it did not become such a public issue again until the end of the 1920s and early 1930s, when the Depression brought long lines of unemployed to the streets, shantytowns in Central Park, and soup kitchens everywhere. Responsibility for the poor shifted from private agencies to city, state, and federal governments. This legacy continued for sixty years until the welfare reforms of the 1990s.

Today poverty persists. It is visible and undeniable. There are homeless to be seen on the streets, huddled in doorways, and camping out in the parks. Poverty is a constant topic of television, radio, newspaper, and magazine reporting. It is impossible for anyone to deny the dimensions of the poverty that exists within the boundaries of New York City.

Between 1991 and 1993 the median income of the poorest one-fifth of the city's residents dropped from $6,600 to $5,800. During the same two-year period the percentage of their income spent on housing

3.

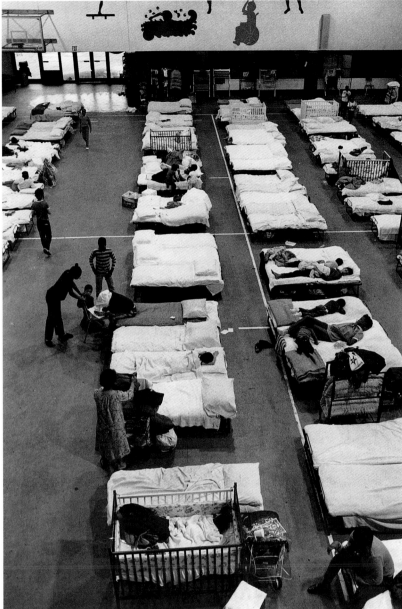

4.

increased from 60 percent to 79 percent, and the number of housing units available for less than $450 dropped. How do these people manage? Two or three families often share two- or three-room apartments. Such crowded conditions are considered more desirable than homeless shelters. In January 1988, there were 17,800 homeless persons. In the early 1990s the city opened fifteen shelters for men and twelve for women, providing for eleven thousand people.

1. Recent immigrants from Mexico, Juana Castillo, Lucio Gaspar, and their children, 1996; photograph by Fred Conrad, NYT. As Juana Castillo lies sick in the family bed, her children with no place to go gather around her.
2. Homeless woman in front of Bergdorf Goodman, 1989; photograph by David Grossman.
3. Demonstration in support of the homeless at Columbus Circle, 1989; photograph by David Grossman.
4. Temporary lodging at the Roberto Clemente Shelter in the Bronx, 1987; photograph by Stephanie Hollyman.

1.

Private Schools

Since the nineteenth century, in addition to the city's public and parochial schools there have always been a number of private schools, some for boys, some for girls, and some coed. Today the Independent Schools Association of Greater New York lists 124 member schools; however, not all private schools are members of this group. Located throughout the city, with most on the Upper East Side and Upper West Side, some are k–12, and others are preparatory for distant boarding schools. They vary widely in philosophy and student body. Most stress academic excellence; some follow specific educational philosophies. There are Catholic schools, Chinese schools, French schools, Italian schools, Jewish schools, Greek Orthodox schools, Muslim schools, and United Nations schools. Admission is highly com-

petitive at most of these schools, especially those that promote academic excellence and those that offer social status. There is an annual trauma in which thousands of parents participate. They present their children for admission, hoping that they will be accepted at the private schools of their choice. Some parents seek a nurturing educational environment with small classes. Other parents will gain the satisfaction of knowing that their children have been placed on the right track for either social acceptance or Ivy League colleges.

2.

St. Nicholas Society

At the beginning of the nineteenth century some people from New England moved to New York and became financially successful. They appeared to be a threat to established New York families. To separate themselves from the new arrivals, in 1835 Washington Irving founded the St. Nicholas Society, an organization restricted to New Yorkers with continuity in the city. Today its membership is open only to males who can demonstrate maternal or paternal ancestry dating back to 1784 in New York State. Among its many members have been men from these families: Astor, Beekman, de Peyster, Duer, Goelet, Jay, Lorillard, Rhinelander, Roosevelt, Stuyvesant, Van Buren, Van Wyck, Varick, and Verplanck.

1. Buckley School class, late 1970s; BS.
2. The 162d Annual St. Nicholas Society Dinner at the Colony Club, 1996; photograph by Leonard Freed, MAGNUM. In a traditional ceremony, at the end of the dinner white clay church warden pipes and tobacco are distributed. From left to right: D. Campbell McCrary, Jennifer Osborne, Clark Reiner, and Eric P. Widing.

1.

Fine Food and Cigars

New York has been a restaurant town since the Delmonico brothers opened their first eating establishment on William Street in 1831. Their successors created restaurants with legendary names that have since vanished: Louis Sherry, Rector's, and Shanley's. Prohibition gave birth to some new places like "21." The 1939–1940 World's Fair introduced Americans to a variety of European cuisines. Henri Soulé, maître d' of the fair's French pavilion, remained to establish his own restaurant, Le Pavillon, which served as a training ground and set standards for outstanding French-inspired food for a generation. Later came Lutèce and Le Cirque, which maintained French dominance.

By the late seventies restaurant madness had set in. Great new restaurants with inspired chefs, in many cases Americans,

were opening in midtown, downtown, and all over town; some, the Gotham Bar and Grill and Chanterelle, survive. It continued in the eighties with An American Place, Aureole, Bouley, Le Bernardin, Lespinasse, San Domenico and Union Square Café. French dominance began to wane, and the Italians took over. Nearly every place that served food became a *ristorante*. The explosion of the eighties continued in the nineties with Daniel, Jean Georges, and Le Cirque 2000, where grandeur and opulence reign. Along with the restaurants came the food store explosion: Balducci's (a Greenwich Village tradition), Dean and Deluca in SoHo, Grace's Marketplace on the Upper East Side, and the Union Square Greenmarket. Food consciousness reached the level of passion.

1. Italian-born Tony May, at head of table, holding court at Sandro, his first New York restaurant, 1985; photograph by Lou Manna. One of the most influential Italian restaurateurs, he created San Domenico, New York's premier Italian restaurant.

2. Club manager Philip Darrow and Culbro Corporation president Edgar Cullman, Jr., at Club Macanudo, 1996; photograph by Paula Court. The club is named after the famed Jamaican stogie manufactured by the Culbro-owned General Cigar Corporation.

3. Lyons-born Daniel Boulud, owner and executive chef of the restaurant Daniel, 1994; RD. Boulud was first with Roger Vergé in Mougins, then in Copenhagen, Washington, and New York at Le Régence and Le Cirque before he opened Daniel, where the excellence of his food is esteemed.

1.

2.

3.

A World Fashion Center

Until the end of World War II Paris was the undisputed fashion capital of the world. As American artists, musicians, and writers were gaining international acclaim, American designers of women's clothing were creating a new niche for themselves in the fashion world. Paris meant couture, and New York meant ready-to-wear. Manufacturers' brands traditionally adopted the names of their owners. In the French tradition, American designers began to give an identity to their creations under their own names. What emerged was a panoply of clothing and accessory lines carrying the names of individual designers. When individual department stores and specialty shops expanded into shopping malls, merchandising changed.

Seventh Avenue continued to be the cen-

ter of the fashion industry but transformed its profile from commerce to glamour. By the late 1980s Seventh Avenue names had become synonymous with Hollywood names. Designers became stars, and their products were sold around the world under their names. Today New York, along with Paris and Milan, is one of the principal fashion capitals of the world.

4.

1. "Seventh on Sixth," 1996; FG. The fashion industry developed a collective approach to presenting new fall and spring lines. Recently refurbished Bryant Park was used as the site; large tents were erected, and individual designers presented their new lines here rather than in their showrooms.
2. Presenting a new line in the Calvin Klein showroom, 1996; FG. In attendance were buyers and fashion reporters.
3. Presenting a new line in the Perry Ellis showroom, 1996; FG. Such presentations have become media events.
4. Ralph Lauren being applauded by his models after presenting a new line, 1996; FG.

1.

2.

Zip Code 10021

Stretching from Fifth Avenue to the East River between Sixty-first and Eightieth Streets, this enclave is home to some of the richest people in the country, if not the world, but not all of New York's wealth is concentrated here.

On the East Side, there are zip codes 10022, 10028, and 10128, and on the West Side, it is Central Park West. All of them reflect affluence in certain areas; however, it is 10021 where the lifestyle of the rich is most evident. There are spacious apartments on Fifth Avenue and Park Avenue that sell for millions. There are brownstones that sell for more. Some of the most expensive restaurants are on the side streets. Madison Avenue has become a par-

adise for the wealthiest shoppers. It is no longer necessary to go to the Place Vendôme in Paris or to the via Monte Napoleone in Milan to shop; branches can be found on Madison Avenue.

1. Brooke Astor, philanthropist and benefactor of the New York Public Library, with Dr. Paul Leclerc, its president, 1995; photograph by Star Black.

2. Managing director of Christie's New York Patricia Hambrecht, 1996; photograph by Brad Trent. Christie's, along with its competitor Sotheby's, houses regular multi-million-dollar auctions of art, antiques, and assorted memorabilia.

3. Interior designer Mario Buatta 1986; photograph by George Lange. Buatta's list of past and present private clients includes the superrich and famous: Nelson Doubleday, Charlotte Ford, Henry Ford II, Malcolm Forbes, Mr. and Mrs. S. I. Newhouse, and Billy Joel, among others.

4. Carroll Petrie, socialite, hostess, and art collector, in her apartment, 1995; photograph by Brad Trent .

1.

A Galaxy of Cultural Magnets

Some people say that they live in New York to take advantage of Broadway, Carnegie Hall, Lincoln Center, the Metropolitan Opera, the Metropolitan Museum of Art, the Museum of Modern Art, the Guggenheim Museum (uptown and downtown), Off Broadway, the Brooklyn Academy of Music, and the myriad cultural institutions offering exhibitions, concerts, dance programs, lectures, and film programs. Millions of people come to New York every year to participate in the city's incredible display of cultural riches. No other city in the world equals New York in the number and variety of its cultural presentations. Culture is bigger business than sports.

According to the Alliance for the Arts, in the fiscal year 1995 nonprofit cultural orga-

nizations with 40,723 employees generated $1,682,100,000, commercial theater with 10,733 employees generated $540,800,000, and commercial galleries and auction houses with 6,211 employees generated $437,700,000. Cultural institutions could not flourish without artists. Living and working in New York are actors, dancers, directors, filmmakers, musicians, opera singers, painters, poets, sculptors, writers, and tens of thousands of other artists. Their passion for creative activities becomes a contagious commodity. Collectively they contribute to an ambiance brimming with independent thinking and nonconformist lifestyles.

1. A Chorus Line, *1984; photograph by Martha Swope, TI. One of Broadway's longest-running musicals, it was conceived, directed, and choreographed by Michael Bennett, with a book by James Kirkwood and Nicholas Dante, music by Marvin Hamlisch, and lyrics by Edward Kleban.*

2. *The Metropolitan Museum of Art, 1979; CB. Home of the blockbuster exhibition, the Met has shown major exhibitions drawing on the treasures of museums and private art collectors throughout the world. The museum's front steps have become a congenial resting place for weary tourists and culture-hungry New Yorkers.*

3. *Postperformance reception of the Mark Morris dance company's* Orfeo and Euridice, *at the Brooklyn Academy of Music, 1997;*

photograph by Elena Olivio. On the left is dance company director Mark Morris, and on the far right is Harvey Lichtenstein, BAM president and CEO. For more than twenty-five years Lichtenstein has been New York's most innovative impresario. Under his direction BAM has hosted groundbreaking performers from around the world.

4. *Midnight swing, dancing on the plaza at Lincoln Center, 1997; photograph by Stephanie Berger, LCA. The nation's premier performing arts center is a daunting complex of independent yet affiliated organizations: Metropolitan Opera, New York City Ballet, New York Philharmonic, New York City Opera, Chamber Music Society of Lincoln Center, Film Society of Lincoln Center, Lincoln Center Theater, School of American*

Ballet, City Center of Music and Drama, Juilliard School, and the New York Public Library's performing arts library.

1.

Hollywood on the Hudson

New York was the birthplace of the motion-picture industry in the United States. Before the streets were paved, Thomas Edison had a studio in the Bronx at Decatur Avenue and Oliver Place. The Biograph Company had a studio on 175th Street near Marmion Avenue in the Bronx. Vitagraph's 1908 *Romeo and Juliet* was filmed in Central Park, and Mack Sennett's Keystone Film Company was at 150 West 14th Street. Adolph Zukor's Famous Players Film Company had offices on West 26th Street. Seeking better weather, film production companies sent crews to California, Florida, and Cuba for winter shooting. When New Yorkers Jesse Lasky, Samuel Goldwyn, and Cecil B. DeMille formed the Jesse L. Lasky Feature Film Company, they established their production studio in Hollywood. By

1915 Hollywood had become the dominant film production center although executive offices remained in New York. In 1919, the Famous Players-Lasky Company (later Paramount Studios) constructed a thirteen-building complex (now Kaufman Studios) in Astoria, Queens. Throughout the twenties, thirties, and forties New York continued to be the scene, but not the production location, of Hollywood-made films, some of which were Broadway plays and musicals converted into films. In 1922, 12 percent of motion-picture production was based in New York with 84 percent in Hollywood.

With the breakup of the studio system in the 1950s, New York became a center for independent filmmaking. Although the Hollywood studios continued to be the locus of decision making and distribution, New

2.   3.

York began to evolve as a related yet separate entity in the American film industry.

In the late 1960s and early 1970s a new generation of filmmakers made New York its base: Woody Allen, Milos Forman, Sidney Lumet, and Martin Scorsese. In the 1980s Jonathan Demme and Spike Lee joined this constellation. New York has also become a favored scene for countless television series of sitcoms and good cop, bad cop shows.

In 1996 the film and television industry generated $2,227,000,000 in revenue with seventy-eight thousand people employed. In the same year 201 films, mostly independent productions, were made on location in New York. The ubiquitous location vans with their crews, lights, sound booms, and cameras testify to the film industry's place in the city's economy. The annual Lincoln

Center film festival provides a worldview of filmmaking. The New York University and Columbia University film departments have trained outstanding directors. Bicoastal actors, directors, and producers maintain homes in both Los Angeles and New York. And there are even guidebooks telling where the stars live in New York.

1. Liza Minnelli, Martin Scorsese, and Robert De Niro at the premiere of their film New York, New York, *Alice Tully Hall, Lincoln Center, 1977; CB.*

2. Woody Allen and Diane Keaton in a scene from Annie Hall, *1977; CB.*

3. Milos Forman, Czech-born director, filming Taking Off, *on location in the East Village, 1970; CB.*

1.

Global Financial and Communications Capital

Everyone in the world has heard of Wall Street, knows what it is and where it is. Both loved and reviled, it is synonymous with entrepreneurship, capitalism, and money. The New York Stock Exchange is the nerve center of Wall Street and the barometer of the global economy, which operates around the clock. What happens in Tokyo, London, Paris, and Milan is heard on Wall Street, and what happens on Wall Street is heard in Tokyo, London, Paris, and Milan. Computers have transformed the methods and speed of financial transactions. SuperDot 250, an electronic order-routing system, links member firms to specialists' posts on the trading floor. Today more than 98 percent of the orders using SuperDot are executed and reported back to the originating firm within twenty-eight seconds.

Perhaps what seems an anachronism in the age of sophisticated telecommunications, transactions still take place on a one-to-one basis whereby a member goes to a trading station with buy and sell orders. As more Americans have become stock market investors, the volume of transactions has soared to a peak of 684,580,000 shares on January 23, 1997.

Are New Yorkers more wired than anyone else in this country or the world today? No one has done a statistical survey, but the answer is probably yes. Computer nerds from Silicon Valley might dispute this; their approach to being wired is one-dimensional, the computer screen. In New York one finds that communications technologies intersect with millions who have a hand in one or more technologies as either originators or

2.

users. In New York one finds everything in more abundance than any place in the world: 15 local television broadcasting stations and 6 networks, 20 cable television channels, 15 AM radio stations, 22 FM radio stations, 23 local newspapers, 199 magazine publishers, 43 book publishers, and 183 Internet servers.

"The Metropolis strives to reach a mythical point where the world is completely fabricated by man, so that it absolutely coincides with his desires. . . .

"Through this pervasiveness, its existence has become like the Nature it has replaced: taken for granted, almost invisible, certainly indescribable. . . . Manhattan . . . generated its own metropolitan Urbanism—a *Culture of Congestion*. . . .

". . . the Metropolis needs/deserves its own specialized architecture, one that can vindicate the original promise of the metropolitan condition and develop the fresh traditions of the Culture of Congestion further."
REM KOOLHAAS, *DELIRIOUS MANHATTAN*

1. *Trading floor of the New York Stock Exchange, 11 Wall Street, 1992; NYSE.*
2. *Control room for* CBS Evening News *at CBS Production Center, 524 West Fifty-seventh Street, 1997; CBS.*

1.

2.

3.

Champs!

With three championships in the 1990s New York was America's most winning sports town. The Giants won Super Bowl XXV in 1991. The Rangers won the Stanley Cup in 1994 and the Yankees won the World Series in 1996.

Over the years, New York teams have been champions time and again. The Yankees with Babe Ruth and Lou Gehrig in the twenties, Gerhig and Joe DiMaggio in the thirties, and DiMaggio in the forties, had a stellar record. Between 1949 and 1960, Casey Stengel's Yankees with Mickey Mantle, Whitey Ford, and Yogi Berra took ten pennants and seven World Series. The Dodgers, when they were still in Brooklyn, won National League pennants in 1947, 1949, 1952, 1955 (their only World Series

win) and 1956, all against the Yankees in the historic Subway Series. In 1957 the Dodgers defected to Los Angeles. In 1962 the Mets became New York's new National League team winning two World Series in 1969 and 1986 and the pennant in 1973. In 1977 Reggie Jackson hit three successive home runs, each on the first pitch, each off a different pitcher, to give the Yankees their first World Series win in fifteen years. The Yankees won again the next year.

In basketball, CCNY, St. John's, and LIU have been triumphant. In 1950, Nat Holman's CCNY team won both NIT and NCAA titles. The Knicks won NBA championships in 1970 and 1973. In 1969 there was the Jets historic Super Bowl III upset. In the old Madison Square Garden on Eighth

4.

Avenue, college track and field drew huge crowds as New York University and Manhattan contested Georgetown and Villanova.

5.

6.

1. Charlie Hayes catches a foul ball hit by Atlanta Braves' Mark Lemke, and the Yankees win the World Series, 1996; photograph by Ron Frehm, WW.
2. Yankee outfielder Roger Maris hit his sixtieth home run to tie Babe Ruth's single season record, 1961; WW. On the last day of the 162-game season, October 1, 1961, Maris hit his sixty-first home run to pass Ruth's mark of sixty in a 154-game season.
3. In one of the Subway Series, Brooklyn left-hander Johnny Podres is seen pitching to the final Yankee batter, Elston Howard, 1955; photograph by Frank Jurkoski, CB. Podres shutout the Yankees, 2–0, to give the Dodgers their first World Series.
4. Captain Willis Reed gives the victory sign in the locker room as the New York Knicks

take their first NBA championship with a seventh-game rout of the Los Angeles Lakers, 1970; WW.
5. New York Jets quarterback Joe Namath drops back to pass in Super Bowl III, played in Miami's Orange Bowl, 1969; WW. The Jets defeated the Baltimore Colts 16–7.
6. The New York Rangers celebrate their victory over the Vancouver Canucks in the Stanley Cup finals played at Madison Square Garden, 1994; photograph by Keith Torris, NYDN. This was the Rangers' first Stanley Cup since 1940.

1.

An African-American Mayor

When David Dinkins was elected mayor of New York City in 1989, he was the first African-American to hold this office. Since a majority of Democratic voters had decided to end the Koch era, there was the opportunity to elect a black mayor. Regarded as a nice guy, Dinkins epitomized mainstream Democratic organization politics. Coalitions were formed among blacks, Puerto Ricans, and whites to provide the kind of support necessary to elect Dinkins. He defeated Mayor Ed Koch in the primary and went on to win the November election against Rudolph Giuliani. He was a one-term mayor, losing to Giuliani in the 1993 campaign.

1. Mayor David Dinkins leading a march in Harlem, accompanied by Spike Lee, Melba Moore, and Denzel Washington, 1989; photograph by Harvey Stein.
2. Mayor Ed Koch campaigning at Polish function, 1989; photograph by Harvey Stein.
3. Mayor Rudolph Giuliani with his son, Andrew, watching the World Series at Yankee Stadium, 1996; NYDN.

Jewish and Italian Mayors

Ed Koch, veteran Democratic politician, had risen from Greenwich Village district leader to city councilman and then to congressman representing the Upper East Side. In the September 1977 primary he ran against Abe Beame, Bella Abzug, Mario Cuomo, and Manhattan Borough President Percy Sutton. Defeating them, he went on to be elected mayor in November. Reelected three times, he left office in 1989. Former U.S. Attorney Rudoph Giuliani, who made a name for himself as a relentless and successful crime fighter, ran against Dinkins in the 1989 election on the Republican ticket. He ran again against incumbent Dinkins in 1993, defeating him by a narrow margin.

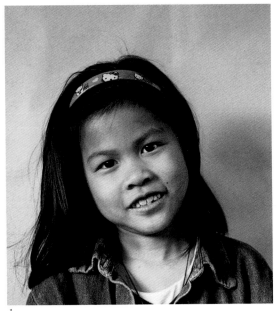

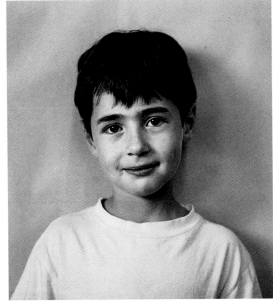

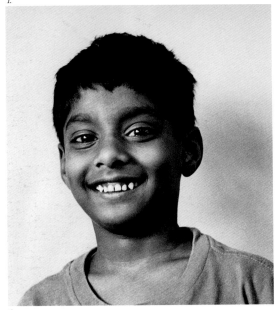

The Faces of New York's Future

Between 1990 and 1994, 560,000 new immigrants settled in New York City. Of that number, 33 percent came from the Caribbean, 3.3 percent from Central America, 12.3 percent from South America, 21.7 percent from Europe, 26.1 percent from Asia, and 2.2 percent from Africa. These statistics begin to suggest what the future population of New York will be: fewer Caucasians from Europe and more people of color from the Caribbean, Mexico, Central America, India, China, the Middle East, and Africa.

According to Board of Education statistics for the 1995–1996 year, public school enrollment was 1,075,605, of which 36.4 percent were black, 37.3 percent Latino, 16.5 percent white, 9.5 percent Asian/Pacific Islander, and 0.4 percent Native American/Alaskan Native. Throughout the entire system students represent 193 countries. In the 1995–1996 year there were 44,926 immigrant students entering the system.

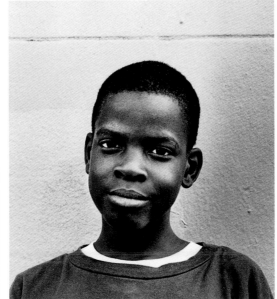

6.

8.

10.

7.

9.

11.

Third-grade children from the Borough Park neighborhood of Brooklyn, 1997; all photographs by Ethel Wolvovitz. 1. Jennifer, age six, Chinese; 2. Samik, age eight, Indian; 3. Danny, age six, Albanian; 4. Jennifer and Stephanie, age seven, Puerto Rican/ Dominican; 5. Pamela, age 7, Polish; 6. Ho Yan, age seven, Chinese; 7. Candace, age seven, American; 8. Luis, age six, American; 9. Atiba, age nine, Trinidadian; 10. Rabia, age seven, Pakistani; 11. Julian, age seven, Colombian.

THE MAYOR SPEAKS

"New York, more than any other city, has been built by the dedication and dreams of new Americans. . . .

"New York's immigrant population is an economically diverse group, with substantial numbers in professional, managerial, administrative and blue-collar occupations. Census data show that immigrants in New York work and own businesses in slightly higher percentages than U.S. citizens. They bring new ideas, new energy and an appreciation for American values and ideals. Immigrants challenge us to do better, and we all benefit from their industry and prosperity."

RUDOLPH GIULIANI, JANUARY 9, 1997

Preceding pages: Fireworks celebrating the Centennial of the Statue of Liberty, July 4, 1986; CB. Among those involved in planning this event were Lee Iacocca, Chairman and Chief Executive Officer of The Statue of Liberty–Ellis Island Foundation, and Stephen Briganti, Executive Vice-President of the Foundation. The International Fireworks spectacular was produced and directed by Tommy Walker and Omar Lerman. It was sponsored by Abraham & Straus and Bloomingdale's. The fireworks were presented by a triumvirate of leading American fireworks companies: Fireworks by Grucci, Zembelli, and Pyrospectaculars.

Author's Afterword

I have been a New Yorker, as a full-time resident, part-time resident and visitor, for most of my life. In 1939, at the age of thirteen, I came to New York for the first time with my parents to see the World's Fair. In Cleveland, I knew about the city from the Sunday edition of the *New York Times* which my father, who had been raised on the Lower East Side, in Harlem, and in the Bronx, read religiously. We stayed at the then Taft Hotel located at Seventh Avenue and Fifty-first street, went to the fair, visited friends and relatives on the Lower East Side, in Brooklyn, and in the Bronx, and saw my father's elementary school on Houston Street.

Four years later I went to Yale and became a frequent weekend visitor staying at my aunt and uncle's converted carriage house artists' studio in Brooklyn Heights. Although I benefited from my education at Yale, I always considered myself to be a social outcast. Life at Yale in the 1940s was predominantly upper-class white Protestant. I had classmates whose names ended in III's and IV's, proclaiming their American heritage. My father was born on the outskirts of Vilna and my mother was the first child in her family to be born in this country. I didn't qualify to wear white buck shoes nor was I welcome at "their" tables in the dining hall.

I knew that I had to find out who I was, so on my weekend excursions I began to wander the streets of the Lower East Side, searching for my roots in this country. This was not the Lower East Side of my father's youth where he had been a *schlepper* carrying garments from one sweatshop to another. It was beginning to change as some of the tenements were replaced by public housing and as Jews moved out and Puerto Ricans moved in. But there was enough nostalgia remaining to abet my identity problem. I realized that as a member of a gigantic nuclear family—my mother had eight siblings—I had been raised in a protective Jewish cocoon. There were the Jews and there were *goyem*; perhaps there was some commercial interchange, but there was no socializing. However, New York was different; there were so many Jews that you didn't have to worry about being ostracized.

At this point in my life, in my early twenties, I decided that I was a New Yorker. It was the only place I had found, as a member of a minority group, where I felt comfortable. Continuing my studies at Yale, I got a graduate degree and then entered into one of those rebellious episodes of one's life that seems to be a concomitant of maturation. I decided to abandon my professional training and get a commercial job in New York. It wasn't as easy as I thought. I discovered that the Yale Club had an employment agency and assumed that they had only good jobs to offer. So, I took a job as a junior salesman for the Royal Typewriter Company and reported to their office at Two Park Avenue every morning before going from door to door in office towers trying to sell typewriters. A week on the job, I realized that I had made a horrible mistake and I decided to extract myself. It took me a year to find a job at the San Francisco Museum of Art and I was on a career track.

Fourteen years later, I returned to New York with my wife and our two kids to take another job that turned out to be a disaster. After that. I began to write for Clay Felker when *New York* magazine was a Sunday supplement in the *New York Herald Tribune*. My wife and I went to dinner at Elaine's with a friend and bumped into an acquaintance who told me of a job at The Jewish Museum, the then current hot art spot. She said that they were looking for an assistant director. I got the job and was informed by the director that there was an exhibition idea floating around that no one wanted to do. It was an exhibition on The Lower East Side. He asked me if I was interested in doing it. I came home and told my wife what happened and said that the day that the exhibition opened, there would be crowds stretching from the corner of Fifth Avenue and Ninety-second Street to Madison Avenue. There were. The exhibition was so popular that they presented it again six months later.

Despite the success of the Lower East Side exhibition—it was the first exhibition in a museum to incorporate the use of films and sound—the museum's trustees decided to fire me. Fortunately, I found a job at the then nascent New York State Council on Arts. While there, I met Tom Hoving who had just been appointed director of The Metropolitan Museum. Basking in the recent success of The Lower East Side exhibition,

I proposed doing an exhibition on Harlem at the Met to Tom Hoving. He bought the idea instantly. In the late 1960s civil rights was a national concern. After two year's preparation, "Harlem On My Mind" opened under a cloud of controversy. It was a gigantic mulitmedia presentation with video, projections, and sound proclaiming Harlem as the cultural capital of black America. Although I continue to meet African-Americans who describe the significance of the exhibition in their lives, it was vilified in the media making it the most controversial exhibitions presented in an American art museum in the twentieth century.

Having created two major exhibitions with accompanying books, I realized that I had found my metier—interpreting the culture of America's ethnic groups. Since that time, I have continued to create books and exhibitions on this theme. I did another exhibition about the history of Jews in the United States, which was shown first at The New York Public Library and later at Ellis Island. Later I did an exhibition about Italian-Americans, which opened in Italy and came to Ellis Island. More recently, I was co-curator of an exhibition at the Municipal Art Society on new immigrants.

All of that was preparation for this book. Everyone tells me that this must be a labor of love. If there is such a thing, this is it for me. I have devoted the last two years of my life totally to this book and have loved every minute of it. One of my colleagues said that it is a loving portrait of the city. I don't deny that. For me, New York is the greatest city in the world. Although I doubt that I will ever be able to explore every neighborhood and every street, working on this book has provided me with the opportunity to expand my knowledge of this universe called New York City.

This is my interpretation of the city. Someone else will see it differently and make another kind of book. When I first came upon John Kouwenhoven's *The Columbia Historical Portrait of New York*, which had been published in 1953, I decided to create a book that would update his monumental work, but one that would focus more on the people. This is it.

January 1998

Acknowledgments

Although I am the author and designer of this book, it would have been impossible to complete it without the active participation of the many people who have assisted me over the last two years.

Foremost is my editor, James Mairs, whose support, expertise, and enthusiasm have contributed immeasurably. I have never experienced working with an editor of his stature both as a professsional and as a human being. He has been my collaborator, not my editor.

Massimo Vignelli prefers to call himself design consultant; he is the architect of the book's format. He came up with a brilliant solution to integrate images and text. Pictures are the cinematic frames, captions are the sound track. I tried to follow his concept as I selected, organized, and scaled images, and later as I wrote text and captions. Massimo reviewed every page to be certain that I had had executed his concept faithfully.

Four other people were virtual collaborators through all phases of the book's evolution. My wife Mary reviewed every page as I finished it. My son Abe made a number of significant recommendations. John Mollenkopf checked every page and read every word. Gina Webster produced the final type and computer-generated pages.

Recognizing that this book's breadth of content required specialized scrutiny, I assembled a group of readers whose knowledge of New York City's ethnic groups would supplement my own. They included Roscoe Brown, Jr., of the CUNY Graduate School and University Center, Sushan Chin, archivist, Museum of the Chinese in the Americas, William Johns, Director of the New York Genealogical and Biographical Society, Karl Katz, former Director of The Jewish Museum in New York and Israel Museum in Jerusalem, Irvine MacManus, Jr., Vice Chairman of El Museo del Barrio, John Mollenkopf of the CUNY Graduate School and University Center, Edward O'Donnell, History Department, Hunter College, Remigio Pane, Professor Emeritus of Rutgers University, and Russell Tallchief of the Smithsonian Institution's Museum of the American Indian. Two other readers in specialized areas were Lenore Benson of the Fashion Group International and Stephen Wheeler, archivist of the New York Stock Exchange. Each of them read sections that corresponded to his or her area of expertise. Their insightful comments and recommendations have refined the content of this book in many ways.

From its inception, this book required additional funding. Joan Davidson, President of Furthermore, the publication program of the J. M. Kaplan Fund, provided initial grants, which made it possible to begin research. Later grants from the Susan and Elihu Rose Foundation and Seymour Durst Old York Foundation assured completion. Financial support from the Emigrant Savings Bank along with exhibitions in its branches and its MTA advertisements have guaranteed that the people of the city will know about this book. City Lore and the New York Foundation for the Arts served as agents for grants.

I was a constant visitor at a number of New York City archives. I want to thank those who were most helpful to me: Museum of the City of New York—Eileen Kennedy and Peter Simmons; The New-York Historical Society—Lisa Berger and Dale Neighbors; The New York Public Library—Sharon Frost and Julia Van Haaften; Old York Library—Eva Carrozza; and Queens Borough Public Library, Long Island Collection—William Asadorian. I was a less frequent visitor at other archives and want to thank those who assisted me: Don Bowden of Wide World Photos; Carrie Chalmers at Magnum Photos; Norman Currie and Sarah Partridge at Corbis-Bettmann; Krysia Fisher at the YIVO Institute for Jewish Research; Pedro Juan Hernandez of the Centro de Estudios Puertorriquenos at Hunter College; Aimée Kaplan and Dan Wishnoff at the CUNY LaGuardia and Wagner Archive; Bill Martin of the New York Daily News Photo Archive; Allen Reuben at Culver Pictures; Jeff Rosenheim of the Department of Photograpy at The Metropolitan Museum of Art; and Mary Yearwood of the Schomburg Center for Research in Black Culture, New York Public Library,

There were others who lent family photographs or directed me to relatives who provided them. I want to thank John Milnes Baker, Jack H Bloom, Francis L. Kellogg, Daisy Marks, Paula Sarnoff Oreck, Ethel Wolvovitz, and Peggy Zorach.

This book draws upon the research that I assembled for four other books. Although I was responsible for most of the image and text research myself, I did have assistance from others. In Washington: Athena Angelos and Diane Hamilton. In New York: Kristen Case and Craig Kayser, who also served as fact checker.

Although there are a number of photographers whose work is represented here, there are several who deserve special thanks. They are: Leonard Freed, Matt Harnett, Harvey Stein, and Ethel Wolvovitz who labored for months over the photographs of the Brooklyn elementary school children. Charles Traub of the Graduate Program in Photograpy at the School of Visual Arts provided insights and advice of inestimable value.

At W. W. Norton, Managing Editor Nancy Palmquist bent schedules and procedures to help get this book out on time. At Modernage Photographic Services, Kenneth Triano and Joe Smith provided the highest quality copying under rush conditions and Arthur Vitols was willing to travel to archives in all parts of the city to make photographic copies.

At Arnoldo Mondadori Editore I would like to thank Daniela Novati and Sergio Brunelli and their attentive colleagues whose concern for the production details of this book have assured the quality of its reproduction.

There were a number of others who helped in a variety of ways and I want to thank them. They are Harold Augenbraum of the Mercantile Library, Tracy Calvan of the Muncipal Art Society, Barbara Cohen and Judith Stonehill of the recently closed New York Bound bookstore, Jenny Dixon of the Lower Manhattan Cultural Council, Mary Holloway of the Associaton for a Better New York, Harvey Horowitz and Kenneth Jackson of the History Department, Columbia University, Harris Lewine, Vicki Gold Levi and Ellen Libretto of the Queens Borough Public Library, Harry Macy, Jr. of the New York Genealogical and Biographical Society, Tony Marro, Editor of Newsday, Roberta Newman, and the Learning Alliance whose programs on multiculturalism enouraged me to undertake this book.

Suggestions for Further Reading

There is no complete bibliography of the history of New York City. It is much needed. Listed below are those works that I have found to be valuable in compiling this book.

General Works

I. N. Phelps Stokes: *The Iconography of Manhattan Island, 1498-1909* (New York: Robert H. Dodd, 1918); Kenneth T. Jackson, ed.: *The Encyclopedia of New York City* (New Haven: Yale University Press, 1995); John Kouwehoven: *The Columbia Historical Portrait of New York* (Garden City: Doubleday & Company, 1953); Ellen M. Snyder-Grenier: *Brooklyn! An Illustrated History* (Philadelphia: Temple University Press, 1996); Ira Rosenwaike: *Population History of New York City* (Syracuse: Syracuse University Press, 1972); Thomas Bender: *New York Intellect* (Baltimore: Johns Hopkins University Press. 1987); James E. Buck, ed: *The New York Stock Exchange, The First Two Hundred Years* (Essex: Greenwich Publishing Group, 1992); Mark Girouard *Cities & People* (New Haven: Yale University Press, 1985); Richard B. Morris, ed.: *Encyclopedia of American History* (New York: Harper & Row, 1970); Stephan Thernstrom, ed.: *Harvard Encyclopedia of American Ethnic Groups* (Cambridge: Harvard University Press, 1980); Morris U. Schappes, ed.: *A Documentary History of the Jews in the United States, 1654-1875* (New York: Schocken Books, 1976); Jacob Rader Marcus, ed.: *The American Jewish Woman: A Documentary History* (New York: Ktav Publishing House, 1981); Allon Schoener: *The American Jewish Album, 1654 to the Present* (New York: Rizzoli, 1983); Allon Schoener: *The Italian Americans* (New York: Macmillan, 1987); Philip S. Foner, ed.: *The Voice of Black America* (New York: Simon and Schuster, 1972); Martin E. Dann, ed.: *The Black Press* (New York: Capricorn, 1971); E. Franklin Frazier: *The Negro in the United States* (New York: Macmillan, 1966).

Chapter One

W. P. Cumming, R. A. Skelton, D. B. Quinn: *The Discovery of North America* (New York: American Heritage Press, 1972); Joyce B. Goodfriend: *Before the Melting Pot, Society and Culture in Colonial New York City, 1664-1730* (Princeton: Princeton University Press, 1992); Shane White: *Somewhat More Independent, The End of Slavery in New York City, 1770-1810* (Athens, Georgia: The University of Georgia Press, 1991); Robert Brilliant: *Facing the New World, Jewish Portraits in Colonial and Federal America* (New York: The Jewish Museum, 1997).

Chapter Two

Robert Greenhalgh Albion: *The Rise of New York Port, 1815-1860* (Boston: Northeastern University Press, 1984); Robert Ernst: *Immigrant Life in New York City, 1825-1863* (Syracuse: Syracuse University Press, 1994); Edward K. Spann: *The New Metropolis, New York City, 1840-1857* (New York: Columbia University Press, 1981); Ralph K. Andrist: *The Erie Canal* (New York: American Heritage, 1961); Stanley Nadel *Little Germany, Ethnicity, Religion and Class in New York City, 1845-80* (Urbana: University of Illinois Press, 1990); Ronald H. Bayor and Timothy J. Meagher, ed.: *The New York Irish* (Baltimore: Johns Hopkins University Press, 1996); Iver Bernstein: *The New York City Draft Riots* (New York: Oxford Univeristy Press, 1990); Herbert Asbury: *The Gangs of New York* (New York: Paragon, 1990).

Chapter Three

Jacob A. Riis: *How the Other Half Lives* (New York: Dover Publications, 1971); Abraham Cahan: *The Rise of David Levinsky* (New York: Harper & Brothers, 1960); Allon Schoener, ed.: *Portal to America, The Lower East Side, 1870-1925* (New York: Holt, Rinehart and Winston, 1967); Irving Howe: *World of Our Fathers* (New York: Harcourt Brace Jovanovich, 1976); Stanley Nadel *Little Germany, Ethnicity, Religion and Class in New York City, 1845-80* (Urbana: University of Illinois Press, 1990); Ronald H. Bayor and Timothy J. Meagher, ed.: *The New York Irish* (Baltimore: Johns Hopkins University Press, 1996); Leon Stein, ed.: *Out of the Sweatshop* (New York: Quadrangle, 1977); Leon Stein: *The Triangle Fire* (Philadelphia: J.B. Lippincott, 1962); James Weldon Johnson: *Black Manhattan* (New York: Da Capo Press, 1990); Seth M. Scheiner: *Negro Mecca, A History of the Negro in New York City, 1865-1920* (New York: New York University Press, 1965); Herbert Asbury: *The Gangs of New York* (New York: Paragon, 1990); Luc Sante: *Low Life* (New York: Farrar-Straus-Giroux,

1991); David Nasaw: *Going Out, The Rise and Fall of Public Amusements* (New York: Basic Books, 1993); David McCullough: *The Great Bridge, The Epic Story of the Building of the Brooklyn Bridge* (New York: Simon and Schuster, 1972); Lloyd Ultan & Gary Hermalyn: *The Bronx in the Innocent Years, 1890-1925* (New York: Bronx County Historical Society, 1991); William Lee Younger: *Old Brooklyn in Early Photographs, 1865-1929* (New York: Dover, 1978); Vincent Seyfried and William Asadorian *Old Queens, N.Y. in Early Photographs* (New York: Dover, 1991); David C. Hammack: *Power and Society, Greater New York at the Turn of the Century* (New York: Russell Sage Foundation, 1982); Robert A. M. Stern, Gregory Gilmartin and John Montague Massengale: *New York 1900, Metropolitan Architecture and Urbanism, 1890-1915* (New York: Rizzoli, 1983); Elliot Wilensky and Norval White: *AIA Guide to New York City* (New York: Harcourt Brace Jovanovich, 1988); Page Smith *The Rise of Industrial America* (New York: Penguin Books, 1990).

Chapter Four

The WPA Guide to New York City (New York: Pantheon Books, 1982); *New York Panorama* (New York: Pantheon Books, 1982); Robert A. M. Stern, Gregory Gilmartin, Thomas Mellins: *New York 1930* (New York: Rizzoli, 1987); Robert A. Caro *The Power Broker, Robert Moses and the Fall of New York* (New York: Alfred A. Knopf, 1974); Allon Schoener: *Harlem On My Mind, Cultural Capital of Black America* (New York: The New Press. 1995); James Weldon Johnson: *Black Manhattan* (New York: Da Capo Press, 1990); Claude McKay: *Home to Harlem* (Boston: Northeastern University Press, 1987); David Levering Lewis *When Harlem Was in Vogue* (New York: Alfred A. Knopf, 1981); Deborah Dash Moore: *At Home in America, Second Generation New York Jews* (New York: Columbia University Press, 1981); Beth S. Winger: *New York Jews and the Great Depression* (New Haven: Yale University Press, 1996); Jenna Weisman Joselit: *The Wonders of America, Reinventing Jewish Culture, 1880-1950* (New York: Hill and Wang, 1994); Albert Fried: *The Rise and Fall of the Jewish Gangster in America* (New York: Holt, Rinehart and Winston, 1986); Ronald H. Bayor and Timothy J. Meagher, ed.: *The New York Irish* (Baltimore: Johns Hopkins University Press, 1996).

Chapter Five

J. A. S. Grenville: *A History of the World in the Twentieth Century* (Cambridge: Harvard University Press, 1994); Jean Gottman: *Megalopolis, The Urbanized Northeastern Seaboard of the United States* (Cambridge: The M.I.T. Press, 1963); Robert A. M. Stern, Thomas Mellins, David Fishman: *New York 1960, Architecture and Urbanism Between the Second World War and the Bicentennial* (New York: Monacelli Press, 1995); Saskia Sassen: *The Global City, New York, London, Tokyo* (Princeton: Princeton University Press, 1991); Allon Schoener: *Harlem On My Mind, Cultural Capital of Black America* (New York: The New Press. 1995); Nancy Foner, ed.: *New Immigrants in New York* (New York: Columbia University Press, 1987); Philip Kasinitz: *Caribbean New York, Black Immigrants and the Politics of Race* (Ithaca: Cornell University Press, 1992); Gabriel Haslip-Viera and Sherrie L. Baver: *Latinos in New York* (Notre Dame: University of Notre Dame, 1996); John Mollenkopf, ed.: *Power, Culture and Place, Essays on New York City* (New York: Russell Sage Foundation, 1988); *The Newest New Yorkers, An Analysis of Immigration into New York City During the 1980s* (New York: Department of City Planning, 1992); *The Newest New Yorkers 1990-1994, An Analysis of Immigration to NYC in the early 1990s* (New York: Department of City Planning, 1996).

Illustration Sources

AC, Author's collection; AJA, American Jewish Archives; AJHS, American Jewish Historical Society, BB, Brown Brothers; BCHS, Bronx Country Historical Society; BHS, Brooklyn Historical Society; BML, Biblioteca Medicea Laurenziana, Florence; BRS, Brearley School; BS (page 333), Black Star; BS (page 386) Buckley School; BURNS, Burns Collection; CAS, Children's Aid Society; CB, Corbis-Bettmann; CBS, CBS, Inc., Photo Archives; CEP, Centro de Estudios Puertorriquenos, Hunter College, CUNY; CMI, Congregation Mikveh Israel, Philadelphia; CP, Culver Pictures; CSI, Centro Studi Emigrazione, Rome; DM, Daisy Marks; EB, Emigrant Savings Bank; EK, Eileen Kennedy; EW, Ethel Wolvovitz; FD, Frank Driggs Collection; FG, Fashion Group International; FLK, Francis L. Kellogg; FM, Ferruccio Malandrini; HIAS, Hebrew Immigrant Aid Society; ICP, International Center of Photography; JHB, Jack H Bloom; LAA, Louis Armstrong Archive, Queens College, CUNY; LC, Library of Congress; LCA, Lincoln Center Archives; LGWA, LaGuardia and Wagner Archives, CUNY; MA, Municipal Archives, City of New York; MAGNUM, Magnum Photos; MCA, Museum of the Chinese in the Americas; MCNY, Museum of the City of New York; MERCY, Sisters of Mercy Archives; MMA, The Metropolitan Museum of Art; MMA/WEA, The Metropolitan Museum of Art, Walker Evans Archive; MOMA/FS, The Museum of Modern Art, Film Stills Collection; MOMA/PC, The Museum of Modern Art, Photographic Collection; NA, National Archives; NCEY, National Committee on Employment of Youth; NEWS, Newsday; NYDN, New York Daily News; NYHS, New-York Historical Society; NYPL, The New York Public Library; NYPL/SC, The New York Public Library, Schomburg Center; NYSE, New York Stock Exchange; NYT, The New York Times; OYL, Old York Library; PARKS, New York City Parks Photo Archive; PC, Private Collection; PHW, Photo World; PML, Pierpont Morgan Library; PI, Poppenhusen Institute; PS, Peter Schweitzer; PSO, Paula Sarnoff Oreck; PWW, People's Weekly World; PZ, Peggy Zorach; QBPL, Queens Borough Public Library, Long Island Collection; RC, Rockefeller Center, Inc.; RD, Restaurant Daniel; RMP, Railroad Museum of Pennsylvania; SI, Smithsonian Institution; SIHS, Staten Island Historical Society; TC, Trinity Church; TM, New York Transit Museum; 3M. Fototeca 3M, Milan; TI, Time, Inc.; TL, Life Magazine; UC, Union Club; WW, Wide World Photos; YIVO, Yivo Institute for Jewish Research.

INDEX

Numbers in italic refer to illustrations.

0401LG 515
PA
07-05-07 161623 DU 晉Group